The Humanism of Milton's
Paradise Lost

DAVID REID

EDINBURGH UNIVERSITY PRESS

Edinburgh University Press Limited
22 George Square, Edinburgh

Typeset in Lasercomp Ehrhardt 11/13 pt
by D S C Corporation Ltd, Falmouth and
printed and bound in Great Britain by
The Redwood Press, Melksham

A CIP record for this book is available from the British Library

ISBN 0 7486 0401 4

CONTENTS

CONTENTS

Acknowledgements

I wish to thank Professors Jan de Bruyn and Ian Ross of the University of British Columbia for their help and encouragement at an early stage of my researches and Dr John Hale of the University of Otago for the knowledge and understanding which he put into reading the manuscript and suggesting corrections. Thanks are due to the University of Stirling for a sabbatical in which I worked over the ideas of the book. Some of the material in Chapters III and IV appeared in a different form in 'Tasso and Milton on how one sees oneself', *Milton in Italy: Contexts, Images, Contradictions*, ed. Mario di Cesare, Medieval and Renaissance Texts and Studies (Binghamton, New York, 1991), pp. 445–61. I have discussed most of the ideas in this book with my wife; some of the ideas are hers and there is also the matter of intellectual example.

Quotations of Milton's poetry are taken from *The Poems of John Milton*, ed. John Carey and Alastair Fowler (London, 1968), and of his prose from *Complete Prose Works of John Milton*, ed. Don M. Wolfe et al., 8 vols (New Haven, 1953–82), cited throughout in the abbreviated form *CP*.

For Susan Reid

Introduction

Strictly, a humanist is one who studies and imitates classical literature with a view to making it new. David Daiches is perhaps the only writer on Milton to keep to this sense of humanism in his inquiries into the classical and biblical strains in Milton's work.[1] My inquiry is looser, and I shall enlarge the term, as others have done in other ways. I shall apply it to a study of literature which includes the neoclassical humanism of Milton's day but which has at once developed and contracted since. Broadly understood like this, humanism supplies me with my critical position. I aspire to writing about *Paradise Lost* as a humanist myself, but it would be foolish to speak of more than aspiration. Genuine humanist criticism is 'hard and rare'.

In the broad sense in which I shall speak of them, humanists are students of literature who consider their study useful in that it shows them what humans are like or might be like. But, and this is an important qualification, humanists are human themselves. The humanity they discover in literature is their own, or at least something in which they have a potential share. For humanists, the reflection upon experience that literature sets up is a reflection that helps them to generalise their own experience. In Lawrence's 'Odour of Chrysanthemums', for instance, we recognise the miner's widow's recognition of the otherness of the husband with whom she had struggled blindly while he lived. Our recognition here is of something that in our own experience may have been no more than wraithlike; but the tale fixes it for us with Lawrence's gift of vividness, and our recognition can grow. It is a point of development in our moral consciousness. This sort of experience, and the reflection or widening apprehension of life that follows on it, attend any literature that really speaks to us. We feel our humanity has been enlarged. Humanism, the study of what it is to be human through literature, is a persistent reflection upon such experiences.

Of course, we need not accept the likenesses which literature offers. These may seem false, meagre or half-true, and a rejection or qualification may express a recognition as finely as an endorsement.

> The emotion of Othello in Act V is the emotion of a man who discovers that the worst part of his own soul has been exploited by someone more clever than he; it is this emotion carried by the writer to a very high degree of intensity ... What may be considered corrupt or decadent in the morals of Massinger is not an alteration or diminution in morals; it is simply the

disappearance of all personal and real emotions which this morality supported and into which it introduced a kind of order. As soon as the
emotions disappear the morality which ordered it appears hideous.
Puritanism itself became repulsive only when it appeared as the survival
of a restraint after the feelings which it restrained had gone. When
Massinger's ladies resist temptation they do not appear to undergo any
important emotion; they merely know what is expected of them; they
manifest themselves to us as lubricious prudes. Any age has its conventions; and any age might appear absurd when its conventions get into the
hands of a man like Massinger – a man, we mean, of so exceptionally
superior a literary talent as Massinger's, and so paltry an imagination.[2]
Here, T. S. Eliot's cutting-away of Massinger expresses as sharp a sense of
human likeness as any of his appreciations of other writers.

Though Eliot seems to me to have been a great critic until about 1922, I should
not wish to call him a humanist. His insights were won against the sub-Arnoldian
humanism current when he was young, not to mention the neohumanism of
Babbitt and More. His judgements were subversive, and he avoided respectable
ways of talking about the function of literature. Humanism, however reticent,
however implicit in its formulations, tries to appropriate literature for human
culture; it has a way of institutionalising. Faced with insights as subversive as
Eliot's, an intelligent humanism will attempt to take them over for its own
humanising discourse and in the process remake itself. F. R. Leavis's early
critical work is just such an attempt, and even those least in sympathy with his
criticism will acknowledge how his appropriation of Eliot revitalised the study
of literature.

Leavis's criticism is probably the most impressive twentieth-century
example of what I mean by 'humanism', though I could, for all its crankiness,
also point to the criticism of Yvor Winters. In spite of their differences,
literature is, for both these critics, a means of becoming human. But Leavis is
more to my purpose, for his humanism attempted to lay hold of Eliot and
Lawrence, writers whose work was profoundly subversive when it appeared.
And in making them his modern classics, he was drawn to criticise and remake
what passed for the literary tradition at the universities. No critic was more
conscious of how a literary tradition might betray or falsify the consciousness of
what it is supposed to transmit. His criticism is the best example that I know of
how humanism tries to renew itself by distinguishing between its lethal and its
life-giving strains.

For Leavis, following Eliot, *Paradise Lost* was the classic of the lethal tradition. The issue arose over Milton's verse, and Eliot indeed made a connection
between Milton's verse and Massinger's. Both critics, however, seem curiously
imperceptive about the vigour and inventiveness of Milton's language, and they

can have few followers now. At any rate, I do not mean to take the matter up; my purpose has been to point to the critical movement inside humanism. In the process of bringing literature inside the cooperative task of human culture, humanism also has a way of substituting what we are supposed to be like for what we are really like. It is here that the critical and self-critical impulse of humanism comes in. It is here, too, that the subversive or anomalous work may afford the insights by which humanism revises or renews itself.

For the humanist, the study of literature is a means of realising a more complete humanity than merely one's own. Other sorts of literary study aim at a more absolute point of view, an Archimedean point where the students may prise themselves loose from their humanity and the humanity which they may discover in the work. Sociological and deconstructionist critics alike deplete the literary work of intelligence about experience. They themselves supply the intelligence; the work is the object on which it is demonstrated. Although sociology has a rich tradition of reflection upon how it is itself implicated in social organisation – in Habermas, for example – with sociological literary criticism the issue of self-reference, the point that it is a human rather than an adept who is studying other humans is rarely taken to heart. It is rarely thought necessary that the sociologist's account of literary production should extend to his own production. With deconstructionist criticism, self-reference is all too well understood, and the self-undermining of the critic goes with the general dismantling of the subject. Both these kinds of criticism tend towards reductive accounts of the work. Reductive accounts are often salutary: they may tell us things that humanist criticism, concerned with the humanity of the work and keyed to some possible integration of human consciousness, finds it hard to take in. It would be a dull reader who gleaned nothing from such criticism; but, whatever it has to offer, it is not humanist criticism.

The chief consideration for the humanist study of literature is the work as a criticism of life, a life that the student shares in and is obliged to gather to mind. Such criticism, it may be said, can never be objective. Certainly, if by objectivity we mean the sort of judgement that can be made by dissociating ourselves from our humanity, the charge will hold. The judgements, the attempts to see what things are really like, that humanist criticism can make are indeed provisional, being limited, for example, in the experience on which they are based. However, this need not imply complete subjective or historical relativism. Experience is only to be had by individuals in time; but a literary work that is a criticism of life is an enlarging and generalising of experience. Because the work shows a likeness of things, it invites comparison with the reader's own sense of what things are like. This provides an opportunity for detachment from mere time-bound subjectivity, an opportunity for the education of experience. Such criticism will be provisional and probably fumbling; yet, in the work of the great humanist critics (notably Johnson and Arnold in addition to Leavis), amid so much that is impermanent or half-true, there occur enduring insights and problems. One keeps returning to these critics to get one's bearings. It might be thought, perhaps, that Johnson's critical judgements are timebound, of interest only to the historian of taste. Yet his judgement of *Paradise Lost*, far from being the echo of the prevailing Miltonolatry, aroused indignation when it was published. What Johnson did was to take the established reading of the poem and ask how it measured up as a criticism of life. Here his judgement was adverse: *Paradise Lost* was too sublime to have much bearing on human experience. While this judgement is in my opinion mistaken, it remains valuable. The quality of his affirmation of the humanist concern with the criticism of life cannot be passed by; and his judgement is fair that *Paradise Lost*, read more or less as Addison had read it, is wanting. Johnson's judgement, then, is of its time in its acceptance of what Addison had seen, but it goes beyond Addison's by no means negligible understanding to a greater clarity about what had been seen. There, Johnson poses the central problem for the humanist criticism of *Paradise Lost*: how can a poem that is so taken up with imagining things outside experience reflect on the concerns of experience? Johnson's achievement here is an example of what humanist criticism may aim for: the winning of a partial clarity about the reflection of a literary work on life.

So much, then, for a general characterisation of humanism. Neoclassical humanism – the humanism of the Renaissance and the seventeenth and eighteenth centuries – thought of literature in ways different from ours, as will be explained. The broad characterisation of humanism offered here, however, holds for its essential concerns, indeed for the essential concerns of humanism in any age.

Paradise Lost poses a problem for humanist criticism. To formulate it rather differently from Johnson: *Paradise Lost* is religious in such a way that one asks whether its religious concerns exclude, or at least damage, a concern with the study of humanity. Like *Paradise Regained* and *Samson Agonistes*, *Paradise Lost* turns rather on obedience to God than on an issue of ordinary morality.

I doubt whether Milton would have found it paradoxical to distinguish between morality and the will of God. At any rate, while presumably he held that obedience to the will of God included ordinary morality, he chose to treat extraordinary cases of obedience to the will of God not included in ordinary morality. The Christ of *Paradise Regained* may exemplify temperance, and other virtues besides, but these are incidental to His singular calling from God to recover Paradise. He has to distinguish in His temptations, not between general good and evil, but between what is of God and what is not, in terms of His divine mission. The crux comes when He rejects with asperity the learning of Athens, the basis of humanistic culture. As for Samson, he may exemplify a development of the spirit from despair to a regained confidence in his own worth, but Milton presents that development not as a general human experience but as a special waiting on a divine summons and a rejection of all those motions which are not that. When the summons comes, it is to the performance of an act hard to square with ordinary morality. In *Paradise Lost*, too the issue is a divine command. The eating of the apple may feature a range of failings, as Milton himself argues in the *Christian Doctrine*[3]; yet it is from the transgression of God's prohibition that the general failing follows in terms both of the epic's moral logic and of the plot's narrative unfolding. *Paradise Lost* seems to be concerned with divine rather than human morality, and there are points where the divine morality seems not merely arbitrary but even at odds with a morally developed human nature. In *Paradise Lost*, there is the additional difficulty that the creation and the innocence of humanity are not matters of experience, but belong to a revealed or mythical narrative that represents a state of affairs we can imagine but not know.

The difficulty raised here is certainly not new. The problem of how the religious scheme of the poem bears on human concerns has, in one form or another, occupied most serious criticism of *Paradise Lost*. A brief historical sketch of how the problem has been met may be found in the Appendix. The writers treated there fall into two classes: critics whose humanist concerns prompt them to translate, negotiate or reject Milton's theological scheme, and literary historians who describe Milton's Christianity and his humanism within what they take to be his intellectual context. My aim is to combine these two approaches, at once placing *Paradise Lost* historically in terms of neoclassical humanism and discussing the poem in terms of the sort of humanism that thinks of literature as the criticism of life.

Ideally, history should amend criticism and vice versa. At one extreme, a criticism without history would be out of touch with the terms in which the poem was conceived; at the other, a history without criticism would be out of touch with those present concerns that are our only entry into interpreting the past. How the two might work together is best explained by an example. In his *Poetry and Humanism in Early Tudor England*, H. A. Mason takes it that his humanism and the humanism of Erasmus and More have at bottom the same concern to realise 'a central, a truly human' culture.[4] Since he shares the concern, he is trained to enter into what they achieved and to pick out what is significant in it and directed to those ends of humanism that emerge in historical perspective with a certain permanence. At the same time, he is in a position to point out where the humanism of Erasmus and More wins through to a finer conviviality or a more lively and intelligent appropriation of classical culture than could be found in the conventional humanism of their time. Here, for him, is the impulse of genuine humanism, at once critical and creative, to refashion itself according to more searching and generous ideas of human life. And then, informed as he is, not only by the best that Erasmus and More achieved, but also by the achievment of the four and a half centuries of humanism that have succeded, he is able to bring out where they fell short of their best, where their humanism is defective or mechanical. Mason's book shows what can be done in the way of a critical – historical account of humanism. I have cited it only to illustrate the general approach I shall follow; I admire it too much to think I have imitated it in my actual critical practise.

The critical – historical approach has no magical solutions to the humanist difficulty with Milton's religious scheme. 'Christian humanism', for instance, might seem to offer a tidy way of dealing with the problem, a synthesis of Christian and humanist concerns, which Milton and his predecessors were able to enjoy. But it will not work. As intellectual history, it smoothes over the differences between Milton's sort of Christianity and the cultural concerns of neoclassical humanism. As criticism, it evades the question of whether Milton's religious scheme can represent human life for us. In the end, I do not think that the religious framework of *Paradise Lost* can be entirely digested into humanist concerns. The surprising discovery, however, is that Milton's religious frame-work contains a moral psychology of the will that perhaps speaks more directly to our own humanism than the concerns of neoclassical humanism. That, at any rate, is the view which this book sets out to unfold at once critically and historically. Less summarily, what it has to say is as follows.

In the first place, *Paradise Lost* belongs to neoclassical humanism, not just by conforming to orthodox views about the function of literature, but also by sharing in its critical development, in which the scope and object of humanist study were defined sharply against those concerns that distracted from them. Not only Milton's treatment of forbidden knowledge but also the whole mag-nificent sweep and focusing of his imagination on 'this punctual spot' are ways of feeling for what is human and distinguishing it from those notions that hide or alienate ourselves from ourselves. 'The discovery of the world and of man', Burckhardt's expansive phrase for one impulse of the Italian Renaissance, still applies in the later phases of neoclassical humanism. In *Paradise Lost* and the moment of humanism to which it belongs, the discovery is of those limits within which we are human. It is characteristic of all neoclassical humanism that it should suggest a sense of possible sublimity in human nature. It is characteristic of the critical development in which *Paradise Lost* has a place that the human powers that are celebrated consist in an incisive attention to our humanity. In *Paradise Lost*, free will is the power that the epic celebrates. The fate of the world depends on how it is exercised. It is the faculty that makes humans godlike. Yet, as Milton sets it up, its true exercise is to choose what really concerns our human nature. The task of Adam and Eve is to stand in the nature in which they have been created, and not to exceed it, far less to fall below it.

The standing is precarious; it can be kept or lost by the reason that 'also is choice', and the critical act of such free will is to discriminate between those courses that fall beyond and away from our humanity and those that maintain it.

In its concern to distinguish what is truly human from what is not, *Paradise Lost* belongs to the humanism of its time and to the critical movement within that humanism. Its sense of the precariousness of human nature, the epic importance which it gives to the attention of mind by which the human measure is kept – these things look forward to the Augustans. Yet the central interest of *Paradise Lost* is something that neoclassical humanism never satisfactorily took in, namely, those motions of the will – error, guilt, repentance – that Christianity made its particular study and that evangelical Protestantism took hold of with peculiar intensity. These are what the human action of *Paradise Lost* consists of, and on them the rest of the poem opens up a universal perspective. It is there, above all, that Milton has a grasp of what it is to be human. No Renaissance humanist commentary that I know of manages more than a conventional interpretation of the Christian study of the motions of the will. What humanists such as Erasmus have to say is usually sensible, even inspiriting, but not very close to the subject. In this matter, they are generally content to speak of what we are supposed to be like, not what we are really like. By far the most penetrating neoclassical humanist account of the motions of the will is Montaigne's 'Du Repentir'. However, while this remarkable essay has memorably shrewd things to say about false repentance, it makes a mystery of true repentance: 'il faut que Dieu nous touche le courage'.[5] At the point where a humanist interpretation of the motions of the will might begin, Montaigne relinquishes the matter to the special language and operations of Christianity. In this, as in other things, he showed the course neoclassical humanism would take as it defined its interests more sharply. The Christian study of the will was left to the sphere of religious devotion separate from humanist culture.

Far from giving grand expression to what was generally believed, to a 'Christian humanism' in which Christian and humanist concerns are supposed to be at one, Milton effected a bold and original appropriation of religious concerns for humanist treatment. The focus of his epic upon the Fall, the continuing process of evil in guilt and the return of the will upon itself in repentance, owes more to Protestant ideas about the freedom and bondage of the will than to humanist discussion, let alone humanist epic. In the eighteenth century, *Paradise Lost* was rated very highly, but Milton's achievement in representing the motions of the will was not what was admired. That lay outside the humanism of Milton's time and was not taken up in the succeeding age.

This book initially characterises neoclassical humanism by discussing two general topics. Chapter 1, on volition, distinguishes the Protestant and the humanist interests in the matter, while Chapter 2 examines the humanist concern with human creatureliness as a sort of myth picture inside which a truly human point of view might emerge. The last two chapters turn to how these topics bear on *Paradise Lost*, but in the reverse order. So, Chapter 3 compares *Paradise Lost* with *Jerusalem Delivered* and *Absolom and Achitophel* to show how the universal design of Milton's epic focuses on what makes us human. Chapter 4 then discusses how that focus brings out a study of the will that marks *Paradise Lost* out among neoclassical humanist poems.

Notes

1 David Daiches, *Milton* (London, 1957), pp. 8–9, 151, 227.
2 T. S. Eliot, 'Philip Massinger', *Selected Essays, 1917–1932* (London, 1932), pp. 213–4.
3 *Christian Doctrine*, 1, 11, CP, 6, 383–4.
4 H. A. Mason, *Humanism and Poetry in the Early Tudor Period* (London, 1959).
5 *Montaigne, Œuvres Complètes*, ed. Albert Thibaudet and Maurice Rat (Paris, 1962), p. 795.

Chapter 1

The Study of the Will

The Protestant Reformation differed from neoclassical humanism on the study of the will, but, as I shall argue, *Paradise Lost* crosses the line between the two. 'Neoclassical humanism' is a broad term referring to a type of literary culture extending from the Renaissance to the late eighteenth century. 'The Protestant Reformation' is equally capacious; what it refers to took many shapes from the start, and, by the time of *Paradise Lost*, had been complicated and altered by a century and a half of sectarian and scholastic controversy. For some purposes, the fine print of these complications and alterations is important. Just where Milton stood among the Arminianising Independents, for instance, can be made to tell us a lot about the theology of free will in *Paradise Lost*. The purpose here, however, is to inquire into what lay between the Reformation and humanism in the matter of volition, and so a broader strategy is needed. This inquiry, itself a humanist undertaking, has to resist the vermiculate questions into which Protestant scholasticism and sectarianism crumbled their matter. It begins by returning to the sources, to the exchange between Erasmus and Luther over free will, for it is there that the division between the Reformation and neoclassical humanism emerges clearly and with a surprising finality; the various adjustments of religious conviction and of literary culture that followed did not overcome it, unless in some way *Paradise Lost* does so.

Renaissance humanists made much of volition. Rhetoric was their basic discipline, and on their belief that it might change the world by shaping the wills of its hearers they founded their ambitious claims for literary culture as a humanising and civilising institution. Eloquence, their ideal of discourse, addressed itself not just to reason but to the whole human being – appetitive, striving, volitional, as well as rational.[1] Even humanist recommendations of a contemplative life as against an active one discussed the matter as a choice of life, a course to be embraced, a matter in which the will as much as the mind was engaged.[2] The will, then, is a characteristic concern of the humanists, whether they write as philosophers or theologians or, more strictly in character, as orators, poets and men of letters.

Yet if we turn to those motions of the will that Christianity, especially evangelical Protestantism, made peculiarly its own, to sin, guilt and deliverance, it is striking how conventional the humanist interpretations of these matters are.

In the clash between Luther and Erasmus on free will, it is in fact the theologian who has the insights about how people work, while the humanist is unable to escape theological commonplaces. Their debate brings out how matters lie between neoclassical humanism and Christianity. For though Erasmus's *Diatribe on Free Will* is an essay in theology, its shortcomings as well as its virtues are characteristic of the way neoclassical humanists talked about the will; and though Luther does not speak for all Protestants, let alone all Christians, he shows a knowledge of the motions of the will generally closed to neoclassical humanists. He cast his insights into paradoxical and repellent doctrinal forms, and it was with this that Erasmus took issue. Certainly, nothing seems more inaccessible, more locked up in the special language of theology, than Luther's doctrine of the bondage of the will, a doctrine given more exact and terrible formulation by Calvin. The insights are present in the crannies of Luther's exposition, in the escapes of thought which his eruptive style allows, in these and in the connections of thought we can draw between *The Bondage of the Will* and *The Freedom of a Christian*. But they exist, and they lay hold of the Pauline account of the motions of the will, which neoclassical humanism did not thoroughly take in, or sheered away from.

I have no theological axe to grind, but write as a humanist inquiring even of theological literature what it has to report about human experience. From that point of view, Luther seems to stand out among the Protestant writers. Among Milton's contemporaries who treated the freedom and bondage of the will, Leighton, Sterry, Bramhall and Taylor wrote with distinction, but none disclosed the human issues as Luther did at the outset of the Reformation.

Erasmus had long been pressed to come out against Luther. When finally he did so in his *Diatribe on Free Will*, he criticised Luther's views on the will – the crux, as Luther himself said, of his quarrel with Rome. However, while Erasmus was writing as a theologian who submitted his ideas to the old church, he was at the same time expressing his commitment to a humanist culture that Luther's views seemed to annihilate.

To see why he should have dismayed Erasmus, we need only run through the views which Luther expressed in *The Bondage of the Will*, his answer to Erasmus's criticisms and both a recapitulation and a development of the doctrines which Erasmus had attacked. Free choice counts for nothing in matters of salvation or of the spirit. Morally or civically, one may indeed act virtuously.[3] But this has nothing to do with acquiring merit in the eyes of God; as far as God is concerned, one can do nothing out of oneself. What free choice achieves by its own endeavours, even if it achieves 'the sanctity of angels' (p. 307), is worthless. To rely on it is sin; it is only faith that saves. By faith, Luther means entire trust that God will save one, that His promise of salvation is meant for oneself. The faith that saves is the faith that one has been saved. Why some are saved and others damned is a mystery. It is certainly not on account of their virtues or vices. Luther is emphatic about that, putting forward the paradox of the justified sinner, *simul justus et peccator*.[4]

Morally, the implications of Luther's dogmatic position are distressing, and he drew them out recklessly. To convey the impotence of the will, he had recourse to the notorious image of the beast of burden.

> If God rides it, it wills and goes where God wills ... If Satan rides it, it wills and goes where Satan wills; nor can it choose to run to either of the two riders or to seek him out, but the riders themselves contend for the possession and control of it. (p. 140)

Equally disheartening is his treatment of how we should understand God's commands. As Erasmus pointed out (p. 87), a command supposes the power to carry it out, and so the many commands in Scripture imply that the believer is free to obey or not. Luther replies with a logical quibble that 'ought' need not imply 'can', and with the illustration that we could command a man with his arms tied to stretch out his hand in order to taunt him with his powerlessness. That, says Luther, is how God's commands work. He commands not so that we should obey freely but that we should despair of our powers to obey (pp. 192–3). Quite apart from the repulsive picture that Luther draws of God the taunter, Luther raises awkward questions about God's justice. 'It is difficult', Erasmus remarks in his mild way, 'to explain how it can be a mark of [God's] justice (for I will not speak of His mercy) to hand over [those] to eternal torments in whom He has not deigned to work good works since they have no free choice, or if they have, it can do nothing but sin'.[5] Luther's reply to this 'difficulty' is to embrace it as a paradox and the supreme test of faith:

> When God makes alive He does it by killing, when He justifies, He does it by making men guilty, when He exalts to heaven, He does it by bringing men down to hell ... This is the highest degree of faith, to believe God righteous when by His own will He makes us necessarily damnable. (p. 138)

Luther comes over here as something of a moral desperado.

Luther's doctrines not only offended Erasmus's good sense and his belief in God's justice; they also struck against his idea of Christian culture. Erasmus attempted to combine humanist and Christian ideals in what he called 'the philosophy of Christ'. By that he meant, in the first place, heartfelt piety issuing in a good life. For him, Christian faith made better human beings. While the otherworldly ends of Christianity were clearly present to him, Erasmus wrote with most edge about Christianity as an institution that civilised and humanised. In that that cultural task of humanising and civilising, *bonae litterae* had a key part to play, supplementing the Bible itself with patterns of human goodness and religious idealism.[6] Luther's doctrine of the bondage of the will is profoundly subversive of this Erasmian attempt to reconcile cultural and religious ends. It makes human effort and human goodness vain as far as a Christian life is concerned. Luther, in fact, saw the relation between the human order and the divine as war: 'It is the unvarying fate of the Word of God to have the world in a state of tumult because of it ... For the Word of God comes, whenever it comes, to change and renew the world' (*Bondage*, p. 129). As Luther exalts the power of the word of God to renew the believer and the world, he disparages the power of the merely human words of Erasmus's *bonae litterae*, classical literature and his own writing inspired by it. 'You reek', Luther tells him, 'of nothing but Lucian, and you breathe out on me the vast drunken folly of Epicurus' (p. 113). This is admittedly pointed at Erasmus's scepticism about whether there can be certainty in matters such as free will and his belief that theological disputes by their very nature contradict the spirit of Christian teaching, not to mention the humanist values of amenity and decorum. However, the general drift of Luther's remarks about Erasmus's humanist learning and skill in *The Bondage of the Will* is patronising and contemptuous, though, amusingly, he ornaments his treatise with far more classical allusions than Erasmus does. In his practice as a reformer, Luther may have allowed humanist studies a place in civic life, but, as a religious teacher, his doctrines of the bondage of the will and the sole efficacy of the word of God where faith was concerned enforce a distinction between civic ends and religious ends and have a way of confounding the effort of humanist culture.

The rebarbative and unreasonable tone of Luther's doctrines and their hostility to humanist culture are secondary matters, however. The dispute is about the will. Here, Erasmus has little of interest to say: stalemate is good enough for him. Nothing, he feels, can be asserted with any certainty one way or another. It is the sort of topic over which those whom he calls 'Sophists', meaning the schoolmen, dispute. The whole rhetorical drive of his humanism and his piety is to take religious thought out of the realm of professional theological debate and apply it to Christian living. Hence his impatience with a subject that he feels has no bearing on how to live. What can be said for Erasmus's performance is that it has the freedom and balance of the man of culture. There is something admirable in his superficiality. He could see what was under his nose, the damaging implications of the bondage of the will for the justice of God. His good sense could not relinquish at least a modicum of free will: his formula was that the will is free to cooperate with grace or not (*Free Will*, pp. 81–5). Unfortunately, he lacked the theological exactness and finesse required to set out his position satisfactorily, and Luther found it easy to make his ideas look incoherent.[7]

At bottom, Erasmus conceives the will in terms of rhetoric. Free will is for him a matter of temperance or self-control, the power our rational or spiritual self has over our lower, appetitive self. He divides the human being in the *Enchiridion* into three parts: the spirit, which may make us divine, the flesh, which is appetitive and earthly; and in between. the feeling human soul, which is mutable and may turn to either.[8] In line with this, he allegorises the Paradise story as a parable of the fall of this tripartite creature. Adam represents the mutable soul, and the Fall is his inclination to Eve, the flesh.[9] The mutable soul has to be nudged, prompted and encouraged away from the flesh toward the spirit. Accordingly, it is the rhetorical task of the *Enchiridion* to persuade the soul to incline to the spirit. In this connection, Erasmus uses the old figure of the warfare of the spirit against the vices of the flesh to give a heroic and inspiriting image to the quarrel of a higher, rational part of ourselves with a lower, sensual one. In the *Diatribe on Free Will*, Erasmus divides the self in the same way. Our lower nature is the flesh; our higher, rational nature is the spirit; and somehow in between is an unstable part, which may incline to either.[10] Pictured like that, humans are open to the promptings of rhetoric, above all of the divine rhetoric of Christianity that would confirm the soul in its upward motions toward the spirit and God.[11]

A good system of life that involves other people would impose self-control, the sort of freedom Erasmus has in mind. However, Erasmus's thought makes this freedom oppressive. He may sound more liberal in his *Diatribe on Free Will* than Luther in his *Bondage of the Will*; but in the *Enchiridion*, where his ideas have more scope, the war of the higher self upon the lower self locks the freedom of the will up in self-division. It is hard to pin down so fluctuating and diverse a creature as Erasmus, but his platonising idea of free will does not apear to escape from a self-enclosed, monastic ideal of freedom into a world where freedom is to be exercised among other people.

Luther takes up the freedom of the will in a more interesting way. Erasmus's tripartite human being suited the rhetorical cast of his humanism. Rhetoric has a design upon us: it works on us by urging a higher self upon us or by presenting images to us of what we are supposed to be like. It tries to improve us according to the desires of the mind, to stamp a good character or shape an inner statue in us. Luther goes below that to a less conventional and in some respects truer account of what we are like. His ideas are not shaped by rhetoric; the word of God, for him, is not a kind of divine eloquence. In *The Freedom of a Christian*, he imagined it as Christ Himself. The soul clings to the word and is touched by it and healed. Perhaps thinking of the wine that is Christ's blood, Luther adds that the soul is intoxicated by it.[12] In *The Bondage of the Will*, he imagined it as a prophetic and revolutionary force bringing the human order under judgement. In either case, he deals with a biblical rather than a classical idea of the active power of the word. If Erasmus, according to the rhetorical ideas of Renaissance humanism, writes as an orator, then Luther writes perhaps as a prophet but certainly as a man who, despairing of himself, has undertaken a spiritual journey passing through a place of transformation in order to arrive at where he really was all the time, but now can be so freely and at one with himself. This is at least one explanation of his violent, eruptive and paradoxical style, the style of a man who has come through. It is also a style in some ways shaped by the Bible, especially by Paul, whose Epistle to the Romans, the classical utterance of the man who has come through, Luther judged the chief part of the New Testament.[13]

What Luther came through to was an idea of freedom, not as Erasmian free will, that is the freedom of self-control or free obedience, but as the freedom of spontaneity, freedom from constraint. For him, the freedom of a Christian consisted in being impelled by the love of God:

> Neither the divine nor the human will does what it does, whether good or evil under any compulsion, but from sheer pleasure or desire, as with true freedom; and yet the will of God is immutable and infallible and it governs our mutable will, as Boethius sings, 'Remaining fixed, Thou makest all things move'. (*Bondage*, p. 120)

From this point of view, the freedom of a Christian is one aspect of the bondage of the will. Clearly, a divine impulse might set the believer free from social and political constraints. Luther, however, tried to contain the revolutionary impulse of his own doctrines in a fairly conservative ecclesiastical reformation, though it escaped and took over in the radical reformation. For him, the overthrowing of the human order was to be above all an inward and spiritual one. The constraints from which the divine impulse freed one were above all the constraints of self-division. It is here that his criticism of Erasmian free will, the freedom of self-control, has its cutting edge.

In an ambivalent way, Luther allowed that one had Erasmian free will or power over oneself (*Bondage*, p. 143), but he did not think that that freedom mattered. We might do what we were commanded to do or what we told ourselves to do; but 'in relation to God or matters of salvation or damnation a man has no free choice, but is captive, subject and slave either of the will of God or the will of Satan' (p. 143). We have no freedom there, because in the religious sphere what counts is the spirit. Outward compliance and inward grudging are not freedom, and those are all that Luther thought we are capable of from ourselves. We cannot will to act spontaneously and without constraint. The more we try, the more we tie ourselves in knots. We do the right thing for the wrong reason, out of fear or out of a desire to acquire a good character. In this sense, our good works are hypocrisy, and in this way the word of God expressed as commands, so far from prompting us to goodness as a divine rhetoric might, simply arouses crooked desires. It was here that Luther talked of the incurved nature of the self, which, even in its highest efforts, even in its worship of God, would seek itself.[14] His 'incurved man' is an image not just of self-enclosure but also of self-division, of being bent against oneself as well as on oneself. And so where the relation with God is concerned, Erasmus's free will, with its division of flesh and spirit, turns out to be, in Luther's terms, the incurved man, the man closed in on himself, unable in making war on himself to act freely and without constraint. He dismissed Erasmus's platonising interpretation of flesh and spirit. The biblical distinction, as he pointed out, is not between a higher and a lower self at war with each other but between two states of the entire human being. The flesh is the entire self divided against itself and at war with God; the spirit is the entire self at one with itself and impelled by the love of God (*Bondage*, pp. 270–7). For the same reason, he rejected platonising allegories (like Erasmus's) of the Fall.[15] He considered Eve as complete a human being as Adam.[16] Where Luther makes a parable of the garden state in the *Freedom of a Christian*, it is to illustrate the freedom from constraint of the believer restored by faith to paradise (p. 360). Like Adam's work, the believer's good acts are not something forced on a lower self to acquire spiritual merit, but are something done ungrudgingly from the gratitude of the whole being.

An ideal system of life would feature not just the freedom of self–control but also freedom from constraint. We need to be not just responsible for our actions but also not in our responsibility alienated from ourselves. This goes some way to explain why Christian liberty, that protean term to which Luther gave such forceful definition, haunted Protestant Europe as an ideal and was still working itself out in Milton's England. It also helps to explain the force of Luther's criticism of Erasmus's ideal of freedom. Certainly, Luther delighted in extreme formulations and in a Pauline crushing of human pretensions; but as far as the crookedness of the will is concerned and how it may be used in a false, self–defeating way, his insights are human, not just theological. His ideal of freedom from constraint has told us something about how we really work, not just about how we are supposed to work.

Nevertheless, Luther understood the crooked will as a religious problem. It was only in relation to God and to justification in the eyes of God that he considered freedom with absolute seriousness as a condition for right action. For him, it required a religious transformation for us to act freely:

> If God works on us, the will is changed, and being gently breathed upon by the Spirit of God, it again wills and acts from pure willingness and inclination and of its own accord, not from compulsion, so that it cannot be turned another way by any opposition, nor be overcome or compelled even by the gates of hell, but it goes on willing and delighting and loving the good, just as before it willed and delighted in and loved evil. (*Bondage*, p. 140)

I have tried to translate Luther's ideas of freedom and bondage out of his own religious language into talk of freedom from constraint. However when it comes to the actual Pauline transformation from the old man to the new about which Luther writes so turbulently and movingly in his *Freedom of a Christian*, translation has to become a much more tentative affair. No ordinary language of moral psychology can do justice to the power of his religious language. Erasmus as a Renaissance humanist was unable to lay hold of the Pauline transformation from flesh to spirit, and, with hindsight, we may connect that with the limitation of his rhetorical ideas of human culture. The late twentieth-century humanist is not in a much better position, but he may, without knowing exactly what it is that would render the enterprise vain, be prudent enough to realise that he cannot entirely squeeze the sense out of Luther's religious transformation. There are various secular analogues. Carlyle's conversion from the everlasting No to the everlasting Yes in *Sartor Resartus* and the Sartrean embracing of nothingness come to mind, but those conversions are as locked up in their special languages as Luther's. It may simply be that transformations from old to new can only work symbolically. If that is so, the humanist attempt to unfold, generalise, decontaminate and make over to human culture would disperse their power. They would take place only while their language remained in some sense sacred. Whatever the case, I find myself capable of only a limited interpretation of the transformation from bound to free in Luther.

At this point, it will be helpful to narrow the terms of discussion and talk of guilt and forgiveness instead of, as before, self-division and wholeness. This has an obvious bearing on the subject matter of *Paradise Lost* and perhaps approaches Luther more closely.

Guilt is the discovery that one has fallen foul of the law and that freedom with respect to the law has returned upon one in blame. Guilt means the impotence of the will to free itself from consciousness of wrong. The will is curved in upon itself in an infinite regress into unfreedom such as Milton's Satan and Adam suffer.

> St Paul speaks of existence 'shut up under guard of the law'. The guilty conscience is shut in first of all because it is an isolated conscience that breaks the communion of sinners. It 'separates' itself in the very act by which it takes upon itself, and upon itself alone, the whole weight of evil. The guilty conscience is shut in even more secretly by an obscure acquiescence in its evil, by which it makes itself its own tormentor. It is in this sense that the guilty conscience is a slave and not only consciousness of enslavement; it is the conscience without 'promise'.[17]

At this point good sense will break in with objections. The preoccupation with sin or guilt is a sterile preoccupation and an exaggerated self-preoccupation. This objection is of course just, but unhelpful. It is exactly the impotence of guilt that its efforts are sterile and that it is a state of self-torment. The consciousness of being preoccupied with a self whose efforts are sterile is part of the torment of guilt. The world of guilt is unreal, but it is a miserable thing to fall into the unreal and know it.

What brings about the transition from the crooked will to the free will is an act of forgiveness. This is the act of grace that the unfree will is unable to do by itself, and is the means of deliverance that can only be grasped by faith. One cannot forgive oneself; someone else has to do that, and this may explain why one cannot repent out of oneself. Repentance, the return of the will upon itself, is not complete unless it is met by the forgiving of the other.[18] It is the other's forgiving that cuts through the entanglement of the crooked will in its past to make a new beginning possible. And for the other, 'forgiving is the only reaction which does not merely react but acts anew and unexpectedly unconditioned by the act which provoked it and therefore freeing from its consequences both the one who forgives and the one who is forgiven'.[19]

There is something anomalous in forgiving. It contradicts the strict moral logic of freedom, responsibility and guilt, or of fault and retribution.[20] It not only sets the guilty party free but also takes the offence to itself and so discharges it. That roughly is how the transaction of forgiving works on a human level. Luther, like Paul, is concerned with a religious transaction. But the outlines of human forgiving can be discerned there, and, perhaps most important for the self-enclosure of guilt, the operation is a transaction involving another person, even if it takes place in the inner world of faith and the other person is God.

The religious account brings out the anomaly of forgiveness in the most disturbing way. God's mercy is imagined as contradicting his anger and the contradiction is resolved in the sacrifice of Christ. How the sacrifice is supposed to work is not clear to me. It is a divine act or miracle, but it does not work like magic without some answering motion of those for whom it is done. According to Paul, the sacrifice is 'effective through faith' (Romans 3, 25, *NEB*). Luther follows him, holding that faith consists partly in the recognition of guilt and the impotence of the will to free itself out of itself.[21] This first motion of repentance is what he is chiefly concerned with in *The Bondage of the Will*. For the transaction to be complete, however, repentance must meet forgiveness, and, as to how faith lays hold of forgiveness through the sacrifice of Christ the best account is in *The Freedom of a Christian*:

> The third incomparable benefit of faith is that it unites the soul with Christ as a bride is united with her bridegroom. By this mystery, as the Apostle teaches, Christ and the soul become one flesh [Eph. 5:31–2]. And if they are one flesh, ... and there is between them a true marriage ... it follows that everything they have they hold in common, the good as well as the evil. Accordingly the believing soul can boast of and glory in whatever Christ has as though it were its own, and whatever the soul has Christ claims as his own. Let us compare these and we shall see the inestimable benefits. Christ is full of grace, life, and salvation. The soul is full of sins, death, and damnation. Now let faith come between them and sins, death, and damnation will be Christ's, while grace, life, and salvation will be the soul's; for if Christ is a bridegroom, he must take upon himself the things that are his bride's and bestow upon her the things that are his. If he gives

her his body and very self, how shall he not give her all that is his? And if he takes the body of the bride, how shall he not take all that is hers? *(Freedom of a Christian,* p. 351)

This passage probably comes as close as possible to explicating the Christian idea of sacrificial atonement in a way that suggests the transaction of forgiving. For the sacrifice, instead of being put in the morally puzzling terms of vicarious expiation and mediation, is put as a marriage or mutual exchange of persons. Christ's death means His giving up his guiltless self to accept the guilty self of the believer; the believer's dying to his dead or guilty self, his dying with Christ, means his giving up his guilty self to accept the guiltless and therefore free self of Christ. With this exchange, the offence or injury vanishes. The guilt has been taken away from the guilty self and the injury has been cancelled when it is accepted by the injured or guiltless person. In this way, the transaction between persons in the marriage figure can be read as what happens in repentance and forgiving.

As for the freedom of action gained through forgiving, Luther thinks of it as a freedom directed to doing right. Although freedom of action was regained by a kind of evasion of the logic of the law, the freed will is free in order to do what the law commands, not bound by the law and so grudgingly, but filled with gratitude and therefore spontaneously and lovingly. Strikingly, Luther speaks of this freedom expressing itself actively outwards in the world as a giving of oneself as a Christ to one's neighbour, and so repeating by oneself the unconstrained divine goodness that had set one free.[22] At this point, for Luther, Christian liberty becomes Christian love.

The rift between neoclassical humanism and evangelical Protestantsim epitomised here in the representative contending figures of Erasmus and Luther is more a difference than a true conflict. Though they disagree about biblical teaching, Erasmus and Luther are really talking about different things. Erasmus's ideas, in accordance with the rhetorically-based neoclassical humanism, picture the will as self-control, temperance, the rule of a higher self over a lower self. He thinks of Christian philosophy and good literature as prompting the higher self in the right direction and helping to confirm it in virtue. The rhetorical frame of his ideas assumes that the will is free to attend or not to attend to the call to a life directed towards God, and that the will has some power in itself to act on the call. Luther's idea of the word of God, whether read or preached, confounds rhetoric and its moral and civilising designs. Its effect on its hearers is consternation. It finds them out on a far deeper level than the words of even the most divinely-inspired rhetoric, and makes demands for wholeheartedness and purity of intention that cannot be answered by efforts of self- control. The demands of the word of God can only be met by a transformation from self-division to freedom from constraint that may be at least partially understood as a transaction of forgiveness and repentance. Neoclassical humanism never satisfactorily interpreted the transformation about which Luther speaks. With its rhetorical designs, it could not really admit the impotence of the guilty will and so could not suggest what was implied in the Protestant doctrines of the freedom and bondage of the will.

That, summarily, is how matters lay between neoclassical humanism and evangelical Protestantism where the will was concerned. However, some further clarification is needed. A humanist might be an evangelical Protestant but then his humanism would be one thing and his religion another as he could not very well blend the two in an Erasmian Christian philosophy. Melanchthon is an interesting case. Under Luther's influence, his *Loci Communes* roundly affirms the bondage of the will. Yet, as a humanist, he was committed to the value of human traditions in shaping an intelligent civil order. He made a sharp distinction therefore between the religious sphere, where human effort did not count and only the word of God was a force, and the civil sphere where human effort did count and humanistic education was a moral and civilising force.[23] In practice, this division cannot have been easy to keep up. Nevertheless, the division running through Melanchthon between religious and humanistic concerns marks the real state of affairs between neoclassical humanism and evangelical Protestantism. Their concerns were different.

Even those who did not draw Melanchthon's distinction acknowledged something like it in effect. The Erasmian compromise between *bonae litterae* and Christian faith meant pushing neither too hard. Its humanism was conventional in its treatment of those motions of the will that Christianity laid hold of, and its Christianity did not lay hold of Paul's ideas with Luther's seriousness. The compromise was on the surface; the deeper concerns might still diverge. There are, of course, other motions of the will than those that Christianity made its peculiar study. Neoclassical humanists give a great deal of attention to mixed or self-deceiving motives and emotional conflict. In the *Secretum*, Petrarch examines the withholdings and disguises by which he cheats himself into believing that his repentance is wholehearted. The *Secretum* contains, besides, an account of *accidia*, memorable for its unadjusted picture of the experience of depression, memorable also for the practical advice which Petrarch receives from St Augustine as to what he should do about his condition.[24] However, Petrarch's distinction as a student of the inner life lies in the directness of his representation of a will that cannot be at peace with itself not in an analysis of sin, guilt and repentance. It was an inspired choice that led him to compose 'Penitential Psalms', essays in a genre peculiarly suited to the expression *de profundis* of the clamour of unresolved spiritual conflict, but he does not get beyond conflict. A man who can express his longing for God as 'If only I could hate myself enough to love thee' has clearly nailed himself to self-division.[25] If we turn from the beginning to the close of the period of neoclassical humanism,

Pope's 'Eloisa to Abelard' makes a brilliant, if rather repellent, display of self-division and self-deception.[26] These are not the motions of the will in question; and, while it has much to say about Christianity as a civilising force or as a social institution, in its maturity, neoclassical humanism left the analysis of error, guilt and repentance outside its scope.

This limitation might take a pietistic form as a distinction between the man of culture and the man at prayer. Such a distinction lies behind Johnson's feeling that Milton's subject, the Fall, is not really suitable for poetry:

> Of the ideas suggested by these awful scenes, from some we recede with reverence, except when stated hours require their association; and from others we shrink with horror, or admit them only as salutary inflictions, as counterpoises to our interests and passions. Such images rather obstruct the career of fancy than incite it.[27]

Johnson's religious gloom was peculiar to himself. The line he drew between religious and literary concerns, however, is not merely a personal judgement but summary, as so many of his judgements are, of a whole tradition. From the other side, Luther had drawn the same line at the outset.

Milton manages to straddle this line between humanism and the Christian, especially Protestant, study of the will. In *Paradise Lost*, he treats error, guilt and repentance with a grasp of how people work unequalled in other neoclassical epics. His insights into the unfreedom of the crooked will and into repentance owe much to the Protestant and Pauline understanding of these things. To represent such motions of the will as a human action with genuine understanding, Milton had to step outside the conventions of humanism governing neoclassical epic. In addition Milton straddles another line. His treatment of the Fall implies free choice, and we know from his theological writing, where he wrote not merely as a Protestant but as a radical, that he rejected those doctrinal formulations of predestination and grace in which the magisterial Reformation, stemming from Luther, had cast its ideas of the will. As far as his poem is concerned, Milton's doctrine of free will allows him to represent the Fall as a choice. This he could hardly have done if he had held orthodox Protestant views on the bondage of the will. If the wills of Adam and Eve had been bound, they could not have chosen; if they were free to choose only before the Fall, then we, who come after, could find nothing of ourselves in their freedom. Either way, there would be no room for the human and moral interest of Book IX of *Paradise Lost*.

Milton has managed then to combine the sort of understanding of guilt and repentance that is locked up in Protestant doctrines of grace and the bound will with a study of choice that could only go with a belief in free will. We shall not find his originality or his greatness in his ideas but in his poem. Still, the doctrinal framework tells us something about *Paradise Lost*.

Like Erasmus and unlike Luther, Milton is partly concerned to justify God.

If Adam were not free, God's providence would be responsible for the Fall. So in both *Christian Doctrine* and *Paradise Lost,* Milton takes up the Arminian position that, although the human will can accomplish nothing without grace, it could at least sin by itself. The Father in *Paradise Lost* is quick to point this out:

> So will fall
> He and his faithless progeny: whose fault?
> Whose but his own? Ingrate, he had of me
> All he could have; I made him just and right,
> Sufficient to have stood, though free to fall.
>
> (III, 95–1)

There is more for Milton in free will than justifying the ways of God to man. From the time of *Areopagitica* he expressed an intense belief in free will as the hinge of human worth. Both there and in *Paradise Lost* he thinks of free will in terms of temperance. 'Temperance' itself and its cognates are scattered throughout the poem. The basic notion is of harmoniousness, as in Bach's well-tempered clavier. The angels 'tempered soft tunings' (VII, 598) to celebrate creation. Eve tempers creams from nuts to mix and blend tastes for Raphael's palate (V, 347). Such uses of 'temper' for an act of skill or art suggest that the virtue of temperance is not so much abstinence as judicious balancing and moderating and that connects it with the divine harmony and blending of contraries that sustains Milton's universe. 'Temperance' also has a severer sense: etymologically, it stems from the Latin 'temperare', whose root meaning is of cutting, dividing, separating, setting bounds. The process of creation in *Paradise Lost* is not just a harmonious blending but also a cutting and setting bounds to things. The cut that sets humanity free from mere nature is the prohibition of the fruit; that is, the word that completed human nature by bestowing rational freedom on it. It is in this severer sense of imposing a limit that Raphael twice enjoins temperance on Adam. When Adam asks about the creation of the world, Raphael warns him about intellectual appetite: 'Knowledge is as food and needs no less / Her temperance over appetite, to know / In measure what the mind may well contain' (VII, 125–8). 'Temperance' here means restraint of an appetitive self based on knowledge of human limits. Similarly, when Adam confesses to being too fond of Eve, Raphael, assuming he means he is too fond of sexual pleasure warns him against letting physical appetite overcome his judgement. While Raphael does not use the word 'temperance' here, his admonishings to a rational life through the subjection of passion imply the control of a lower by a higher self. One may still think of temperance as an art of balancing or poise: some things are too high for human rationality, some too low; temperance means holding the balance through self-knowledge of the human measure, by an art of rational discrimination. However in taking Adam to task, Raphael also implies a restraint to be imposed and a limit not to be transgressed, and this gives 'temperance' its severer cast. We think not so much of poise as of firmness. After such warnings the fall itself can be and often has been read as a failure in temperance.[28] Michael in his short history of the world, names the 'inabstinence of Eve' as the source of those diseases which follow from excess (XI, 476), and he traces human servitude to evil masters back to Adam's original lapse from the rational command of his passions (XII, 82–90).

Temperance only takes us so far with the motions of the will in *Paradise Lost*. At the very least, more than the psychology of a self-enclosed individual is involved. Adam and Eve choose objects outside themselves. At the Fall, Adam does not choose his lower nature; he chooses Eve. Milton's Eve, unlike Erasmus's, is not a personification of Adam's sensuality. His temptation is not just a psychomachia, a conflict of reason and passion. It is a test of his powers of rational discrimination of right and wrong outside himself. It is there that he is free to choose. 'Temperance' has a way of turning the choice outside in and trivialising it. We must not let Raphael tell Book IX.

A choice of right and wrong outside the self is not actually inconsistent with the idea of temperance. To account for the fall in terms of temperance is not wrong, but is inadequate both with respect to the field of freedom outside the self in which choices are made, and even when it is a matter of describing the inner form of freedom of the will in *Paradise Lost*. The inner check for Milton's characters is more than self-restraint or poise; it is obedience to God. The word of God in *Paradise Lost* comes above all as a command. After that it comes as a warning and, to the fallen, as a call. Such a word seems to imply the freedom of the will to obey or disobey, just as Erasmus's exhortations imply a will free to heed or not. At least it seems closer to Erasmus's rhetorical sense of the word of God than Luther's of world-confounding judgements and promises. Yet Milton's whole stress is so different from Erasmus's as to give free will an entirely different character. The obedience required in *Paradise Lost* finds its way deeper into the recesses of the conscience than the command of one's higher nature over one's lower nature. It strikes home in a way that temperance does not.

With Milton's conception of free will as obedience to a divine command, there also went his idea of human dignity. The other that one obeys is God, not a fellow creature, and one serves him freely in the sense that one can withdraw one's service. A lofty sense of this sustains Abdiel in the face of Satan's scorn. One's standing in the eye of God, meaning 'not falling', guarantees one's standing, meaning 'worth' or 'status'. Both senses come out in Raphael's declaration to Adam about angelic standing:

> Myself and all the angelic host that stand
> In sight of God enthroned, our happy state
> Hold, as you yours, while our obedience holds
> On other surety none; freely we serve who serve
> Because we freely love, as in our will
> To love or not; in this we stand or fall.
>
> (V, 535–40)

The connection between freedom of the will and dignity through obedience is peculiar to Milton's ethical imagination. Pico, in his *Oration on the Dignity of Man*, finds human dignity in freedom, but for him it is freedom from finite creaturely nature, the freedom to rise upward through the scale of creation through spirit to God himself, that makes human dignity.[29] For Milton, by contrast, human dignity lies not in infinitude but in the free holding to the limit which God has marked out by His command for being human.

Milton's idea of free will, the reason which is also choice, has its own imaginative colouring, but all the same falls within the general scheme of temperance. There is also a side to Milton's thought on free will that stresses dependence on God. Erasmus and Arminius have much to say on that subject too,[30] but in Milton the doctrine is not merely a pious conviction but an imaginative conviction. He does not, however, give dependence on God such unlimited sway as Luther. For Milton, the human will 'can something' in relation to God out of itself. It can swerve away from God. Nevertheless, the power it has to accomplish good, even the impulse to good itself, comes from God. So, Adam and Eve in Paradise are turned to God by the divine energy that passes into their human natures and sustains them.

On the one hand, in the free obedience of Adam and Eve in Paradise, Milton develops and deepens an idea of free will as temperance, to be found in Erasmus. On the other, in his imagining of how they move in the enormous bliss of the state of innocence, he gives expression to an ideal of being impelled by God as freedom from constraint that one can find not only in Luther but also in the radical reformation of Milton's own day.

Fallen humanity, for Milton, is equally dependent on God, if less comfortably, for the power that makes it free. God makes it possible for man to return, 'Yet not of will in him, but grace in me / Freely vouchsafed' (III, 174–5). In case this seems divine exaggeration, we have in the Son an example of how God does everything, and the Son is not a fallen creature. The Son becomes the Father's 'effectual might' (III, 170) by emptying himself of himself so that he may be filled with God. The defeat of the rebel angels, the creation and the deliverance of humanity are all accomplished by perfect dependence on the Father's power. The Son's acts are more than human and ideal. On a human level, and altogether more subtly, the restoration of Adam and Eve works out the pattern of self-abandonment and divine filling in the despair and repentance of Adam and Eve. Their recovery from hatred, self-hatred and guilt in repentance is, we are told by God, the effect of grace, 'The speediest of [his] winged messengers' (III, 229), working in them. Milton represents the action of grace so soberly as a human action in the guilt and repentance of Adam and Eve and with so little in the way of supernatural machinery that it comes as something of a surprise to learn at the beginning of Book XI that a more than human power had brought about the human restoration. Nothing else, though, would fit in with his general understanding of free will, which is that the will has power to act for good only from God. Here, his views come close to Luther's, with this difference that for Luther what is important is the love and trust of the believer in his dependence on God, whereas for Milton the important thing is power revitalising the will, setting it free from the self-entanglement of guilt and enabling it to act, confident that it is doing the will of God.

I said earlier that an ideal system of life would have to combine freedom as self-control and freedom from constraint. In a fugitive and partial way, Milton's Paradise does perhaps realise that utopian combination. Where volition is concerned, however, the point is that Milton's combining of the two ideas of freedom makes room for his representation of the motions of choice of error, guilt and repentance. It is not, however, his combining them as ideas that is remarkable (much greater mental agility than his had been spent on that), but, to repeat, his working the combination out as a human action. It is there that he enlarged the scope of neoclassical humanism.

Notes

1   Hanna H. Gray, 'Renaissance Humanism: The Pursuit of Eloquence', *JHI*, 24 (1963), pp. 497–514; Paul O. Kristeller, 'Humanism and Scholasticism in the Italian Renaissance', *Studies in Renaissance Thought and Letters* (Rome, 1956), pp. 563–6; Charles Trinkaus, *In Our Image and Likeness: Humanity and Divinity in Italian Humanist Thought*, 2 vols (London, 1970), shows how eloquence may be thought of as the principle behind Italian humanist culture.

2   See e.g. Milton, 'Prolusion 7', *CP*, 1, 291–2; Trinkaus, 2, p. 712ff.

3   *On the Bondage of the Will*, in *Luther and Erasmus: Free Will and Salvation*, ed. E. Gordon Rupp and Philip S. Watson (London, 1959), p. 313.

4   'When [God] justifies, he does it by making men guilty', *The Bondage of the Will*, p. 138. The Latin formula is generally accepted as epitomising Luther's position; see Anders Nygren, *Eros and Agape*, tr. Philip Watson (New York, 1969), p. 687, and Heiko A. Oberman, 'Simul Gemitus et Raptus: Luther and Mysticism', *The Reformation in Medieval Perspective*, ed. Stephen E. Ozment (Chicago, 1971), p. 239.

5   *Diatribe on Free Will*, in *Luther and Erasmus*, ed. Rupp and Watson, p. 88.

6   Erasmus, Dedication of the Colloquies to Johannes Froben, *The Colloquies of Erasmus*, tr. Craig R. Thompson (Chicago, 1965), p. 3, supposes 'this little book [will make] better Latinists and better characters'; in his *Enchiridion* (London, 1533), Cap.ii, he talks of classical literature as one 'of the weapons to be used in the warre of a chrysten man,' and in 'The Godly Feast', *Colloquies*, pp. 65–8, makes the famous defence of pagan literature, as a moral education for Christians.

7   Neither Rupp in his introduction, *Luther and Erasmus*, pp. 1–12, nor Harry J. McSorley, Luther, *Right or Wrong: An Ecumenical - Theological Study of Luther's Major Work*, 'The Bondage of the Will' (New York, 1969), pp. 277–93, feel that Erasmus grasped the issue clearly from the point of the professional theologian. But see Heiko Augustinus Oberman, *Masters of the Reformation: The Emergence of a New Intellectual Climate in Europe*, tr. Dennis Martin (Cambridge, 1981), p. 107ff., for a more sympathetic account.

8   *Enchiridion militis christiani*, tr. Charles Fantazzi, *Collected Works of Erasmus*, vol. 66 (Toronto, 1988), p. 52.

9   *Enchiridion*, p. 25.

10   *Freedom of the Will*, pp. 76–85.

11   Erasmus's is a rhetorical theology; he interprets the Bible as a kind of sacred rhetoric: 'What is the point of so many precepts, so many threats, so many exhortations, so many exhortation; if of ourselves we do nothing, but God in accordance with his immutable will does everything in us' (*Freedom of the Will*, p. 87). See Marjorie O'Rourke Boyle, *Erasmus on Language and Method in Theology* (Toronto, 1977), pp. 33–57, and *Rhetoric and Reform: Erasmus' Civil Dispute with Luther* (Cambridge, Mass., 1983).

12   *The Freedom of a Christian*, tr. W.A. Lambert, rev. and ed. Harold Grimm, *Career of the Reformer*, I, *Luther's Works*, vol. 31 (St Louis, 1957), p. 345.

13   'Preface to the Epistle of Paul to the Romans', *Words and Sacrament*, I, ed. Theodore Buchanan, *Luther's Works*, vol. 35 (St Louis, 1960), p. 365.

14   'Our nature has been so deeply curved in upon itself because of the viciousness of original sin that it not only turns the finest gifts of God in upon itself and enjoys them (as is evident in the case of legalists and hypocrites), indeed it even uses God himself to achieve these aims, but it also seems to be ignorant of this very fact that in acting so iniquitously, so perversely, and in such a depraved way, it is even seeking God for its own sake' (*Lectures on Romans*, ed. Hilton J. Oswald, *Luther's Works*, vol. 25 (St Louis, 1972), p. 291.

15   Luther, *Lectures on Genesis*, ed. Jaroslav Pelikan, *Luther's Works*, vol.1 (St Louis, 1958), p. 159.

16   *Lectures on Genesis*, pp. 37–8. Luther was not entirely consistent on the matter of Eve's equality with Adam; see James Grantham Turner, *One Flesh: Paradisal Marriages and Sexual Relations in the Age of Milton* (Oxford, 1987), pp. 121–2.

17   Paul Ricoeur, *The Symbolism of Evil*, tr. Emerson Buchanan (Boston, 1969), p. 146.

18   See *Lectures on Genesis*, pp. 177–8.

19   Hannah Arendt, *The Human Condition* (Garden City, N.Y., 1959), p. 216.

20   Arendt, p. 216.

21   E.g. *Freedom of a Christian*, p. 46: 'The moment you begin to have faith you learn that in all things you are altogether blameworthy, sinful, and damnable'.

22   *Freedom of a Christian*, p. 387; cf. Erasmus's much weaker formulation of the same idea in *Enchiridion*, Fifth Rule.

23   See Adolf Sperl, *Melanchthon zwischen Humanismus und Reformation* (Munich, 1959), p. 159ff.; Wilhelm Pauck, Introduction to *Loci Communes*, Melanchthon and Bucer (Philadelphia, 1969), pp. 8, 12–14.

24   *Opera omnia* (Basle, 1496), b2 – b4. The account of depression is still remarkably exact even if, with Hans Baron, *Petrarch's 'Secretum': Its Making and its Meaning* (Cambridge, Mass., 1985), pp. 215–18), we wish to play down the centrality of the experience in Petrarch's biography.

25   '*O si mihi sic irascar ut te diligam*', 'Psalmi Poenitentiales', I, in Petrarch, *Psalmi penitentiales: Petrarque, les psaumes penitentiaux*, ed. and tr. H. Cochin (Paris, 1929), p. 40. This reading seems to me preferable to the '*o si mihi sic irascar in peccatis meis*' of Amerbach, 1496, and Henricpetrina, 1581.

26   Eloisa's wonderfully incisive self-analysis of the hide-and-seek of the emotions in repentance rather supports than confutes my argument ('Eloisa to Abelard', (ll.188–96). It analyses the inability of the natural woman truly to turn back on her passional self. It belongs therefore with Montaigne's essay 'Du Repentir', to the analysis of false or hypocritical repentance.

27   'Life of Milton', *Lives of the Poets* (London, 1906), l, 126.

28   See Denis Saurat, *Milton: Man and Thinker* (London, 1944), pp. 129–38, and more recently and baldly Fredson Bowers, 'Adam, Eve, and the Fall in *Paradise Lost*', *PMLA*, 84 (1969), pp. 264–73. Similar moral schemes may be found in Edwin Greenlaw, 'A Better Teacher than Aquinas', *SP* 14 (1917), pp. 196–217; Douglas Bush, '*Paradise Lost' in our Time: Some Comments* (New York, 1945).

29 Giovanni Pico della Mirandola, 'Oration on the Dignity of Man', tr. Elizabeth Livermore Forbes, in *The Renaissance Philosophy of Man*, pp. 223–54.
30 See *Christian Doctrine in Complete Prose*, 6, pp. 151–202; also Maurice Kelley's introduction pp. 81–6, and Dennis Danielson, 'Arminianism in *Paradise Lost*', *Milton Studies*, 12 (1978), pp. 47–73 and for Arminian currents in Milton's time, Danielson's, *Milton's Good God* (Cambridge, 1982), p. 79.

Chapter 2

Finite Man

Whereas in Chapter 1 the aim was to bring out how Milton's understanding of the motions of the will goes against the grain of neoclassical humanism, this chapter turns to how *Paradise Lost* belongs to one of its main lines of development. This line of development bears on Milton's treatment of forbidden knowledge and his picture of human finitude. The notion of forbidden knowledge seems obscurantist. The rage and scorn of the following lines are peculiarly Satan's, but his questions are surely everyone's:

> knowledge forbidden?
> Suspicious, reasonless. Why should their Lord
> Envy them that? Can it be sin to know,
> Can it be death? And do they only stand
> By ignorance, is that their happy state,
> The proof of their obedience and their faith?
> (IV, 515–20)

It turns out in *Paradise Lost* that the forbidden knowledge of good and evil is not really knowledge at all but consciousness of guilt, the empty knowledge of having transgressed a limit. The apple does not enlarge the minds of Adam and Eve: the belief that it might was a delusion. Nevertheless, the delusion is tempting, and much of *Paradise Lost*, especially the talk with Raphael, is taken up with clarifying what is wrong about wanting forbidden knowledge. The fruit becomes a symbol, not so much of a divine 'No' to the human mind, as of a limit to what makes human sense. It marks the difference between knowledge that fits inside the human frame and knowledge that escapes or violates it. Epics are expansive poems: they stretch the issues they treat over the universe. What concerns Adam and Eve looks as if it concerns the whole world, not just because they are the first human beings, but also because it is in the nature of an epic that its heroes should appear to be engaged in some grandly representative task of human culture. Milton draws that epic task out of the calling of Adam and Eve to obey the command about forbidden knowledge, and he does so in terms of the cultural effort of neoclassical humanism to distinguish the true subjects of human knowledge from empty ones, the proper from improper studies of mankind.

Other lines converge here. Protestant thought turns on a sense of creaturely finitude in the face of an infinite God, with all that that implies for human knowledge of divine matters. Baconian thought also made much of the human limits within which useful knowledge can be pursued, and frequently interpreted the Fall as a parable of the folly of applying the mind in a way that ignored those limits and could issue only in vain learning. Baconian epistemology was in the air in the later seventeenth century, the air in which Milton wrote his poem. In the eighteenth century, Pope gave allusions to *Paradise Lost* a Baconian slant, as if it might be taken for granted that Milton and Bacon lent authority to a cultural consensus distinguishing the narrow limits within which humanity might escape absurdity. Milton was not a Baconian, not in the significant way of Davenant or Cowley, and no more will be said here about the Baconian line on human finitude, though it serves as a useful indicator that Milton's treatment of forbidden knowledge falls in with the advancement of learning.

The Reformation and Human Creatureliness

Luther broke with earlier accounts of the relation between God and humanity in which some divine spark, or capacity, or infusion in human nature stirred up an appetite for God and separated a spiritual man fit for God from a sinful earthly residue.[1] The idea of justification which Luther developed in *The Bondage of the Will* ruled out such a separation. He did not think that one somehow earned justification in the eyes of God by becoming a more spiritual being. Rather, God, by an unconditional act of love and forgiveness, took the entire human being to Himself, as a justified sinner. It was that act of grace and not any affinity for God or propensity towards Him that linked humanity with God. The spiritual human being was not some higher part, a soul, a spirit, strained out of the whole creature, but someone in his creatureliness living by faith in the promises of God.

With this radical setting-apart of divine and human went a criticism of what passed for knowledge of God. Given that human nature and human reason had nothing divine in themselves, they could not arrive by themselves at an adequate idea of God. They had rather to depend on what God chose to say about Himself. So, true knowledge of God for Luther was biblical; ideas of God arrived at by speculation, on the other hand, were for him human fabrications and delusory. As a consequence, Luther despised the effort of the schoolmen to synthesise Aristotle with Christian teaching: 'The whole Aristotle is to theology as darkness is to light'.[2] He considered that the two could have nothing to do with each other, and dismissed the schoolmen in *The Bondage of the Will* as 'Sophists' and reason, meaning speculative philosophical reason intruding on Christian doctrine, as 'Madame Reason'.[3] For him, the sole authority in matters of faith was the word of God, which speaks to us in our creaturely condition, while philosophy, which speaks about God on the authority of human reason or even attempts to raise us out of our creatureliness to the contemplation of God, was an attempt to steal God for ourselves:

> The people of Israel did not have a God who was viewed 'absolutely' … in the way the inexperienced monks rise into heaven in their speculations and think about God as he is in himself. From this absolute God everyone should flee who does not wish to perish, because human nature and absolute God … are the bitterest of enemies …
>
> A Turk, a hypocrite, or a monk says, 'Have mercy on me, O God'. This is as though he had said nothing. He does not take hold of the God he names as he is veiled in the sort of mask or face that is suited to us; but he takes hold of God and invades Him in His absolute power, where despair, and Lucifer's fall from heaven into hell, must necessarily follow.[4]

Not all the reformers followed Luther exactly. Calvin, for instance, held that natural reason has no excuse for not arriving at a fair notion of the Creator from Creation. However, sin deflects it, especially if we are philosophers, and so revelation is required.[5] Calvin emphasises sin rather than human creatureliness as that which limits reason and renders vain its attempt to know God out of its own resources. Yet Calvin, like Luther, dismisses speculation for humanity as a way to divine knowledge and turns to scripture as the authoritative source of knowledge of God.[6]

To this severely anti-speculative tradition, Milton himself belonged.

> When we talk about knowing God, it must be understood in terms of man's limited powers of comprehension. God as he really is, is far beyond man's imagination, let alone his understanding … God has revealed only so much of himself as our minds can conceive and the weakness of our nature can bear … It is safest to form an image of God in our minds which corresponds to his representation and description of himself in the sacred writings. (*Christian Doctrine*, 1, 2, *CP*, 6, 133)

With this idea of the limits to human understanding of God went a general belief in the creatureliness of the entire human being, but with a particular Miltonic stress. In *Paradise Lost*, the limits cannot originate in sin: Adam, Eve and Raphael talk about forbidden knowledge before the Fall. It seems to be the rule, not just in *Paradise Lost* but in his other mature work as well, that Milton's idea of the limited powers of the mind goes not with a sense of sin but with a sense of the unity of the human creature, body and soul. He did not think that a human was a finite physical body enclosing an infinite soul or mind but that the entire human was a finite living form. This biblical view of the soul he puts forward in his *Christian Doctrine*:

> Man is a living being, intrinsically and properly one and individual. He is not double or separable: not, as is commonly thought, produced from and composed of two different and distinct elements, soul and body. On the

contrary, the whole man is the soul, and the soul the man: a body, in other words, or individual substance, animated, sensitive, rational. The breath of life mentioned in Genesis was not part of the divine essence, nor was it the soul, but a kind of air or breath of divine virtue, fit for the maintenance of life and reason and infused into the organic body. For man himself, the whole man, I say, when finally created, is specifically referred to as a *living soul*. (1, 7, *CP*, 6, 318)[7]

So, when Adam and Eve first appear in Book IV, it is their naked forms, 'godlike erect', that are the image of God. It may seem for a moment that, except with the hair he so lovingly dwells on, Milton concentrates on the human face divine as 'the image of their glorious Maker' (line 292), for he describes their looks as the expression of abstract qualities, 'Truth, wisdom, sanctitude severe and pure' (line 293), qualities one usually reads into a face rather than a body. Yet I think the whole body is to be imagined. There is a striking example of Milton's picturing the attitude of the entire body as the expression of moral qualities in his sonnet on his dead wife, when she appears to him with veiled face: 'Love, sweetness, goodness in her person shined / So clear, as in no face with more delight'. It is as if her body smiled with the qualities which death veils from him in the face. The 'looks divine' which Satan sees are probably like that, not just facial, but a shining of the whole organism.[8] Satan says that he could have loved Adam and Eve,

> so lively shines
> In them divine resemblance, and such grace
> The hand that formed them on their shape hath poured.
>   (IV, 363–5)

The word 'grace' turns beautifully in the line that follows from divine grace into physical grace, and it is the entire physical being, not just the face, which shines with God's loveliness. It is true that Milton does not visualise with great distinctness what a paradisal being looks like in the flesh. In a way, the soul is the garment of the body for him. The poetry of Paradise is all like that, however, transforming divine energies into various forms of life and breath and back again rather than fixing on material particulars. It is in this way that Milton's idea of the union of body and spirit becomes more than an idea – a felt imaginative intuition about the creaturely being of the 'living soul'.

Milton's feeling for the unity of the body and soul has something in common with Luther's insistence on human creatureliness, but he draws something distinct from it – the dignity of the whole human being. Adam and Eve are 'godlike erect' as naked forms. It was a commonplace of classical thought that an upright stance enabled human looks to 'correspond with heaven' (VII, 511). In *Paradise Lost*, though, the physical uprightness of Adam and Eve is not their already rising heavenward on two legs but their standing attentive to the will of God. It is in this way that their whole living form reflects God. Broadly, Milton's ideas of forbidden knowledge and of creaturely finitude lie within the scheme of Protestant thought; but, in tying them up with human dignity, he gave them a peculiar twist, a twist that made his story suitable for epic treatment and fitted it to the preoccupations of neoclassical humanism.

Neoclassical Humanism

It is in the nature of religious thought that it should come up with an idea or even a philosophy of human nature, an 'anthropology' in the Kantian sense. There seems no reason, though, why humanism, that is, *litterae humaniores* or literature conscious of itself as a civilising and humanising institution, should do so.[9] Humanism in that sense does not seem to imply any particular philosophy of human nature, let alone a moral-metaphysical picture of human finitude. Yet, if we look into neoclassical humanism, we shall find a strain that is as insistent as Luther on human creatureliness, though on different grounds. This strain develops the ideal of eloquence to the point where neoclassical humanist ideas about the human acquire critical edge. It first emerges clearly in Italy with Valla and reaches maturity in France with Montaigne and in England with the Augustans, most distinctly in Swift and Pope. It is with this strain of neoclassical humanism that the important connections with *Paradise Lost* are to be drawn.

The Augustans coopted *Paradise Lost*, as for different reasons Blake and the Romantics did later. They found an epic unfolding of the order of things rather than a visionary poem. They fastened on its representation of a universe informed by divine energy and the heroic but precarious condition of humanity in its middle state, rather than on Satan and the poem's cosmic flights and invocations.[10] Even if it gave them back the image of their mind, what they found was there. *Paradise Lost* contains more disparate energies than they allowed, certainly; but as far as the neoclassical humanism is concerned, its impulse might be called proto-Augustan. The usual line to the Augustan mode is traced from Jonson and Marvell, and quite rightly with urbanity and wit. *Paradise Lost*, however, satisfied the ambition of English humanism for a native epic worthy to stand beside the classics and so also worthy of literary appropriation through imitation, allusion, parody and critical reflection. Above all, it invested the idea of humanity in its creaturely middle state with a heroic pathos, and this, where it did not actually inspire, looked forward to Augustan satire and moralising, with its characteristic sense of possible sublimity within creaturely limits.

Talk of 'man' or 'finite man' or 'human creatureliness' has an archaic ring to it. The movement of mind that cast its thought into *An Essay on Human Understanding*, *An Essay on Man* or *A Treatise of Human Nature* both summarised and extended one preoccupation of neoclassical humanism. But no-one now would set out, as Hume did, to study human nature as the shape or bounding line that determines the possibility of all exact knowledge. The rules by which things make sense and the limits within which they do so are now sought in the medium, the language or the system they work with. 'Man' as an idea no longer works as a defining form for thought. It is much grander and more general than any currently viable humanist, let alone philosophical or sociological, idea of the human. So, while this chapter will trace how the idea of finite man as neoclassical humanism developed it was a vessel for what we can recognise as genuine humanist concerns, it will be an essay more in the history of ideas than in humanist criticism.

Neoclassical humanism made two assumptions about literature that distance it from us historically. The first is that the literature of classical antiquity is the fullest literary reflection on the human world. That is why we may talk of neoclassical humanism. Not to copy, though, but to translate, to make new, to equal, to overgo – these were the ways in which neoclassical humanism took hold not only of the classics but also of its own business of interpreting the world.[10]

We can see now all sorts of continuity between the intellectual traditions of the Middle Ages and the Renaissance. John of Salisbury's humanism has something in common with Petrarch's. In its picture of itself, however, the humanism of the Renaissance makes a break with its present and its immediate past in order to establish a link with antiquity. That break is the origin of the humanists' sense of history and the story which they made of it. The story was that civilisation had been interrupted; the period between antiquity and themselves was a Dark Age of barbarism and ignorance, but with them a truly human culture was in the process of being restored.[11] All humanism is perhaps at odds with the world in which it finds itself. There is always a struggle between an ideal of a complete human culture and the actual cultural achievement of any given time, hence that embattled frame of mind that Paul Fussell notes as characteristic of Augustan humanists.[12] The embattled mind and the war between civilisation and barbarism, light and darkness, are there from the beginning in the neoclassical humanists' story of a Renaissance from the Dark Ages. Milton himself, when he sketches what he conceives as a liberal education, quarrels in this tradition with the curriculum of 'universities not well recovered from the Scholastick grossnesse of barbarous ages'.[13]

For the discussion of human finitude, however, it is the second basic assumption of neoclassical humanism that is important: literature – poetry, history, moral philosophy, as well as oratory – is eloquence.[14] The Renaissance humanists did not call themselves 'humanists' but 'orators and poets', and rhetoric, which included the study of the classical authors, was their basic discipline.

With eloquence, the problem of talking about dead ideas comes up most acutely. All humanist traditions have their classics, and, if ancient literature furnished the classics for neoclassical humanism, we can after all make the adjustment. But we cannot really free ourselves from the Romantic and post-Romantic distrust of rhetoric with its overt designs to persuade and move, in however good a cause. To us, eloquence suggests something mechanical or meretricious. The function of literature for Wordsworth, Arnold and Leavis, to take three distinguished post-neoclassical critics, is moral, but for them the morality of literature involves a scrupulousness about language and a faithfulness to the genuine imaginative apprehension of things that rule out anything we normally call eloquence.[15] Faced with a poem like *Absalom and Achitophel*, which is a sort of political eloquence, not to say propaganda, we can appreciate its excellence without difficulty, but on grounds other than its rhetorical effectiveness. When we come to think of it in terms of eloquence, then the idea of eloquence will have to be much reformed in the course of argument until it becomes what 'eloquence' least suggests, the act of a mind tempering its ideas to experience, and even then we may only fitfully have a full sense that we are talking about something real. To talk of a humanism founded on eloquence is at best to engage in reconstruction of thought that is no longer thought rather than to clarify what we really think and feel ourselves. The discussion that follows will be subject to that limitation.

Eloquence addressed to the whole human being, passionate and volitional, not just ratiocinative, implies an idea of human culture that in the end finds itself in images of human finitude. Neoclassical humanist ideas about creatureliness come down in the end to eloquence. That emerges clearly in the humanists' quarrel with the schoolmen.

The Humanist Quarrel with Scholasticism

The humanists took issue with the schoolmen over the right use of language, and so raised questions about the sort of knowledge that fits the nature of a talking animal. For the schoolmen, the basic intellectual discipline was logic, which was their method for the articulation of truth. For the neoclassical humanist, the basic discipline was rhetoric, the art of speaking or writing well. The complaint of the humanists about the schoolmen, endlessly reiterated, was that they neither spoke nor wrote well.

> Hem, hem gud-day sirs, gud-day. Et vobis, my masters. It were but reason that you should restore to us our bells; for we have great need of them. Hem, hem, aifuhash. We have often times heretofore refused good money for them of those of London in Cahors, yea and of those in Bordeaux in Brie, who would have bought them for the substantific quality of the elementary complexion which is intronificated in the terrestreity of their

quidditive nature, to extraneize the blasting mists and whirl-winds upon our vines, indeed not ours but these round about us.[16]
Such is the eloquence of Master Janotus de Bragmardo of the Sorbonne in the opening of his oration to Gargantua for the recovery of the bells which the young giant has playfully taken from Notre Dame. This humanist lampoon charges the schoolmen not just with unbecoming delivery and ignorance, but also with a misuse of language that goes far beyond the ungrammatical and barbarous Latin with which Master Janotus later ornaments his speech. Talk of 'the substantific quality of the elementary complexion which is intronificated in the terrestreity of their quidditive nature' means no more than a 'sort of something'. Rabelais is logofascinated, but the verbal freaks are satirically pointed here. For though scholastic discourse was not in reality empty, as Rabelais would have us think, it did rely on jargon such as 'entitas' and 'haecceitas', a sign that its thought had lost touch with the common sense of language.[17] This is at least one reason why humanists, like Erasmus in his *Diatribe on Free Will*, called the schoolmen 'sophists'.[18] Rabelais himself calls Master Janotus '*sophiste*', not orator.[19] For the humanist, the language of the schoolmen expresses thought that cannot really be thought at all by the human mind. Their learning is vain learning.

Janotus gets the bells back, but only because Gargantua has a good laugh at him. His speech fails to move in any other way. That was the chief humanist complaint about scholastic discourse: it lacked eloquence, language in its power to move the passions and the will, as well as the mind, to right action. This is, of course, an extraordinarily ungenerous view of the achievement of scholasticism. The humanists' disparagement frequently suggests little understanding and less wish to understand what they dismissed. It is true, all the same, that scholastic discourse addressed a rational faculty withdrawn from the world. 'Man's ultimate happiness', wrote Aquinas, 'consists in the contemplation of truth. For this operation alone is proper to man, and none of the other animals communicates with him therein. Again this is not directed to anything further as its end: since the contemplation of truth is sought for its own sake'.[20] That is the view of someone for whom philosophy is a way of life. Later nominalist schoolmen might have dissented from Aquinas's contemplative ideal, but, even if in despair of arriving at ultimate truth they turned to evangelical activity, their learning still consisted in dialectical pursuits.[21] Humanist learning, by contrast, was committed through its ideal of eloquence to addressing the whole human being, not a rational fragment, and not so much to the contemplation of truth or disputing about its nature as to seizing its bearing on life and making it prevail in the world.[22] In this tradition, when Milton praises Spenser in *Areopagitica* as a better teacher than Scotus or Aquinas, he is contrasting the humanist eloquence of *The Faerie Queene*, which could represent movingly the active engagement of the warring Christian against temptation, with scholastic knowledge of virtue, which he thinks fugitive and cloistered and withdrawn from the field of moral life (*CP*, 2, 516). In their quarrel with scholasticism over human discourse, the humanists distinguish learning that applies to human life and cultivates it from learning that, aspiring to a rationality outside the human condition, leaves human life untended and falls into triviality. Eloquence in this way takes shape in a cultural ideal of human finitude.

Milton's 'Third Prolusion: Against Scholastic Philosophy' has at least the 'what oft was thought' part of true wit. His rehearsal of the stock humanist criticisms sounds surprisingly old-fashioned. His schooling at St Paul's, which Colet had founded in consultation with Erasmus, must have given him a proud feeling of having a humanist pedigree. Perhaps he expected to go on to advanced humanist studies at university, only to find at Cambridge a basically scholastic curriculum still in possession of the place. At both the universities, indeed, the scholastic curriculum had been at most infiltrated but not overturned by humanist studies.[23] We should also bear in mind that scholasticism, however it figured in humanist propaganda, far from being a relic of the Dark Ages, was the current form of academic philosophy. Humanism offered no philosophical discipline that could replace it,[24] and so the study of scholastic logic and theology continued. Ramist logic made some headway for a time, and the Reformation had some effect on the teaching of theology; but the scholastic curriculum persisted along with scholastic logic and disputation, nor were they driven out even when Bacon's ideas made themselves felt in the course of the seventeenth century.[25] Even in 1728, Pope could still ridicule the scholastic establishment at the universities:

> Broad hats, and hoods, and caps, a sable shoal:
> Thick and more thick the black blockade extends
> A hundred head of Aristotle's friends.[26]

Milton may have pieced his 'Third Prolusion' together out of humanist commonplaces, but he was not flogging a dead horse. It voiced strident discontent with the continuing scholastic tradition at Cambridge. One of his complaints was that scholasticism was not concerned with centrally human matters, but split hairs and indulged a curiosity detached from life.

> The supreme result of all this labour is to make you a more finished fool and cleverer contriver of conceits, and to endow you with a more expert ignorance: and no wonder, since all these problems at which you have been working in such torment and anxiety have no real existence at all, but like unreal ghosts and phantoms without substance obsess minds already disordered and empty of all true wisdom.
>
> For the rest, even were I silent, it is amply clear to you how little these trivialities contribute to morality or purity of life, which is the most important consideration of all. (*CP*, 1, 245–6)

As the humanists saw it, the scholastic refinement of ideas went with monastic withdrawal from life instead of the application of ideas to life through eloquence, and so Milton refers to the 'disputations of sour old men, which reek ... of the monkish cells in which they were written' (*CP*, 1, 241). Scholastic logic and dialectic were arts of disputation. Milton is suggesting that the human temper brought out by such arts must be bad temper produced by a crabbed, inhuman, monastic way of life; as he puts it in his 'Seventh Prolusion', 'Its teachers are not like men at all but like finches which live on thorns and thistles. "O iron stomachs of the harvesters" ' (*CP*, 1, 301). The following passage gathers together the various humanist charges against scholasticism of barren subtlety, vain altercation, uncivilising style and human meagreness:

> But these useless and barren controversies and bickerings lack all power to affect the emotions in any way whatever; they merely dull and stupefy the intellect. Further they bring delight to none but those of a rude and boorish disposition, inclined by some innate tendency to quarrels and dissension, prating fellows moreover, and such as detest and ever turn away from sound and wholesome wisdom ... These studies are as fruitless as they are joyless, and can add nothing whatever to true knowledge. If we set before our eyes those hordes of old men in monkish garb, the chief authors of these quibbles, how many among them have ever contributed anything to the enrichment of literature? Beyond a doubt, by their harsh and uncouth treatment they have nearly rendered hideous that philosophy which was once cultured and well-ordered and urbane, and like evil genii they have implanted thorns and briars in men's hearts and introduced discord into the schools. (*CP*, 1, 244)

Humanism informed by an ideal of eloquence distinguished between a pursuit of knowledge that really concerns and enlarges our human existence and one that draws us away from it and makes us not more but less than human.

The Humanists, however, went further and attacked scholastic philosophy not just as defective human learning but also as defective Christian teaching. When Erasmus talks of the 'philosophy of Christ' in his *Paraclesis*, he is glancing ironically at the claims of scholastic philosophy.[27] He means Christ's teaching as it is to be found in the Bible, not in speculative philosophy. He wishes to restore the plain sense of the Bible so that it can speak with its own direct eloquence and move believers to a Christian life. With this intention, he went back to the sources and translated the New Testament from the Greek. In this restoration of the text from mistranslation and misunderstanding, his humanistic philological skills were employed. More than textual criticism was involved, however: he was challenging the competence of philosophical theology to interpret the Bible, and was implicitly recommending a scriptural theology. He was not the first humanist to do so. Valla, in his *Dialogue on Free Will*, was dismissive of the efforts of philosophers to settle Christian doctrine, and went back to biblical teaching.[28] His *Annotations on the New Testament* showed how accepted doctrines reared on mistaken readings or corrupt texts might be subjected to philological criticism. Erasmus was less radical than Valla. When he criticised Luther's doctrines of the bondage of the will, for all his protests about 'Sophists', he took up the question in terms that the schoolmen had thrashed out, and his biblicism was cautious.[29] Still, his humanistic concern with the authority of a good text and with allowing the text to speak for itself unobscured by philosophical commentary anticipates the Protestant doctrine of the authority of Scripture. Milton's remarks in his *Christian Doctrine* about how theology should be scriptural have already been cited in order to illustrate his Protestant thought about the limits of creaturely understanding. They could equally have been cited here to illustrate a humanist rejection of metaphysical theology in favour of the language of the Bible directed by God to finite human minds. In this, Protestant and humanist concerns actually coincide in a shared hostility to the schoolmen; eloquence, like faith, might insist on the limits of human understanding in matters of religion, though for different reasons.

Towards the close of the period of neoclassical humanism, Pope drew in *The Dunciad* a satirical cartoon of vain learning among churchmen. It mordantly summarises humanist criticism of scholastic theology. Aristarchus, Pope's grand-type of anti-humanist pedantry, congratulates the goddess, Dulness, on the persistence of her empire over divinity:

> See! still thy own, the heavy Canon roll,
> And Metaphysic smokes involve the Pole.
> For thee we dim the eyes, and stuff the head
> With all such reading as was never read:
> For thee explain a thing till all men doubt it,
> And write about it, Goddess, and about it:
> So spins the silk-worm small its slender store,
> And labours till it clouds itself all o'er.
>
> (IV, 247–54)

Metaphysical divinity obscures the way to heaven. The pole, the imaginary point where the universe touches heaven, is blotted out by the disputes of scholastic theologians. The pun on 'canon' equates theology with strife and makes articles of dogma sound like the artillery of theological warfare. There follow lines with which no-one who has tried to write more than ten pages to the point can feel at ease, closing with the wonderful simile of the silkworm, an allusion to Bacon's comments on the vermiculate learning of the schoolmen.[30] In a typical deflating cosmic sweep from pole of the universe to insect, Pope has juxtaposed the celestial pretensions of scholastic theology with the subhuman product of their labours. The schoolmen try to be more than human, only to produce something less than human. Their learning is unfit for the human mind. By Pope's time, more clearly than in Erasmus's, the humanist concern with Christianity has concentrated on its power to civilise and humanise. Pope admires divines who advance the arts of civilised life and despises those whose learning is useless and belligerent. Yet even Pope, when he wants to express most forcefully the objections of humanist culture to scholastic theology, turns to quasi-religious images of the middle state of humanity in the cosmos. What is wrong with scholastic theologians is suggested by their rising above the human condition to make war in the heavens, while sinking below it to spinning webs out of themselves. The play of one inhuman extreme against the other implies the central, truly human point of view and invests it with a religious sense of creaturely finitude.

Though I have been arguing that neoclassical humanism tends to ideas of finite man by virtue of eloquence, its informing principle, it must be added that the tendency is by no means clear in many neoclassical humanists, ambiguous in others and late in emerging in unmixed form. The mature Milton, as we have seen, points to the limits of creaturely understanding as a reason for rejecting human speculation about God. The young Milton, though, while rejecting scholastic learning as inhuman and distasteful, still entertains the most unlimited imaginings about the powers of eloquence to transport humanity beyond itself. The young Milton is also not untypical of neoclassical humanism in its earlier stages.

The Divinising of Man and the Condition of Incorporated Minds

The strain of humanist thought that turned to ideas of human finitude grew as much out of criticism of ancient speculative philosophy as out of criticism of contemporary scholasticism. Here, though, the criticism was a kind of self-criticism, a refining and clarification within neoclassical humanism of its truly humanist impulses.

In its early phase in the Italian Renaissance, neoclassical humanism took the ancient philosophers to itself in its quarrel with the schoolmen. The ancient philosophers, unlike the contemporary ones, were thought to have combined philosophy and eloquence. The case against scholastic philosophy was fully developed, and yet, before Valla, ideas of human finitude were of little account. Indeed, the master theme of the Italian Renaissance, as Charles Trinkaus argues, was the divinising of man, and the humanists as Christians and as classicists made much of it.[31] As Christians, they characteristically picked for eloquent elaboration doctrines such as the immortality of the soul and the Incarnation that speak of a human capacity for God. This preoccupation also accompanied their study of the classics. They found ready-made in Cicero a humanist treatment of the divinising of man. This was his great theme when he combined philosophy and eloquence, when he added a cultured man's sifting of various ancient traditions of speculative idealism to the *studia humanitatis*. His amalgam of philosophy and literature was a model of how humanist culture might lead towards true religion.[32] Christians like Petrarch, and later Erasmus, though neither were uncritical of him, could feel that Cicero's eloquent, copious and loose treatment of philosophical theism only just fell short of Christianity.[33] The following passage from Cicero's *De Legibus* indicates the sort of treatment of philosophical themes that impressed them:

> He who knows himself will realize in the first place, that he has a divine element within him, and will think of his own inner nature as a consecrated image of God: and so will always act and think in a way worthy of so great a gift of the gods, and when he has examined and thoroughly tested himself, he will understand how nobly equipped by Nature he entered life and what manifold means he possesses for the attainment and acquisition of wisdom ... And further when [the mind] has examined the heavens, the earth, the seas, the nature of the universe, and understands whence all these things come and whither they must return, when and how they are destined to perish, what part of them is mortal and transient and what is divine and eternal: when it most lays hold of the governor of the universe, when it realizes it is not shut in by [narrow] walls as a resident of some fixed spot, but is a citizen of the universe, as it were of a single city – then in the midst of this universal grandeur, and with such a view and comprehension of nature, ye immortal gods, how well it will then know itself, according to the precept of the Pythian Apollo.[34]

Many Renaissance humanists entertained quasi-philosophical Ciceronian ideas of knowing oneself as partly divine. Even Erasmus, whose humanism is more critical and tempered to experience than that of most of his predecessors, can still urge a platonising idea of the soul on the self-knowledge of the reader of his *Enchiridion*. Most significantly, the Renaissance humanist mixture of philosophy and eloquence runs into Florentine Platonism. The idea of self-knowledge that Ficino, for example, approves in Plato is not so very different from Cicero's idea of potential divinity: 'Because [Plato] thought of the mind as a mirror in which the image of God's face reflects itself easily, when he would seek for God through each of his imprints, he turned to the beauty of the soul, understanding the oracle "know thyself" to mean above all that whoever chose to know God should first know himself'.[35]

The Florentine platonists, however, are not humanists in the sense used here. Their classics were not the *bonae litterae* of Erasmus but ancient philosophy, platonic, neoplatonic, gnostic, hermetic, cabbalistic. Their concern was in no sense a reflection on the human world through literature. It was rather to release the divine potential in human nature from its earthbound limits. Instead of looking, as humanism does, for knowledge that fits inside our human being, knowledge that makes us human, that we can test against the experience of our humanity, the knowledge the Platonists were after was knowledge that would transport them from their humanity and make them as God. For such a transport beyond the human condition, soaring to the empyreal sphere is a recurrent image. Here, for example, are Pico's exhortations to mount the sky:

> Who would not wish to be so inflamed with those Socratic frenzies sung by Plato in the *Phaedrus*, that, by the oarage of feet and wings escaping speedily from hence, that is from a world set on evil, he might be borne on the fastest of courses to the heavenly Jerusalem? Let us be driven, Fathers, let us be driven by the frenzies of Socrates, that they may throw us into ecstasy as to put our minds and ourselves in God. Let us be driven by them, if we have first done what is in our power. For if through moral philosophy the forces of our passions have by a fitting agreement become so intent on harmony that they can sing together in undisturbed concord, and if through dialectic our reason has moved in a rhythmical measure, then we shall be stirred with the frenzy of the Muses and drink heavenly harmony with our inmost hearing. Thereupon Bacchus, the leader of the Muses, by showing in his mysteries, that is, in the visible signs of nature, the invisible things of God to us who study philosophy, will intoxicate us with the fulness of God's house, in which, if we prove faithful, like Moses, hallowed theology shall come and inspire us with a double frenzy. For, exalted to her lofty height, we shall measure therefrom all things that are and shall be and have been in indivisible eternity; and admiring their original beauty, like the seers of Phoebus, we shall become her own winged lovers. And at last, roused by the ineffable love, as by a sting, like burning Seraphim reft from ourselves, full of divine power we shall no longer be ourselves but shall become He Himself who made us.[36]

In its maturity, neoclassical humanism represented cosmic flights such as this, with their Faustian expansion of the ego to godhead, as the pursuit of vain learning, vain because it was beyond the creaturely capacity of the human mind. Pope, for example, satirises the presumptuous and vain effort of platonic speculation:

> Go, soar with Plato to th'empyreal sphere,
> To the first good, first perfect, and first fair;
> Or tread the mazy round his follow'rs trod,
> And quitting sense call imitating God;
> As Eastern priests in giddy circles run,
> And turn their heads to imitate the Sun.
>   (*Essay on Man*, Epistle II, 23–38)

Yet, earlier humanists seem to have felt no contradiction between their study of man and Renaissance platonism. Sir Thomas More translated the life of Pico and took him as a pattern, though it must be said that it is the ethical and Christian, not the platonic and enthusiastic, Pico whom he has in mind.[37] Erasmus and Rabelais at least playfully dabbled in hermetic mysteries, and Reuchlin and Lefèvre d'Etaples quite seriously. Ben Jonson and Milton himself entertained neoplatonic lore, poetically if not philosophically. Above all, there are, as Trinkaus has argued, affinities of outlook and cultural style between Florentine platonism and Italian humanism. Florentine platonism is the hypertrophy of the master theme of Italian humanism, the 'divinising of man'. Its uncritical amalgam of ancient theistic traditions with Christianity exaggerates a general tendency among the humanists to assimilate classical philosophy to Christian faith. Erasmus's 'Sancte Socrates, ora pro nobis' is a cautious northern example of this humanist fashion. Finally, Renaissance platonism unites philosophy and eloquence. As the extraordinary rigmarole quoted from Pico's Oration shows, Renaissance platonism was rhetorical. It avoided the exact analysis of propositions practised by the schoolmen,[38] aiming rather at the harmonising of exalting ideas. It reduced everything to signs and allegories of God. Everything led upwards, and platonising eloquence participated in the great return of things to their celestial origin by stirring up an appetite for God.

The Renaissance platonists are, however, so far wide of the genuine concerns of humanism that the phase of neoclassical humanism whose tendencies they exaggerate cannot be very discriminating about its ends. With Valla, however, a truly critical strain emerged in Italian humanism. In him, it became critical of the idealistic philosophical culture too easily taken over from Cicero and too easily sliding into the angelical leanings of Renaissance platonism.[39] In his *Dialogue on Free Will*, Valla has Antonio Panormita confess to longings for knowledge beyond the reach of the human mind. Strikingly, he expresses them as a dream of flying up to heaven.

> Why should I foreswear wings, if I could possibly obtain them by Daedalus' example? And indeed how much finer wings do I long for? With them I might fly not from the prison of walls but from the prison of errors and fly away and arrive not in the fatherland, which breeds bodies as did Daedalus, but in the one where souls are born. (p. 159)

However, the whole course of the dialogue is to correct such Piconian aspirations and to exhort the mind to acquiesce in the limits of human understanding. In particular, Valla sets out to correct the presumption of philosophers. The philosophers here are not the contemporary schoolmen, whom Valla disdains to mention. They are Boethius, who united philosophy with eloquence, and Aristotle, who was supposed by many humanists to have differed from his later followers in doing so. It is not lack of eloquence, the original humanist objection to the schoolmen, that Valla complains of, but more radically the assimilation of Christian faith to philosophical theism and with it the attempt to divinise man through philosophical speculation. Speaking of Boethius, Lorenzo asks:

> What cause was there for a Christian man to depart from Paul and never remember him when dealing with the same matter he had dealt with? What is more, in the entire work of the *Consolation* nothing at all is found about our religion – none of the precepts leading to a blessed life, no mention and hardly a hint of Christ. (p. 179)

To this, a now chastened Antonio replies: 'I believe it was because he was too ardent an admirer of philosophy'.

Valla's criticism of the assimilation of Christianity to philosophical theism fits in with his call for a biblical theology and with his ideas of eloquence as sufficient arbiter of human culture. More to our purpose, however, is the way in which his notion of human finitude turned the mind upon the study of man and away from those flights into the empyrean which are found in their most extravagant form in the writings of the Renaissance platonists and hermetists. In his dialogue *On Pleasure*, he rejects 'Stoic' idealism and elevates pleasure to the true good. Maffio Veggio poses as an 'Epicurean', a libertine, in order to demolish the surly virtue of the 'Stoic' first speaker. He may not mean all he says in defending adultery, defining man as '*animal bibens*' and so forth, but his sallies serve to show how unlike the paragons of classical virtue human beings really are.[40] He brings out in the form of play or wit how humans are appetitive, libidinous and volitional, and suggests that an ethic of self-denial is self-contradiction or self-deception. Veggio's final move is to tempt the 'Stoic' to a dinner that will refute his denial of sensual good. The third book opens after the meal with Antonio da Rho correcting the licentiousness of Veggio's hedonism with a Christian hedonism, which, with its promise of heavenly fruition, appeals not to a 'Stoic' paragon or merely spiritual being but to sensual and creaturely humanity. He pictures a heaven almost baroque in its unendingly various, material and human joys, which include the plea-sures of rank, being admired and seeing one's enemies (the devils) tortured (pp. 309, 291). His heaven is not so much a sublimation of human desires as their enormous gratification. Criticism of the stoic's pride was a common enough humanist theme.[41] What is significant is the contrast which Valla draws between the 'spiritual', self-denying 'Stoic' hero and the human crea-ture, and his preference for the latter. For him, stoical virtues falsify human nature. Perhaps Valla's literary manner is too aggressive, too brilliant, too bent on effect to come up with substantial insights into human nature, but at least, with him, humanism is pointed towards its real object.

Cicero had made it his task to add a knowledge of philosophical speculation to the traditional constituents of culture, the study of literature, history and ethics. In doing so, he substituted as the humanist ideal a rational being for a passionate and appetitive creature, at best *rationis capax*. While this ideal extended the scope of a cultured man's education, it helped to conceal the fluctuating and diverse being from himself. Cicero was himself by no means consistent, nor were the Renaissance humanists in taking over the Ciceronian compromise with ancient philosophy that directed self-knowledge to the spirit, the divine spark within, instead of to the entire creaturely being. Valla, however, made a decisive break, in which an idea of the human being more in keeping with humanist culture made its appearance. Instead of a creature sublimating itself through ascetic virtues and fleeing from itself in speculative mirrors, Valla praises the man who lives according to his creaturely human nature.[42] In Valla, we may detect the first formidable representative of the strain of neoclassical humanism that takes the idea of finite man as its cultural measure.

Platonising philosophy appealed to Renaissance humanists partly because of the divine dignity it accorded to the human spirit. The strain of humanism that emerges with Valla had to renounce that dignity only to rediscover human dignity in finite human nature. A later example of the same discovery is to be found in Rabelais. His giants are giants because they are gigantically human, not because they are humans pretending to be more than human. In the final phase of neoclassical humanism, Swift returns to the same idea in his giants of Brobdingnag. Pope, also, when he urges us to know ourselves as beings 'darkly wise, and rudely great', has a Gargantuan or Brobdingnagian notion of human dignity in mind. However, the Augustans perhaps owed something to another sixteenth-century Frenchman. At any rate, in Montaigne, the strain of humanism that finds the potential dignity of man within creaturely limits is already critically mature. Here, for example, with all the authority of his attempt to know himself behind it, is a passage from the conclusion of his last essay:

> [People want to] be exempted from them[selves] and escape man. It is meere folly, instead of transforming themselves into Angels, they transchange themselves into beastes: in lieue of advancing, they abase themselves. Such transcending humours affright me as much, as steepy, high and inaccessible places. And I finde nothing so hard to be digested in *Socrates* his life, as his communication with Daemones. Nothing so humane in Plato, as that which they say, hee is called divine ...
>
> It is an absolute perfection, and as it were divine for a man to know how to enjoy his being loyally. We seeke for other conditions because we understand not the use of ours: and goe out of ourselves, forsomuch as we

know not what abiding there is. *We may long enough to get upon stilts, for*
be wee upon them, yet must we goe with our owne legges. And sit we upon the
highest throne of the World, yet sit we upon our owne taile. ('Of Experience',
Essayes, Book 3, Ch. XIII, pp. 385–6)

In this passage, Montaigne subverts the attempt to become divine through
transcending our humanity by maintaining that to live according to our
creaturely human nature is in itself to attain 'an absolute perfection, and as it
were divine'. There is a touch of paradox here, an appropriation of stoical
language to profoundly unstoical thoughts. Still, of all neoclassical humanists,
Montaigne comes closest to persuading us that to live according to human
nature is indeed the 'chef d'œuvre de l'homme'.[43] He is much more persuasive
than Erasmus, for instance. The point of the first part of *The Praise of Folly*
is that the human condition is folly and we should enjoy it. Erasmus's geniality
is uneasy, though, and the holy folly praised in the last section is estranged
from the earlier, backhanded, carnivalesque involvement in the creaturely
condition. Erasmus is not by any means a consistent representative of the
strain of neoclassical humanism which I have been trying to isolate. Even if
we turn to Swift and Pope, who are clear and consistent representatives, we
shall find that, in comparison with Montaigne, they are cramped and uncomfortable in coming to terms with creaturely existence. They submit to it as to
something good for them, free chiefly because free from pretence, and enjoyable with difficulty.

Milton's feeling for the middle state is different. He elevates the life of the
body in *Paradise Lost* when he conceives it in terms of the integrity of a living
soul. Montaigne, not to mention Swift, deflates. Admittedly, it is not the
dignity of the body that Montaigne deflates, but the pretensions of the mind
trying to dissociate itself from the body, that inescapable evidence of the
human condition. Hence his reductive wit juxtaposes the bottom with the
lofty spirit that forgets what it sits on, even if in playing off physical nature
against bogus dignity his aim is to hit off a middle state in which we should
be natural and at ease. It is not an epic way of picturing human dignity and
not Milton's way, for all his denouncing of spiritual humbug when he discusses sex in Paradise or angelic digestion. The difference goes further: for
Milton, to live well in one's middle state is a matter of will, of the reason that
also is choice. To fall out of the middle state is to fall into evil and guilt. With
Montaigne, on the other hand, and one might add Swift and Pope, one falls
out of nature into absurdity. With them, the chief business of humanity, living
à propos, is a matter of temper and not of will, a matter of reason, not as moral
choice but as reasonableness, good sense and moderation. Above all, it is a
matter of balance. In *Paradise Lost*, the living soul has a natural temperance
and integrity. With Montaigne, Swift and Pope, humanity is something to be

achieved. The art of being human is to keep body and soul together, to hold in human proportion two sides of our nature, angel and beast, which are always falling apart into disproportionate and deformed shapes. Yet, in spite of these differences, and they are fairly radical differences not just of literary kind but also of sensibility and moral interest, the notion of human creatureliness is what is at stake for Montaigne and the Augustans as for Milton. For all of them, it sets the terms of human possibility. It is indeed the characteristic moral framework of neoclassical humanism in its maturity.

It used sometimes to be said that Milton was the last of the Renaissance humanists.[44] But Milton's concern with human finitude and forbidden knowledge is not backward-looking, a vestige of an earlier, more pious humanism. Human finitude was taken up by Augustan humanists as a measure of things. Johnson, for instance, writes that Raphael's 'reproof' of Adam's aspirations to more than human knowledge about 'the planetary motions' together with Adam's answer about turning our mind to knowledge of our human estate, 'may be confidently opposed to any rule of life which any poet has delivered'.[45] The passage was indeed a favourite one with the Augustans. Nor was it only Raphael's lecture that appealed to them. *Paradise Lost* told the story of the Fall in a way that lent itself to Augustan moralising on the human condition. It showed humans aspiring to godhead and falling out of their humanity, reaching upwards for a knowledge beyond them and entering into a process of error and nonsense. It supplied the Augustans with a fable of the human proportion and of the folly of violating it. So, Pope, in his *Essay on Man*, largely an essay on presumption, supports his argument to 'vindicate the ways of God to man' with what is almost a smart summary of *Paradise Lost*:

> In Pride, in reas'ning Pride, our error lies;
> All quit their sphere, and rush into the skies.
> Pride still is aiming at the blest abodes,
> Men would be Angels, Angels would be Gods.
> Aspiring to be Gods, if Angels fell,
> Aspiring to be Angels, men rebel;
> And who but wishes to invert the laws
> Of ORDER, sins against th'Eternal Cause.
> (Epistle 1, 123–30)

It is not by chance that Pope opens his *Essay* by comparing 'this scene of Man' (*Epistle* 1) to a 'Garden tempting with forbidden fruit'. *An Essay on Man* is by no means Pope's surest, most acute essay on man; but it has to a remarkable degree the knack of summing up the tradition of neoclassical humanist thought on human finitude in pointed images. It is not accidental that these so frequently remind us of *Paradise Lost*. Behind Pope's sense of the precariousness of the human nature and of the discrimination needed to maintain it lies Milton's splendidly articulated version of the original fall of human beings out of their creaturely middle state.

Knowledge within Human Limits in Paradise Lost

Paradise Lost has an odd way of heavily insisting on the bounds set to human understanding and then allowing it generous scope and a liberal education.[46] Clearly, Milton not only felt he had a pious duty to stress the absoluteness of the obedience owed to God's will, but also gloried as a poet in God's authority and power. Yet, with his respect for human dignity and freedom and equally his respect for God's rationality, Milton constantly qualifies the oppressiveness of God's limitation of the human creature and tries not only to make sense of the limitation but also to suggest the scope given to the mind within it. His Paradise is not an anti-intellectual retreat; ignorance is not its enormous bliss. Milton is at pains to show that, though God banned the fruit of the tree of knowledge, He provided in almost every other way for the exercise of the unfallen mind, and that nothing was further from His purpose than to keep Adam and Eve low by keeping them ignorant, as Satan suggests. Only – and this is where the Protestant and humanist traditions about human finitude come together – the knowledge should be apportioned to the human measure.

Milton has given his unfallen man, if not his unfallen woman, remarkable mental powers. Adam is endowed at birth with language and the faculty of discursive thought. His first reasoning leads him to suppose 'some great maker ... / In goodness and in power pre-eminent' (VIII, 278–9), and to wonder how he may know and worship Him. This philosophical conjecture arises from self-knowledge, not self-knowledge of a divine faculty within him of the kind that Cicero taught, but self-knowledge of his finitude: 'How came I thus, how here?/ Not of myself' (lines 277–8). His whole sense of himself standing upright and moving on the 'enlightened earth' (line 274) is creaturely and contingent. Again, when he talks to God in Paradise of his need for a companion, he displays his rationality in distinguishing the creaturely need for the conversation of his likeness from the divine self-sufficiency of the Creator.[47]

The knowledge which Adam displays on these occasions is arrived at by discursive means. Raphael distinguishes for Adam two sorts of reason. 'Discursive, or intuitive; discourse / Is oftest yours, the latter most is ours' (V, 488–9). One of the admirable things about *Paradise Lost* is Milton's representation of the processes of discursive reason, reason engaged not in the elaboration of fixed ideas but in the shifts of conversation and debate. That comes out in the debate in hell, in the conversation between Adam and Eve about gardening apart, and in the temptation scenes. Here we have a development of the humanist interest in the talking animal whose faculty of reason is characterised not so much by its angelic powers of contemplation as by its power of discrimination, prudence, choice of fit and right in the course of a life lived in communication with other humans.

Raphael's distinction between angelic intuition and human discourse must have struck Dryden, for, in his *State of Innocence*, he has Satan memorably expand on the discursive limits of human reason:

> The soul pure fire, like ours, of equal force;
> But pent in flesh, must issue by discourse:
> We see what is; to Man truth must be brought
> By sense, and drawn out by a long train of thought
> By that faint light to will and understand.[48]

The passage brings out wonderfully the condition of 'incorporated minds'[49] in their middle state, which for Milton as much as for Dryden meant a rationality lodged in the fallible processes of argument.

Discursive reason can take one only so far. It leads Adam to suppose a creator, but it cannot actually acquaint him with Him. Given his creaturely and finite mind, it is necessary that God should make Himself known, for 'how can finite grasp infinity'? God therefore appears and asserts His identity: 'Whom thou sought'st I am' (VIII, 316), a form looking forward to the 'I am that I am' by which he chose later to be known. Since Adam's human mind cannot reach knowledge of divine things by its own discursive power, such knowledge has to be revealed to him by God or angels.

Human knowledge about God in *Paradise Lost* is always revealed, never reached by the human mind out of itself. Moreover, the form in which such knowledge is imparted is accommodated to human capacity. When God reveals Himself to Adam, he relaxes some of the mystery with which he surrounds Himself with after the Fall. He comes down to Adam's level and, like Raphael, speaks to him 'as with his friend' (IX, 2). But it is distinctly the friendship of unequals, and however gracious, even jovial, God is in accommodating Himself to the limits of his creature, the gulf between them tells. The 'celestial colloquy sublime' 'strained to the height' (VIII, 454–5) Adam's earthly powers, and, exhausted, he 'sought repair / Of sleep' (lines 457–8). It is easy to be put off by God's condescension to Adam and the bounds which he puts on Adam's understanding. In fact, it took an unusually bold biblical imagination to picture so free a conversation between God and man. As so frequently in *Paradise Lost* Milton represents liberal ideas in the guise of religious restriction.

With Raphael, there is no such absolute distinction of being as between Adam and God. The talk, far from overpowering Adam, seems to invigorate his faculties. It is altogether more like a human conversation. The form in which divine things are accommodated to the human mind here is an inspired adaptation of the humanist *convivium*, the convivial meal at which humanist thinking about eloquence as human discourse took a particularly engaging turn.[50] There, the whole human being is recreated, body and mind, in 'the feast of reason and the flow of soul'. It is not just in the shared eating that heaven comes down to the human creaturely system in *Paradise Lost*, but also in conversation. In colloquy with God, Adam comes out with an ideal of 'conversation with his like' (VIII, 418) as the life of the human mind. Human beings for him become human in conversation with other human beings. The sociability of speech is the condition of discursive rationality. Here, Milton is filling out the Genesis story along humanist lines. Antonio da Rho, in Valla's *Dialogue on Pleasure*, glosses the 'It is not good for man to be alone. Let us make a helpmeet, like unto him' of Genesis with a quotation from Cicero's *De Amicitia*: 'If someone ascended into heaven and contemplated the nature of the world and the beauty of the stars, his amazement would be disagreeable to him instead of most enjoyable, unless he had somebody that he could tell it to'.[51] This hypothetical solitary man rapt to heaven is more or less in Adam's position in Eden wanting somebody with whom to converse so that his humanity may be complete. With Raphael, of course, the conversation is not really like with like. He may talk with Adam 'as with his friend', but only 'as'. He sits with Adam 'indulgent', his affability assumes the vast superiority of archangel to human and, however poised, Adam has to watch his step elaborately. In human terms, the conversation is full of snubs. The meal does not realise the humanist ideal of cultivated, convivial talk among equals.[52] Rather, it boldly translates it to the intercourse of earth and heaven. Conventionally, this is stiff with mystification, ceremony and ascetic discipline; but Milton makes an extraordinary effort to imagine it as paradisaically free and rational conversation. Adam is not strained out of his creaturely being but indulged in it and to some extent shared with.

Milton transposes the convivial meal into a form in which divine matters may be accommodated to the finite human mind. The form of the convivial meal accommodates heavenly matters to the earthly mind graciously. The content of Raphael's talk equally turns on the limits of Adam's understanding; indeed, it rubs them in. Raphael makes great play with the poem's ramifying metaphor of knowledge as food, talking of the 'human measure' and impressing on Adam how the human system may digest only what is fitted to its capacity (VII, 126–30, 640). Again, when about to describe the war in heaven, he asks himself:

> how last unfold
> The secrets of another world, perhaps
> Not lawful to reveal? Yet for thy good
> This is dispensed, and what surmounts the reach

> Of human sense, I shall delineate so
> By likening spiritual to corporeal forms,
> As may express them best.
>
> (V, 563–73)

Raphael is making a point, not just about how he has to adapt heavenly matters so that Adam may take them in (yet perhaps, he adds encouragingly, heaven is not so unlike earth), but about how the particular heavenly matters he has in mind apply to human life. He is thinking of how the war in heaven teaches a lesson in obedience to God. In this way, what he reveals are 'Things above earthly thought which yet concerned / Our knowing' (VII, 82–3).

As for Michael's revelation of the divine plan of human history, there can be no doubt that this concerns the knowing of Adam and Eve. It supplies them with the knowledge of how humanity is to be reconstituted in the fallen world, and so tells them how to live and what virtues are required of them and their race as they go forward to redemption in history. What Michael shows is not the secrets of another world. Yet the visions of human history are properly visible only to God's foresight: they are 'the visions of God' (XI, 377). They also, therefore, have to be revealed; but, instead of being accommodated to Adam's understanding (they take the form of signs to humanity by being made history), Adam's now fallen understanding has to be raised to the divine plan. So, Michael has to purify Adam's 'inmost seat of mental sight' (X, 418) so that he may understand what he is shown. The purification works both medically and as a metaphor for the operations of revelation that must meet with the understanding of faith. The revelation of the relations between God and humanity in history consists in promises, and only by faith can promises be received as knowledge and interpreted. To faith, they are indeed divine knowledge. We are nudged to contrast the bogus divine knowledge that the serpent said was contained in the forbidden fruit with genuine divine knowledge addressed to creaturely limits, when Adam thanks Michael for the vision of the history of his race and declares he has 'my fill / Of knowledge, what this vessel may contain; / Beyond which was my folly to aspire' (X, 558–60).

In all three cases of revelation, divine knowledge is given to humanity in such a way that it insists on the limits of the human faculties. The revelation, whether it is the appearance of God to Adam, or the account of heavenly things opening backwards in time and outwards beyond the visible universe, or the prospect forwards in time into human history, violates the human perspective to insist on it. The poem seizes on the truly human perspective as its epistemological principle. It teaches it as a means of distinguishing knowledge from illusion and implies it in some of its characteristic poetic effects.

Forbidden knowledge violates the truly human perspective in an unprincipled way. It comes into the poem in Raphael's talk with the human couple and in Satan's temptation of Eve. In both cases, forbidden knowledge is not really knowledge at all, since it cannot be known by a human mind. The temptation of Eve concerns us at this point, not as part of the human action, but as a part of a fable about true and false intellectual ambition. The sort of knowledge which Satan seems to hold out is illusory or vain learning. It is he who makes up the idea that the fruit might bring divine knowledge and 'exalt / Equal with Gods' (IV, 525–6). All the knowledge that Adam and Eve obtain from the fruit is to know that they have fallen:

> our eyes
> Opened we find indeed, and find we know
> Both good and evil, good lost and evil got,
> Bad fruit of knowledge, if this be to know,
> Which leaves us naked thus, of honour void,
> Of innocence, of faith, of purity.
>
> (IX, 1069–75)

The forbidden knowledge of good and evil turns out to be knowledge only in a bitter and ironic sense; in every other sense it is an illusion.

Even if the promise of knowledge in the forbidden fruit is a hoax, the temptation to forbidden knowledge is taken seriously. Forbidden knowledge is wrong not just because God has forbidden it. The serpent dangles a kind of knowledge before Eve that is wrong for her in principle as a human being. It goes with rising in the scale of being and attaining godlike understanding. Aspirations to these things cannot by themselves make the knowledge wrong. Raphael has encouraged Adam and Eve with the curious prospect of how human beings will fade away from their earthly natures until they become spiritual body-souls like the angels. In Raphael's account, however, as later in Michael's of how God will take humanity to Himself at the end of time, the human part in the return to God is to stand through attention to one's creaturely being. The whole business of being lifted up to God must be left to God. God will raise one in time if one stands; one falls if one attempts to fly up by one's own efforts. In tempting Eve to rise by disobeying, the serpent deludes her about the way to heaven and how to become godlike. He tempts her not just to sin, but also to a wrong sort of knowledge, wrong because it can be obtained only by transgressing the limits of human understanding.

The epistemological principle at issue seems to be more important than any specific piece of knowledge which one should not try to know. About what Eve will learn, the serpent is vague. He says that, on eating the fruit,

> Thenceforth to speculations high or deep
> I turned my thoughts, and with capacious mind
> Considered all things visible in heaven,
> Or earth, or middle, all things fair and good.
> (IX, 602–5)

Again, pretending to be indignant about God's prohibition of the fruit, he says he feels the power of the fruit 'Within me clear not only to discern / Things in their causes, but to trace the ways / Of highest agents, deemed however wise' (IX, 679–83). He said that eating the fruit gave him a human mind, but in these passages he claims more than that, as if, far from stopping at merely human understanding, he had ascended the whole way to divine being and could now understand the workings of the entire universe.[53] The knowledge which he holds out to Eve, however, is not so much any definite information as the attainment of a god's-eye view of things and a general speculative liberation from the conditions of human knowledge in earthbound human nature. In the dream which he had earlier inspired in her, the sort of knowledge was quite unspecified; a taste of the tree of knowledge was to be enough to set her free from the confines of the earth to fly upwards to heaven and take a place among the gods. There, the temptation was to violate the conditions of human knowledge, a violation whose image was the cosmic flight. The image of flight is less patent in the later temptation. Though the serpent may speak, he has not grown wings; though both Eve and Adam hope to reach a higher state of being, they do not actually experience a flight up through the universe. Nevertheless, Adam, as well as Eve, expresses a hope to attain a higher state of being, and both 'fancy that they feel / Divinity within them breeding wings / Wherewith to scorn the earth' (IX, 1009–11).

If forbidden knowledge violates the human frame of understanding and typically assumes the figure of flight from the earthly condition of the human mind, we can appreciate why Raphael takes pains to warn Adam about his interest in the movement of the sun with its attempt to see the universe as God might see it. Within Baconian limits, Raphael approves of the study of the heavens. Adam may study God's works there, content with wonder, 'which is broken knowledge' and which indeed he has expressed in the prayer at the beginning of Book V.[54] He may also learn practical astronomy, the useful knowledge of God's 'seasons, hours, or days, or months, or years' (VIII, 69), whatever seasons are in Paradise. There remains, however, a study of things above the earth that is not proportioned to the human condition, the study of heavenly motions as they are in God's eye, and not as they appear proportioned to human capacities. Consequently, Raphael plays off the claims of rival systems in order to show that the dispute between them is as irresoluble as the puzzle of whether or not the man goes round the squirrel that goes round the tree trunk. Raphael's exposition passes rapidly from the geo- to the heliocentric hypothesis, and the effect is a confounding of perspective. He deliberately leaves the heavens in this dislocated state, refusing to resolve the contradictory perspectives in terms of the question about heavenly motions, only to settle the matter by affirming the centrality of the human and creaturely perspective. This is both a good example of the play with perspective in the poem and a sophisticated way of asserting that 'heaven is for thee too high' (VIII, 172) and so of admonishing Adam to 'Think only what concerns thee and thy being' (VIII, 174).

To say that Raphael's lecture bears on the temptation to forbidden knowledge is to say not that the serpent holds out the prospect of divine astronomical knowledge but that, like the godlike knowledge of which the serpent speaks, the speculative study of heavenly motions lies beyond the human measure of knowledge. There are, however, good reasons why astronomy should serve as Raphael's example of forbidden knowledge, for the study of things above the earth had been associated with the cosmic flight to divine knowledge.

In the passages quoted from Cicero, the spirit is transported heavenward by contemplating the universe. A more extraordinary example is Bruno's cosmic flight on contemplating the heliocentric system:

> Now here is he who has pierced the air, penetrated the sky, toured the realm of the stars, traversed the boundaries of the world, dissipated the fictitious walls of the first, eighth, ninth, tenth spheres, and whatever else might have been attached to these by the devices of vain mathematicians and by the blind vision of popular philosophers. Thus, aided by the fullness of sense and reason, he opened with the key of the most industrious inquiry those enclosures of truth that can be opened to us at all by presenting naked the shrouded and veiled nature; he gave eyes to moles, illuminated the blind who cannot fix their eyes and admire their own images in so many mirrors which surround them from every side. He untied the tongue of the mute who do not know [how to] and did not dare to express their intricate sentiments. He restored strength to the lame who were unable to make that progress in the spirit which the ignoble and compound [body] cannot make.[55]

In Milton's universe, such flights are flights into nonsense. The heroic vocation is to stand in the fullness of human creatureliness, not to fly. Mounting the universe is satanic, and in humans it ends up, as with Eve's dream or the rising promised by the serpent, in bathos.

Cosmic Flights in Paradise Lost

Yet, all this talk of human finitude goes against what is perhaps the overwhelming impression of *Paradise Lost*. If we try to bring the whole of the poem before our minds, what strikes us first is its cosmic design and, with that, a feeling of being enlarged from the earth. With its sudden views of the whole world at once, the poem seems to set us free from time limits and space limits. We are drawn to Satan's wonder as he looks down into the celestial system, and we are drawn to Eve's wonder and fear as she soars heavenward and looks down from the clouds. To her, the earth appears 'outstretched immense' (V, 85). She has not travelled so far that it is reduced to 'a cloudy spot' (V, 266), yet the sudden revelation of its geographical expanse is equally astonishing. These universal vistas, however, are only partial shots of what God sees when He bends 'down his eye / His own works and their works at once to view' (III, 58–9). It is with such divine, or approaching divine, perspectives on the world that *Paradise Lost* above all arouses the astonishment that an epic was supposed to arouse.

A god's-eye view of things and flying through the universe were always favourite themes of Milton's. When he considers suitable topics for poetry in his undergraduate verses, 'At a Vacation Exercise', he first turns to what 'The deep transported mind' might see, a vision of heaven, and then comes down through the universe to the weather, the mountains and the sea. In other poems, he turns to what platonic methods might do to release him from his earthbound condition. In 'Il Penseroso', he is attracted to unsphering

> The spirit of Plato to unfold
> What worlds or what vast regions hold
> The immortal mind that hath forsook
> Her mansion in this fleshy nook.
> (lines 89–92)

This talk of conjuring up the spirit of Plato at least toys with neoplatonic magic. Admittedly, the platonisings of 'Il Penseroso' quickly give way to other pastimes of the withdrawn mind, such as reading Greek tragedies. Yet, platonic reachings beyond the earth are characteristic of Milton's early poetry. In the 'Arcades', the genius of the wood runs through various pastoral fancies about the natural world before suddenly modulating into a platonising account of how he is attuned to the universal harmony of the music of the spheres. The suddenness of the modulation is typical. As with so much of Milton's early poetry, we start with an imaginary version of the natural world and its vital powers in which the mind can wander as in a Spenserian landscape, only to be surprised with a sudden glorying in a vision of the supernatural and celestial world. In the 'Arcades' the genius of the wood has no trouble in entering into the spiritual world, since he is a spirit. For a human, however, some sort of purification seems necessary to transport him out of his earthly condition. Such at least is the implication of the genius's remark that the universal harmony is something 'none can hear / Of human mould with gross unpurged ear' (lines 72–3); a human, that is, might purge himself of his mortal grossness by ascetic discipline, by something like the 'spare fast' of 'Il Penseroso' and the chastity of *Comus*. In this early poetry, the urge to travel beyond the earth into heavenly regions means paring down the creaturely life of the body; one leaves the physical world by denying one's physical nature.

Cosmic flights are commonplaces of Renaissance literature. Particularly with Italian Renaissance platonism, they are a figure for 'the divinising of man', the release of his spirit, hungry for God, through speculative disciplines. Milton's early flights are comparatively tame; but, even though he seems to have been too sober to enter deeply into esoteric studies and transcendental enthusiasm of the Italian sort, Renaissance platonism of the Cambridge sort clearly touched him as a young man.[56]

By the time he came to write *Paradise Lost*, he had shed asceticism. The heaven of which Raphael tells is likened to unfallen earth, except that heaven's bliss seems to be more enormous. At the banquets there they eat and drink 'secure / Of surfeit where full measure only bounds / Excess' (V, 638–40). As for chastity, the angels conjugate like the slipper animalcule: 'Total they mix, union of pure with pure / Desiring' (VIII, 627–8). There cannot be much room in such a heaven for the 'spare temperance' and 'sage and serious doctrine of virginity' of *Comus* (line 767). These virtues, as far as *Paradise Lost* is concerned, could not draw humans upwards. The space that separates earth and heaven there is not lethal or empty, and it is not to be overcome by alienation from one's creaturely existence. In the passage on Mulciber's fall, it is imagined as a summer's day:

> from morn
> To noon he fell, from noon to dewy eve,
> A summer's day; and with the setting sun
> Dropped from the zenith like a falling star
> On Lemnos.
>
> (I, 742–6)

It is not just the way in which the day elapses from line to line that suggests the enormous fall; it is the height of summer air itself through which Mulciber floats until, approaching earth, he appears to shoot downwards. Mulciber's fall, Milton expressly tells us, was a fable; but, as he pictures it, the real universe is also a height of air, 'soft delicious air' (II, 400), 'pure, marble air' (III, 564), 'buxom air' (V, 270), and the verbs he uses to describe travel through it

('winnows', 'wheels', 'soars') convey a delighted sense of the element, its
resistance and its support of the body. Even of his own poetic flight to heaven,
where he sings 'with so much gravity and ease', he says that he breathed
'empyreal air' (VII, 14).[57]

Yet, if *Paradise Lost* turns from the asceticism of Milton's early poems, it is
at the same time the glorious maturity of his youthful visionary attempts to rise
above the earth. It pictures at once the grandest of all his imaginary versions of
the natural world, enormously and intricately various in the wandering energies
that compose it, and at the same time the most astonishing transports of the
mind beyond this world, above all in the epic flight of the poet himself. The
cosmic flight, however, is the poem's image for aspiring to be as God by means
of forbidden knowledge.

> Heaven is for thee too high
> To know what passes there; be lowly wise:
> Think only what concerns thee and thy being.
> (VIII, 172–4)

These are Raphael's words to Adam, discouraging him from speculative astronomy, and here he gives the poem's general moral about obedience a particular
application: obedience to God means knowing oneself as His creature and
attending to one's creaturely standing. How is it, then, that the poem can ignore
its own teaching so signally in soaring beyond the earth?

In the second half of the seventeenth century, Dryden and Cowley, in
whom we can discern Augustan humanism taking shape, were still able to
write with sympathy for the generous fire that carried the mind above itself.
We must allow something of this to Milton's flights, conveying, as they do,
so much more impressively than Cowley's rather strained and easily translat-
able Pindaric raptures, the sense of being lifted up beyond the world. Nevertheless, Milton does not really exempt himself from what his poem teaches
about transgressing human limits. Leaving aside for the moment the poet's
tremendous flight in the invocations, the other flights of the poem all turn to
the earth as the focus of interest. Satan's flight up from hell and Raphael's
and the Son's down from heaven open up an enormous universal sweep of
height and depth, only to centre on 'this punctual spot' (VIII, 23), the human
stage. The human attempts to mount above the earth are vain. All the real
flights through the universe (apart from Satan's return to hell or Uriel's to
the sun) come down to earth, where the action of the poem is worked out. The
cosmic journeyings in *Paradise Lost* move in the opposite direction from Pico's
or Bruno's heaven-storming flights. They tend to earth and mankind; and in
the end, far from transporting us beyond the world we know, the movements
through space discover a world where everything turns on human choice. In

this way, Milton has changed the direction of those flights beyond the earth that recur so noticeably in his earlier work. Instead of simply exulting in transcendent power, in *Paradise Lost* he bends them to 'the discovery of the world and of man'.

There remains the grandest flight of all, however – Milton's flight as epic poet. In the invocation to Book I, he speaks of his ambition 'to soar / Above the Aonian mount' (line 15). In the invocation to Book VII, he tells us how 'I soar / Above the flight of Pegasean wing' (lines 3–4). In both cases, he is not merely soaring but also soaring above other soarers, and in both cases the peculiar lift in the verse obtained from drawing 'soar / Above' over the line-ending catches the mounting of the mind. Again, in both the invocation to Book VII and the one to Book III, he calls attention to how he has transgressed human limits. He boasts of how 'Into the heav'n of heav'ns I have presumed / An earthly guest' (VII, 13–14), and invokes the power of Holy Light so that he 'may see and tell / Of things invisible to mortal sight' (III, 54–5). Even in his invocations, however, Milton places himself as a human being inside the universal frame of things he describes. A transcendental impulse is there, but equally an urge to human definition, to coming to terms with being human. To see how this is so, we should look at the invocation to Book III.[58]

The invocation is a prayer. About to treat heaven and the world of light, Milton asks for a special privilege so that he, as a human, may imagine those things. Where a mystagogue might have relied on his own divine fury, Milton characteristically asks to be raised as he stands and waits in his finite being by an infinite power outside him. Besides, however lofty his style, Milton says nothing that may not humanly be spoken. He has no photosophical doctrines about the identity of holy light.[59] In his opening salutation, he turns over three possibilities about its nature, but with studious vagueness settles for none. Only one thing is clear, that light comes from God, and Milton invokes it as the active principle of his wisdom. Nor on the strength of this prayer does his following account of heaven violate the terms of knowledge. The ideas which the Father and the Son express may be idiosyncratic in some details, but they are addressed to the common topics of biblical theology. Milton had not arrived at them by special illumination but by straightforward reasoning from the general revelation to the human mind in the Bible. Moreover, they concern human life. The plan of salvation that the Father unfolds, and the doctrine of free obedience, set the terms of human life as Milton conceived it. Even the specific details of the pictures of heaven are mostly drawn from the Bible, Milton's imagination supplying mainly general effects of spatial array, light and power. He has nothing to say about the hangings of the council chamber of the Trinity.

The invocation is not just a prayer, but also a meditation on the course of the poem. Indeed, one of the reasons for the elevation of the passage is that it is a point of vantage from which the conduct of the epic, behind and before, can be surveyed. However, in its thinking about the poem, as in its prayer for power, the invocation looks to the human condition of the poet.

Until this point, the narrative has moved from the infernal regions up through chaos to the realm of light following Satan. After the invocation, the perspective abruptly shifts to heaven and the prospect of the Father looking down into the universe.[60] In Book IV the narrative finally focuses on the earth. Many epics contain some such traverse of height and depth: the first book of the *Davideis*, for example, has scenes in hell and in heaven. The initial unbroken sweep from one extreme of the universe to the other, however, and the coming to rest on earth, are peculiar to *Paradise Lost*. There, the extraordinary shifts of perspective assert the centrality of the human action. This movement from one extreme to another to assert the central concern with the middle state is caught in the invocation to Book III in a special way. Between the satanic perspective of the first books and the heavenly one of the first part of Book III, there is an effect of dislocation, and, for the period of the invocation, the universe is located inside the human mind. For the time, we stop following Satan's progress and the opening-out of the universe, and see these things revolving in the poet's thought about his poem. The narrative is broken, so that we enter into considering how a human can compass it.

The epic is internalised and gathered to mind through the figurative discourse of the invocation. There is first the figure of the cosmic flight itself. Until Book III, the business of the poem was to follow Satan's flight upwards through chaos. In the invocation, this turns into the poet's flight, no longer Satan's flight, but Milton's own epic undertaking in relating it to the point where he can talk of himself revisiting the world of light: 'with bolder wing escaped the Stygian pool'. The imagery of light also turns the epic into something revolved in the poet's mind. Milton is about to treat heaven and earth, where holy light runs through creation: but, though he can feel the sun, he cannot see the 'summer's rose, / Or flocks, or herds, or human face divine' that will come into his poem when he reaches Paradise. The world of light comes home to him as his being cut off from these things by his blindness, the peculiar mark of his share in fallen humanity. Deprivation is one way in which the epic's world of light turns inwards. But Milton wants to put himself in touch with the light whose creative power his poem must describe in a less inverted way. The physical light illuminating creation is only one form of holy light. It can enlighten the mind directly as well, and so Milton prays for a special, compensatory, spiritual illumination:

> So much the rather thou celestial Light
> Shine inward, and the mind through all her powers
> Irradiate, there plant eyes, all mist from thence
> Purge and disperse.
>
> (III, 51–4)

Here, even in its spiritual operation, light works as it does physically in the world which Milton will describe. He asks it to disperse mist from his mind as it will disperse darkness in Paradise in Book V. In glancing forwards to the world of light and backwards to Satan's flight, the invocation brings the course of the epic to mind, with a specific view to the poet in his blind and human condition. For a space, it takes us inside the poem as something being produced by a human mind for all the universal sweep that seems to go beyond it.

Something should be said about the beautiful passage on poetry in blindness that interrupts Milton's lament (Book III, 26–40), where the invocation modulates into something mysterious and touching. Peculiarly Miltonic themes are sounded – his longing for fame and for a sacred transformation of weakness into power, blind man into seer, lonely man into prophet. Thoughts of these things move not only of their own accord, 'voluntary', but also, as the sentence runs over from line 37 to line 38, 'voluntary move / Harmonious numbers'. The movement is, however, tentative, a reaching for the transfiguration of the final prayer for inner illumination without arriving there. The section concludes with the nightingale that 'in shadiest covert hid / Tunes her nocturnal note'. With an odd inwardness, the world's being hidden from the blind poet is inverted in the nightingale's being hidden from the world, but still the nightingale is only a figure for a blind poet, not a divinely-inspired one. The rest of the invocation brings the epic down to Milton's creatureliness with a cosmic sweep, but rather generally. The associative and hesitant progress of this section takes us inside Milton's mind much more intimately. Here, if anywhere, we are assured that it is a human being who is speaking to us.

The invocation to Book III keeps within human bounds, even where it seems to transgress them. Much of its genuine poetic power arises from its holding the urge to transcendent poetic power within human limits and from Milton's turning his mind upon his creaturely human condition. The poetry does not evaporate in the transports of a Pico or a Bruno.

> *O what a vile and abject thing is man* (saith [Senecal]) *unlesse he raise himself above humanity!* Observe here a notable speech, and a profitable desire; but likewise absurd. For to make the handfull greater then the hand, and the embraced greater then the arme; and to hope to straddle more then our legs length; it is impossible and monstrous: nor that man should mount

over and above himselfe and humanity; for, he cannot see but with his owne eyes, nor take hold but with his owne armes. He shall raise himselfe up, if it please God extraordinarily to lend His helping hand. He may elevate himself by forsaking and renouncing his owne meanes, and suffering himselfe to be elevated and raised by meere heavenly means. It is for our Christian faith, not for his Stoicke vertue to pretend or aspire to this divine Metamorphosis, or miraculous transmutation. ('An Apologie of Raymond Sebond', *Essays*, 2 ch. 12, 326)

The spirit of Montaigne's gloomy essay is utterly different from the spirit of Milton's soaring invocation. Surprisingly, though, Milton soars within the same limits as Montaigne urges to deflate the human impulse to get above oneself.

Of those writers who speak of human finitude, Ricoeur makes the following criticism:

It is finite man *himself* who speaks of his *own* finitude. A statement on finitude testifies that this finitude knows itself and exposes itself. Thus it is of the nature of human finitude that it can experience itself only on condition that there be 'a view on' finitude, a dominating look which has already begun to trangress this finitude. In order for human finitude to be seen and expressed, a moment which surpasses it must be inherent in the situation, condition or state of being finite ... The complete discourse on finitude is a discourse on the finitude and infinitude of man.[61]

At first glance, Milton seems open to this charge of transgressing the limits which he sets down as human. In fact, he supplies the complete 'discourse on finitude', which Ricoeur says includes a discourse on infinitude. The finitude of human nature in Milton's scheme of things, as in that of the Augustan humanists, is something precarious. Humans are fallible; they can indeed transgress their limits and fall out of their human being into something else. The whole art or calling of being human consists in maintaining one's finite human nature by means of the reason that is also choice, or by exact discriminations. In the nature of free will or judgement, however, there is a sort of infinitude or undeterminedness, even though its true scope is to choose what lies within human bounds. A free being who chooses what lies within the limits that make us human does so with the power to transgress them.

In *Paradise Lost*, the point is made with peculiar immediacy. The flights of the poem beyond human limits and the way in which they come down to earth in the end are a picture of the freedom that discovers and chooses human limitation. Literally, they supply a 'view on' human finitude by showing the earth from universal perspectives; metaphorically, they discover the human condition, the middle state, in the scheme of things that lies outside it. At the centre of the scheme of things in *Paradise Lost* lies free obedience to the divine command. Here again, there is the same play of infinitude or freedom and finitude or the discovery of a limit. The command not to eat the apple makes human creatureliness explicit. It draws a line between humanity and godhead, but in such a way that it can be observed rationally and freely. For Milton, the rational and free realisation of the creaturely condition is the proper study of mankind, what the mind in the fullest exertion of its powers turns to.

Notes

1   Anders Nygren, *Eros and Agape*, tr. Philip S. Watson (Philadelphia, 1953), pp. 684–91, 700–9. For a precise account of Luther's relation to medieval thought, see Heiko A. Oberman, '*Facientibus quod in se est Deus non denegat gratiam*: Robert Holcot, O.P., and the Beginnings of Luther's Theogy' and '*Simul Gemitus et Raptus*: Luther and Mysticism', in *The Reformation in Medieval Perspective*, ed. Stephen E. Ozment (Chicago, 1971); 'The Shape of Late Medieval Thought: The Birthpages of the Modern Era', *The Pursuit of Holiness in Late Medieval Religion*, ed. Charles Trinkaus and Heiko A. Oberman (Leiden, 1974), pp. 19–25; 'The Augustine Renaissance in the Later Middle Ages', *Masters of the Reformation: The Emergence of a New Intellectual Climate in Europe* tr. Dennis Martin (Cambridge, 1981), pp. 64–110.

2   'Disputation against Scholastic Theology' (1517), ed. Harold J. Grimm, *Luther's Works*, 31 (St Louis, 1957), p. 12. For Luther's relation to nominalism, see Oberman, '*Facientibus quod in se est*, p. 128ff., and David Steinmetz's criticism of Oberman, *Luther and Staupitz: An*

3   *Luther and Erasmus*, ed. Rupp and Watson, pp. 112, 124, for 'sophists'; p. 185, for 'Madame Reason'.

4   'Commentary on Psalm 51', *Selected Psalms*, 1, ed. Jaroslav Pelikan, *Luther's Works*, 12 (St Louis, 1955), p. 313.

5   *Institutes of the Christian Religion*, ed. John T. McNeill (Philadelphia, 1960), 1, 43–9, 51–69.

6   *Institutes*, 1, 69ff. As William J. Bouwsma points out in *John Calvin: A Sixteenth-Century Portrait* (New York, 1988), p. 132, 'Calvin was ... moving toward, though he never quite reached, a conception of the wholeness of the human being'.

7   With this statement concerning the integrity of body and soul, contrast the young Milton's position in 'Prolusion VII', *CP*, 1, 291: 'This eternal life, as almost everyone admits, is to be found in contemplation alone, by which the mind is uplifted, without the aid of the body, and gathered within itself so that it attains to its inexpressible joy, a life akin to the immortal gods'.

8   Cf. Raphael addressing Adam, VIII, 219–21, 'God on thee / Abundantly his gifts hath also poured / Inward and outward both, his image fair'. Calvin, *Institutes*, 1, 188, refuting Osiander's anthropomorphism, allows at least a glow of the image of God to appear in the body, though it is chiefly stamped in the mind or soul. Milton's poetry seems to go further, though one cannot educe a definite theological commitment from it: 'poured' in both passages quoted conveys a divine energy, a passing of one thing into another, rather than the positing of a stable quality. Milton's feeling for the body in *Paradise Lost* has at any rate developed from what he felt when he wrote *Comus*, where only the human face 'is the express resemblance of the gods' (lines 67–8).

9   See Paul O. Kristeller, 'The Humanist Movement', *Renaissance Thought and its Sources*, ed. Michael Mooney (New York, 1979), pp. 21–32.

10   See H. A. Mason, *Humanism and Poetry in Tudor England* (London, 1959), p. 256ff. Hans Baron, 'The Querrelle of the Ancients and the Moderns as a Problem for Renaissance Scholarship', *Renaissance Essays*, ed. Paul O. Kristeller and Philip P. Wiener (New York, 1968), p. 107, points out that *aemulatio*, not *imitatio*, became the cry of the best humanists from Poliziano to Erasmus, and subsequently.

11   The final form of this story can be found in Pope's 'Essay on Criticism' (694–6), where Erasmus '*Stemm'd the Wild Torrent* of a *barb'rous Age* / And drove these *Holy Vandals* off the Stage' (*The Poems*, ed. John Butt (London, 1963), and Gibbon's *Decline and Fall*, where Petrarch's viewing the ruins of Rome initiates the movement to restore civilisation.

12   *The Rhetorical World of Augustan Humanism: Ethics and Imagery from Swift to Burke* (Oxford, 1965), p. 142ff.

13 *Of Education*, *CP*, 2, 374; see also 'Prolusion VII' for the decay of learning, *CP*, 1, 293.

14 For references to the importance of eloquence in Renaissance humanism, see note 1, Chapter 1.

15 For another view, see Brian Vickers, *In Defence of Rhetoric* (Oxford, 1988).

16 François Rabelais, *Gargantua and Pantagruel*, tr. Thomas Urquhart (London, 1929), 1, 44.

17 Cf. Valla's criticism of scholastic language in his *Dialectical Disputations*, on which see Jerold E. Seigel, *Rhetoric and Philosophy in Renaissance Humanism: The Union of Eloquence and Wisdom, Petrarch to Valla* (Princeton, 1968), p. 164. Oberman, 'Shape of Late Medieval Thought', p. 14, and *Masters of the Reformation*, pp. 43–5, connects humanism and nominalism in this respect, but the humanist objection is to terms of art rather than unnecessary verbal entities, and so applies to nominalists as well as realists. Hanna-Barbara Gerl, *Rhetorik als Philosophie: Lorenzo Valla* (Munich, 1974), p. 77ff., discusses the notion of common sense involved in Valla's idea of eloquence.

18 'On the Freedom of the Will', *Luther and Erasmus*, p. 40; as a term of abuse for the schoolmen, it is at least as old as Petrarch; see Charles Trinkaus, *The Poet as Philosopher: Petrarch and the Formation of Renaissance Consciousness* (New Haven, 1979), pp. 6–7. Humanists did not totally reject scholasticism. Erasmus turns to them on a theological issue, the freedom of the will, and contemptuously allows something to Scotus in his 'Letter on Colet and Vitry', ed. John C. Olin, *Christian Humanism and the Reformation: Selected Writings of Erasmus* (New York, 1965), 166. Melanchthon, who admitted the need for philosophical education, thought of himself as a nominalist (Oberman, *Masters of the Reformation*, pp. 29–30).

19 François Rabelais, *Œuvres Complètes*, ed. Jacques Boulenger (Paris, 1951), p. 81.

20 *Summa Contra Gentiles*, tr. English Dominican Fathers (London, 1928), 3, 78, cited by Charles Trinkaus, *Adversity's Noblemen: The Italian Humanists on Happiness* (New York, 1965), pp. 33–4.

21 Oberman, *Masters of the Reformation*, pp. 43–4; Trinkaus, *In Our Image*, 1, 60, and *Poet as Philosopher*, pp. 29ff., calls attention to the connection between nominalist and humanist thought on the grounds of scepticism about the mind's capacity for contemplating ultimate truth.

22 Humanists like Melanchthon, who were not entirely hostile to scholastic philosophy, still maintained the primacy of eloquence because it made reason and the will of God active and current in the human world; see Quirinus Breen, 'Melanchthon's Reply to Giovanni Pico della Mirandola', *JHI*, 13 (1952), pp. 413–26; see also the Danish Melanchthonian, Jens Andersen Sinning, *Oratio de studiis philosophicis, theologiae studioso necessariis* (1591), ed. Eric Jacobsen (Copenhagen, 1991), pp. 29–34, for a defence of dialectic in the study of theology. The youthful Milton, arguing for the excellence of learning as affording a godlike power of contemplation, still maintains that 'Virtue without Learning is more conducive to happiness than Learning without Virtue' and hastily passes from contemplation to learning's social advantages ('Prolusion VII', *CP*, 1, 293ff.). Even in this platonising phase, Milton's man of learning is still an orator (p. 288).

23 See William T. Costello, SJ, *The Scholastic Curriculum at Early Seventeenth-Century Cambridge* (Cambridge, Mass., 1955); Mark H. Curtis, *Oxford and Cambridge in Transition* (Oxford, 1959); Roberto Weiss, 'Learning and Education in Western Europe from 1470 – 1520', *The Renaissance*, ed. G.R. Potter, *New Cambridge Modern History*, vol. 1 (Cambridge, 1964), p. 126; Lisa Jardine, 'The Place of Dialectic Teaching in Seventeenth Century Cambridge', *Studies in the Renaissance*, 21 (1974), pp. 31–52; see also John Aubrey, *Brief Lives*, ed. Anthony Powell (London, 1949), p. 304, for an account of the young Chillingworth at Oxford as disputing machine. For the history of rhetoric and logic in this period see Wilbur Samuel Howell, *Logic and Rhetoric in England, 1500 – 1700* (Princeton, 1956) and *Eighteenth-Century British Logic and Rhetoric* (Princeton, 1971).

24 Kristeller, 'Humanism and Scholasticism', p. 580; Jose Ferrater Mora, 'Suarez and Modern Philosophy', *JHI*, 14 (1953), pp. 528–47. See also *The Autobiography of Richard Baxter*, ed. N. H. Keeble (London, 1974), pp. 9, 109, for a seventeenth-century puritan use of the schoolmen.

25 See Charles Webster, *The Great Instauration: Science, Medicine and Reform, 1620 – 1660* (London, 1975), pp. 115–90, for the interest in the natural sciences at the universities and the chiefly informal provisions for their study.

26 *Dunciad*, IV, 190–2; see also *Memoirs of the Extraordinary Life, Works and Discoveries of Martinus Scriblerus*, ed. Charles Kerby-Miller (New Haven, 1950), pp. 122–4, for jokes about scholasticism, and Kerby-Miller's note, pp. 243–4, on Aristotelian logic at the univerities.

27 Epistle. 1211, to Justus Jonas, tr. R. A. B. Mynors, *Correspondence of Erasmus: 1520 – 1521*, vol. 8 (Toronto, 1988), pp. 226–33.

28 Tr. Charles Trinkaus, *The Renaissance Philosophy of Man*, ed. Ernst Cassirer et al. (Chicago, 1948), pp. 155–82.

29 Erasmus, *On the Freedom of the Will*, Luther and Erasmus, p. 64ff., for figurative and allegorical interpretation of Scripture as distinct from Luther's literalism.

30 *Advancement of Learning, Philosophical Works of Francis Bacon*, ed. John M. Robertson (London: Routledge, 1905), p. 55. See Aubrey Williams, *Pope's 'Dunciad': A Study of its Meaning* (London, 1955), p. 107.

31 *In Our Image*, 1, 320–1; see also Giuseppe Toffanin, *History of Humanism*, tr. Elio Gianturco (New York, 1954), p. 194.

32 See Seigel, *Rhetoric and Philosophy*, to whose discussion I am generally indebted in what follows. See Milton's 'Prolusion III', *CP*, 1, 244, for his ideal of philosophy united with eloquence; also *Comus*, lines 476–8, and, not necessarily deflatingly, *Paradise Lost*, II, 555–61.

33 Petrarch, 'On his Own Ignorance and That of Many Others', *Renaissance Philosophy of Man*, p. 115; Erasmus, 'The Godly Feast', *Colloquies*, tr. Craig R. Thompson (Chicago, 1965), pp. 65–6.

34 I, XXII, 59–61, XXIII, 62, tr. Clinton Walker Keyes (London, 1948), pp. 364–7.

35 Marsilio Ficino, *Théologie platonicienne de l'immortalité des âmes*, ed. Raymond Marcel (Paris, 1964), 1, 35–36.

36 'Oration on the Dignity of Man', tr. Elizabeth Livermore Forbes, in Cassirer, *The Renaissance Philosophy of Man*, pp. 233–4.

37 See George B. Parks, 'Pico della Mirandola in Tudor Translation', *Philosophy and Humanism: Renaissance Essays in Honour of Paul Oskar Kristeller*, ed. Edward P. Mahoney (Leiden, 1976) p. 356ff.; on Erasmus's dabbling in hermetic lore, see S. K. Henninger Jr, 'Pythagorean Symbols in Erasmus's *Adagia*', *Renaissance Quarterly*, 23 (1970), pp. 162–5, and Paul Oskar Kristeller, 'Erasmus from an Italian Perspective, *Renaissance Quarterly*, 23 (1970), pp. 1–13.

38 Pico brought Aquinas and Scotus into his theistic syncretism all the same; see 'On the Dignity of Man', *Renaissance Philosophy of Man*, pp. 243ff.

39 Seigel, p. 141ff.

40 Lorenzo Valla, *On Pleasure*, tr. A. Kent Hieatt and Maristella Lorch (New York, 1977), pp. 107–23; see the interpretation in Lorch's introduction, pp. 28–31, and Trinkaus, *In Our Image*, 1, p. 157ff.

41 For the way in which Cicero attempted to modify stoicism with its transcendental impulse to his civic concern with law and human responsibility, see H. A. K. Hunt, *The Humanism of Cicero* (Melbourne, 1954). Both Boccaccio and Salutati were critical of stoicism; see Toffanin, p. 142. Cf. Erasmus, *The Praise of Folly*, tr. Betty Radice (Harmondsworth, 1971), pp. 75–7, 87–91, 100, and Calvin, *Institutes*, 1, 708–12. For a general account, see William J. Bouwsma, 'The Two Faces of Humanism: Stoicism and Augustinianism', *Itinerarium Italicum: The Profile of the Italian Renaissance in the Mirror of its European Transformations*, ed. Heiko A. Oberman and Thomas A. Brady Jr (Leiden, 1975), pp. 3–60.

42 Valla is putting forward an Epicurean, against a Stoic, ideal of living according to human nature; cf. Montaigne's idea of living '*à propos*' ('De l'expérience', *Essais*, ed. Maurice Rat (Paris, 1967), 2, 568), and H. A. Mason, *Humanism and Poetry in the Early Tudor Period* (London, 1959), p. 133.

43 'De l'expérience', *Essais*, 2, 568.

44 E.g. Douglas Bush, *The Renaissance and English Humanism* (Toronto, 1939), pp. 101–3.

45 Samuel Johnson, 'Milton', *Lives of the English Poet* (London, 1906), 1, 122; for the vogue of Raphael's lecture with Augustan humanists, see Fussell, *The Rhetorical Word of Augustan Humanism*, pp. 15–9.

46 On the dispensation of knowledge in Paradise, see Howard Schultz, *Milton and Forbidden Knowledge* (New York, 1953), pp. 173–83; Kester Svendsen, *Milton and Science* (Cambridge, Mass., 1956), p. 78; Dennis Burden, *The Logical Epic* (London, 1967), pp. 97–123.

47 On self-knowledge, see Lee A. Jacobus, *Sudden Apprehension: Aspects of Knowledge in 'Paradise Lost'* (The Hague, 1976), pp. 22–44.

48 *The State of Innocence*, Act 1, sc. 1, *The Dramatic Works of John Dryden*, ed. Sir Walter Scott, rev. George Saintsbury (Edinburgh, 1882), 5, 131.

49 Samuel Johnson, 'Essay 10', *The Rambler*, ed. W. J. Bate and Albrecht B. Strauss (New Haven, 1969), 2, 222, and Fussell's comment, p. 30, on it.

50 See Olin, *Christian Humanism and the Reformation*, pp. 169, 178; also H. A. Mason's discussion in *Humanism and Poetry*, p. 166 ff. The biblical model of angels eating with men is present alongside the humanist convivium; see John R. Knott Jr, 'The Visit of Raphael, *Paradise Lost*; 5' *PQ*, 47 (1968), pp. 35–42; Jack Goldman, 'Perspectives of Raphael's Meal in *Paradise Lost*, Book V', *Milton Quarterly*, 11 (1977), pp. 31–7.

51 *On Pleasure*, p. 283; the saying comes from *De Amicitia*, 88, and is also cited by Stefano Guazzo, *The Civile Conversation of M. Steeven Guazzo*, tr. George Pettie and Barth. Young (London, 1925), 1, 36; see also Milton, 'Prolusion VII', *CP*, 1, 295, for the convivial ideal of learning.

52 See for example Yvonne Charlier, *Erasme et l'amitié, d'après sa correspondance* (Paris, 1977), p. 44, and 'Amicitia aequalitas' and 'Amicus alter ipse' in *Adages, l*, tr. Margaret Mann Philips, *Collected Works of Erasmus* (Toronto, 1982), p. 31.

53 The 'causes' in line 682 are of the kind Uriel mentions in III, 705–7, where, praising the cherubic Satan's desire to know the works of God, he adds, 'But what created mind can comprehend / Their number, or the wisdom infinite / That brought them forth, but hid their causes deep'. On causes, see Schultz, pp. 182–3, and cf. Bacon, *Advancement of Learning*, p. 45, on study of second rather than first causes.

54 Bacon, *Advancement of Learning*, p. 45.

55 Giordano Bruno, *Cena de la ceneri*, Dialogue. 1, tr. Stanley Jakki, *The Ash Wednesday Supper* (The Hague, 1975), p. 61.

56 See Schultz, *Forbidden Knowledge*, p. 49.

57 M. Mahood, *Poetry and Humanism* (London, 1950), p. 199.

58 In this invocation and others, there is a rough resemblance to du Bartas's poetic course: 'My heedful Muse trained in the true religion / Devinely human keeps the middle region', 'The First Day of the First Weeke', 135–6, *The Divine Weeks and Works of Guillaume Sieur du Bartas*, tr. Joshua Sylvester, ed. Susan Snyder (Oxford, 1976), p. 115. Milton, however, transforms this conventional piety into a strong image of movement through space to find the human place in things.

59 For attempts to identify Holy Light, see William B. Hunter Jr, 'The Meaning of Holy Light in *Paradise Lost*, III', *MLN*, 74 (1959), pp. 589–92, and 'Holy Light in *Paradise Lost*, *Rice Inst. Pamphlets*, 46, no. 4 (1960), pp. 1–14. See also Albert B. Cirillo, ' "Hail Holy Light" and Divine Time in *Paradise Lost*', *JEGP*, 68 (1969), pp. 45–56.

60 See Isabel Gamble MacCaffery, *'Paradise Lost' as Myth*, (Cambridge, 1959), p. 60, on change of perspective.

61 Paul Ricoeur, *Fallible Man*, tr. Charles Kebley (Chicago, 1965), p. 38.

Chapter 3

Paradise Lost *and the Neoclassical Epic*

Epic as Eloquence

Of all the genres, epic answered best to the ideas of neoclassical humanists. The neoclassical critics reduced it to a sort of eloquence, and the poets themselves conceived their epics in rhetorical designs. Epic seemed to offer the best chances to realise humanist ambitions for literary culture as the active, civilising power of the word. Its standing was, in fact, such that, in spite of the authority of Aristotle, whose preference was for tragedy, the neoclassical critics generally held epic to be the highest literary genre.[1] If, then, the humanist concern with rhetoric is connected with the humanist study of human nature in its middle state, that connection should run through the neoclassical epic, the institutional form, one might call it, of neoclassical humanism; and it does run, in the form of a development, as will be shown by juxtaposing *Jerusalem Delivered, Paradise Lost* and *Absalom and Achitophel*. Tasso's theme is the Renaissance one of the divinising of human ends now taken up with the peculiar intensities of the Counter-Reformation. With Milton and Dryden, on the other hand, everything turns on human creatureliness. In this development, *Paradise Lost* was central. It pulled together religious and humanist notions of finite man and supplied a grand outline for Augustan humanism to work with. Yet *Paradise Lost* is also an eccentric neoclassical epic. Though in rhetorical design it is as highly evolved as any neoclassical epic, and though it is the grand treatment of human finitude in English, its human action goes beyond the sort of poetry that can be talked about adequately in terms of eloquence. Though so important in the development of the humanist epic, *Paradise Lost* complicates the story. Its study of the will does not lie conformably with the rhetorical conception of other humanist epics. This fairly sticks out as soon as one tries to match it with *Jerusalem Delivered* and *Absalom and Achitophel*. Milton's treatment of the will, however, requires a chapter to itself, and the rhetorical and universal design of neoclassical epics will be discussed here in order to bring out how *Paradise Lost* belongs to, and not, except summarily, how it departs from, the development of neoclassical humanism.

   The neoclassical humanist theory that literature is a sort of rhetoric goes back to antiquity. In *Pro Archia*, for example, Cicero defends humanist studies on the grounds that they supply a moral education.[2] Literature makes images of moral virtue and gives them heroic lustre. These not only show us what virtue is, but also attract our admiration, and stir up our feelings and wills to imitate them. We shape our self-image in the image of virtue that literature holds up. So, Cicero tells us that he has modelled his character on the ideal figures of literature and, *me consule* (the irresistible topic), was braced by their example to expose himself for the public safety to the Catiline Conspiracy.[3] This is to think of literature as moral eloquence.

The rhetorical notion of the power of the literary example confronts us everywhere in the literary theory of the neoclassical humanists.[4] Sidney's *Defence of Poetry* states it in a spirited and elegant form. His argument for the superiority of poetry over moral philosophy works up humanist commonplaces about the rhetorical power of the literary example or image. Unlike the mere precept of the moral philosopher, the image works on the will.[5] It is here that the poet is superior to the historian as well, even though the historian supplies examples. A historian is tied to what happened, while a poet can invent what he pleases and so make moral ideas appear in a vastly more attractive form than they do in dim historical fact.

It is this idea of poetry's power to forge charming or inspiring fictions that lies behind what sounds like a declaration of entire poetic irresponsibility. Practitioners of other human arts must, according to Sidney, stick to nature.

> Only the poet, disdaining to be tied to any such subjection, lifted up with the vigor of his own invention, doth grow in effect another nature, in making things either better than nature bringeth forth, or quite anew, forms such as never were in nature, as the Heroes, Demigods, Cyclops, Chimeras, Furies, and such like: so as he goeth hand in hand with nature, not enclosed within the narrow warrant of her gifts, but freely ranging only within the zodiac of his wit. Nature never set forth the earth in so rich tapestry as divers poets have done; neither with so pleasant rivers, fruitful trees, sweet smelling flowers, nor whatsoever else may make the too much loved earth more lovely. Her world is brazen, the poets only deliver a golden. (p. 78)

This is to make such claims for creativity that it seems to contradict Sidney's statement that poetry is an imitative art. He seems to be talking about imagination, not imitation; but this is a distinction that he would not have drawn. He does not mean what Aristotle meant by 'imitation', but rather putting the shapes of the imagination into words, making verbal images of them. Still, Sidney does hold that these images copy something, only that what they copy is not human actions, the object of Aristotelian imitation, but ethical ideas. Sidney's poet is one who invents images of virtues and vices, that is, one who furnishes moral examples. This shows in the way in which he distinguishes poets who truly 'imitate' in his sense from a second sort, namely philosophical, astronomical or historical poets:

Betwixt [true poets] and these second is such a kind of difference as betwixt the meaner sort of painters, who counterfeit only such faces as are set before them, and the more excellent, who having no law but wit, bestow that in colours upon you which is fittest for the eye to see: as the constant lamenting look of Lucretia whom he never saw, but painteth the outward beauty of such a virtue. For those [true poets] be they which most properly do imitate to teach and delight, and to imitate borrow nothing of what is, hath been, or shall be; but range, only reined with learned discretion, into the divine consideration of what may be and should be. (pp. 80–1)

From this didactic theory of the image, it follows that poetry is more philosophical than history; it is more universal. Here, Sidney again has recourse to Aristotle's terms for un-Aristotelian thoughts. While Aristotle considered that the universality of poetry lay in its representing a human action according to a general understanding of how people behave, Sidney holds that it is a matter of representing examples of how people ought or ought not to behave. The universality of poetry for Sidney consists in its fashioning images of universal moral ideas (pp. 87–8). In this didactic theory of ideal imitation, the poet's creative freedom that Sidney so enthusiastically celebrates turns out to be his job of inspiring his readers; in the golden world he fashions, images of moral ideas can be arrayed with hyperbolical splendour.

Ideal imitation such as Sidney describes is the standard literary theory among neoclassical humanists.[6] Milton himself shared the rhetorical theory of poetry. In his pamphlet *Of Education*, he suggests that poetry should be taught before the other arts of language, rhetoric and logic, 'as being lesse suttle and fine, but more simple, sensuous and passionate' than they are.[7] 'Simple, sensuous and passionate' – out of context, it sounds a surprising recipe for the author of *Paradise Lost* to put forward. In context, however, it is clear that he means no more than to epitomise the stock view of his time. He is making the conventional distinction between poetry and those other arts of rational discourse, logic and rhetoric. Poetry is not concerned to draw out arguments analytically as logic or rhetoric might. 'Lesse suttle and fine', it puts forward ideas through images, and these are 'simple' because they combine things in shapes we grasp immediately (*pietas*, for example, is a complex idea, and logic or rhetoric would have to make something of its complexities; but think of Aeneas and they all hang together), 'sensuous' because literary images are taken in by the imagination or mind's eye as speaking pictures, and 'passionate' because they arouse our feelings and move our wills to imitation. What is implied, then, in Milton's famous phrase is the neoclassical humanist notion of poetry as ideal imitation. If what he stresses in this place is the difference between poetry and rhetoric (not to mention logic), it is nevertheless clear enough here and elsewhere that he did not set poetry radically apart from rhetoric.

The trouble with ideal imitation is that, as a theory, it provides for the representation of reality very crudely. The poetic imagination is bound to human life only by its intention to improve its readers. As for showing what experience is like or how people work, no more is called for than will at once disguise moral ideas and render them visible to the mind's eye. Not likeness but rhetorical effectiveness is the standard. Neoclassical critics do talk of verisimilitude – but, strikingly, their talk resolves itself into discussions of decorum (what actions and what talk suit conventional characters) or of paralogism (the lively faking of circumstantial details to make the impossible seem probable, or at least imaginatively compelling). Both decorum and paralogism are essentially rhetorical considerations. They ask for no more than conventional ideas of human likeness.[8]

The foregoing attempt to lay bare the rhetorical basis of the theory of ideal imitation has neither tried to do justice to Sidney's *Defence* nor brought out any of the finer points of neoclassical theorising that may indeed be more interesting than the basis on which they stand. However, in case this account seems too reductive, there follow two representative statements from later neoclassical criticism, both about epic poetry and each as bald and summary as anything I have offered.

> The EPOPEA is a Discourse invented by Art, to form the Manners by such Instructions as are disguised under the Allegories of some one important Action, which is related in Verse, after a probable, diverting and surprising Manner.

So Le Bossu in his *Traité sur l'Epopée* of 1675.[9] One notes by the way that the diverting and the surprising are on a level with the probable for him. The second passage is from Johnson's *Life of Milton*:

> By the general consent of criticks, the first praise of genius is due to the writer of an epick poem, as it requires an assemblage of all the powers which are singly sufficient for other compositions. Poetry is the art of uniting pleasure with truth, by calling the imagination to the help of reason. Epick poetry undertakes to teach the most important truths by the most pleasing precepts, and therefore relates some great event in the most affecting manner.[10]

The precepts are pleasing because they are recommended by fiction cast into the form of moral examples. It is hard to imagine a blunter statement of the subordination of poetry to moral design.

Jerusalem Delivered

Theory is one thing, of course, the poetry itself another; but at least in the case of *Jerusalem Delivered*, a neoclassical epic answers all too closely to the rhetorical theory. In the opening invocation to the heavenly muse, Tasso excuses mixing divine truth with poetry on the grounds that poetry sugars the pill, or rather the lip of the cup that contains bitter moral medicine (Book 1, st. 3).[11] Here, in a traditional figure, Tasso gives expression to the didactic view of poetry: poetry seduces the reader to the truth by a kind of high-minded meretriciousness. On the one hand there are moral ideas, on the other hand fictions or images in which they may be rendered attractive. These are in fact the lines on which his poem is built, and for that reason it is exemplary of how ideal imitation works. However, it must be added that what makes it a good example makes it an unsatisfactory poem. Its rhetorical design is too simple to take in the mixed good and evil in which real virtues and vices are involved.

The ideal scheme of *Jerusalem Delivered* comes out immediately we consider the action, the delivery of Jerusalem. For Tasso, Jerusalem is the earthly image of the heavenly city. Its delivery from pagan occupation is the representative task of Christendom, the setting-up of the City of God on earth. More even than Aeneas's mission to found a new Troy, the recovery of Jerusalem is charged with moral idea, and consequently the characters involved in it are polarised into types of good and evil. Those who assist in the great enterprise are champions of good; those who resist or draw back from it are evil. The epic works up this polarity in two ways. In the first place, it treats a war, and so the conflict of good with evil takes on a conventional heroic form in which the virtuous cover themselves in the glory that is supposed to make goodness attractive. It is not enough, for example, that the elderly Raymond, the Nestor of the expedition, should exemplify prudence as a counsellor. He must have an 'aristeia' and exemplify prudence heroically in battle in the way he thwarts and parries the imprudent, that is headlong and furious, onslaught of the pagan Argantes (Book 7, sts 67–98). In the second place, Tasso harnesses the universe to his moral design, involving heaven and hell in his action. An epic, after all, treats not merely a heroic action but one of sufficient moment to interest the powers governing the universe. However, Tasso's supernatural powers, unlike Homer's or even Virgil's, are divided into good and evil. God and all the heavenly powers are for the crusaders, and the devil is against them. Because these supernatural forces of good and evil are behind the war, the conquest of Jerusalem then takes on the aspect of an episode in a cosmic war. This touches the moral images of the epic with a cosmic sublimity over and above the heroic lustre which they have from the human warfare. The virtuous are prompted and irradiated by the countenance of heaven; the vicious are darkened by the shades of hell. Rhetorically speaking, then, Tasso uses the epic form to represent his moral scheme as a universal scheme. By 'universal', I mean not just 'having the general application of a moral idea' but literally 'belonging to the design of the universe'.[12] *Jerusalem Delivered*, and in this it is typical of the neoclassical epic, might claim to be 'more philosophical than history', not just because it shows images of virtue and vice, but because it involves them in the workings of the universe. It fits a human action into the general scheme of things.

We should look at Tasso's images of virtues and vices more closely, for his poem treats the conflict of good and evil in a specific form. The virtues which he pictures all have to do with the idea of right order and the vices with disorder. The pagans from whom Jerusalem has to be delivered are naturally the forces of disorder.[13] Even their most puissant champions, Argantes and Soliman, are examples of ill-governed valour. What works against the overwhelming numbers of the pagan army, as much as the prowess of the Christians, is the former's lack of military discipline. The failure of the pagans' campaign comes from an inability to coordinate their three forces. Conversely, when the Christians are united under Godfrey's command and concerted into a three-pronged attack on the city, the pagan forces are unable to withstand the forces of order.

The simple scheme of conflict between order and disorder has, however, a complication. Although only the Christians exemplify the virtues of order and discipline, not all of them do so all the time. Godfrey is a pattern of a reasonable commander, supported by the good counsel exemplifed in Raymond and guided by the divine counsel whose mouthpiece is Peter the Hermit, but it is only towards the end of the poem that he is able to muster his paladins together to the siege. Until then, his army, divided by faction and distracted by beautiful women, is held up as much by its own disorganisation as by the resistance of the pagans. The forces of disorder lie within the forces of order as well as being ranged against them in the enemy, and disorder has to be overcome within the Christian camp before it can be overcome without. Tasso treats the theme of internal disorder on a public and on a private level. On the public level, Godfrey's generalship has to contend with rumour and jealousy. On the private level, disorder takes the form of personal indiscipline. Here, the action is focused on Rinaldo, who kills a fellow crusader in a fit of ungovernable heroic pique, leaves the Christian army and goes to live with Armida on her delightful mountain-top until two crusaders reclaim him for Christian warfare. The two treatments of the idea of order, public and private, fit together. Rinaldo is fitted to undertake duties under Godfrey's command when he regains his self-command. He then becomes Godfrey's most deadly man of war.

'Good and evil we know in the field of this world grow up together almost inseparably'.[14] Little moral discernment, however, is required of the characters of *Jerusalem Delivered*. Certainly, *Jerusalem Delivered* is not quite as simple as the moral scheme I have made out, but it is morally pretty simple all the same. There is little to admire in the victims of the crusaders' virtues. It is true that Tasso tries to invest some of the pagan army with a sort of nobility, but his attempts are meant to be easily seen through. Soliman and Argantes, for example, are bold, defiant and fierce. Tasso lets them kill minor Christians in droves and even match major ones in doubtful circumstances, though not snatch any glory from them. However, Soliman, and even more Argantes, at best exemplify the rash valour which Virgil had shown in Turnus – and there is more finesse in Virgil's treatment. We regret the destruction of human worth in Turnus; we are meant to accept the destruction of splendid vice in Soliman and Argantes.[15] There are, in addition, three women of epic attractiveness on the pagan side. Strikingly, though, Tasso does not let the pagan men feel attracted; love would make them sympathetic. The only pagan love is the Sultan's for his minion, and we are not meant to be drawn to that. By the end of the poem, the pagans have lost the women and their charms to the Christians. So, Tasso has seen to it not only that all the heroic and divine lustre is shed on Christian exemplars, but also that all the romantic attractiveness is associated with them as well.

There is no real moral ambiguity in the scheme of the poem. Virtue and vice are drawn up against each other on opposite sides. Nor do appearances complicate this simple opposition. There can be little doubt about the virtue of the virtuous or about the evil with which they contend. The virtuous may fall, however, and that does somewhat complicate the simple distinction between virtue and vice. Here the best example is Rinaldo, who falls from being a pattern of military virtue to sensuality and then is restored to military virtue again. The same vigour impels him as soldier or lover, and so he is an ambivalent image, or rather he may present an image of virtue or vice, and, with this ambivalence, personal will enters into the moral ideas which epic imitates.

Tasso's method of showing this ambivalence in images is overtly visual: he opposes one descriptive set piece to another so that there are true and false versions, the figure and its disfigurement. With Rinaldo the best counter-imaging is to be found in the contrast between his figure in eclipse with Armida and his figure restored after he has been brought back to the Christian army and indeed to himself. The fallen Rinaldo appears in two reflections. The first is this:

> Downe by the lovers side there pendant was
> A Christall mirrour, bright, pure, smooth and neat,
> He rose and to his mistresse held the glas,
> (A noble Page, grac'd with that seruice great)
> She, with glad lookes; he with enflam'd (alas)
> Beautie and loue beheld, both in one seat;
> > Yet them in sundrie obiects each espies,
> > She in the glasse; he, saw them in her eies.
> > > (Book 16, st. 20)

If one untwists the eyebeams of this mirror-and-eyes conceit, the picture is that Armida gazes at herself in the crystal while Rinaldo gazes at himelf in the pupils of her eyes. Tasso (not Fairfax) has it that they view in different objects a single object ('*Mirano in varii oggetti un solo oggetto*'). The single object is puzzling. But in the following stanzas, Rinaldo pleads with Armida to gaze at herself in him:

> For painted in my hart and purtrai'd right
> Thy woorth, thy beauties and perfections bee,
> > Of which the forme, the shape, and fashion best,
> > Not in this glas is seene, but in my brest.
> > > (St. 21)

The single object is presumably Armida, whether imaged directly in the crystal or indirectly in Rinaldo, who says he is the true glass of her perfection. At this point, Armida leaves for a moment, and two crusaders, who have been taking a good look at what is going on, hurry in to the rescue. They show Rinaldo another reflection, his image in a diamond shield. Here, there is a contrast between the deceptive mirror of love and the incorruptible mirror of Christian warfare in which Rinaldo sees a shameful image of himself, as Fairfax has it, 'a carpet champion for a wanton dame' (Book 16, st. 32)[16]:

> Vpon the targe his lookes amas'd he bent,
> And therein all his wanton habite spide,
> His civet, baulme, and perfumes redolent,
> How from his lockes they smoakt, and mantle wide,
> His sword that many a Pagan stout had shent,
> Bewrapt with flowres, hung idlie by his side,
> > So nicely decked, that it seemd the knight
> > Wore it for fashion sake, but not for fight.
> > > (Book 16, st. 30)

The effect of this image of himself as amorist is to shame Rinaldo, to stir up the warrior within against his disorderly appetites. He is repelled by an image of vice, so he returns with the knights to the Christian army and is prepared for duty by Peter the Hermit. At this point, Tasso inserts another picture, the image of Rinaldo as Christian restored from Rinaldo as Armida's man. Before entering on his warfare, Rinaldo prays on Olivet while it is still dark, repenting 'the sinnes and errours … / Of mine vnbridled youth' (Book 18, st. 14). As he finishes, it dawns; the light touches his armour and a special heavenly dew is infused upon him:

> The heau'nly dew was on his garments spred,
> To which compar'd, his clothes pale ashes seame,

> And sprinkled so, that all that paleness fled,
> And thence of purest white bright raies outstreame.
>
> (Book 18, st. 16)

In this painterly transfiguration, Rinaldo shines out as the Christian hero restored by divine mercy.

The counter-imaging of the false Rinaldo and the true Rinaldo is a striking way of representing the fall and restoration of a hero of Christian warfare, but it is a limited method when it comes to representing moral ideas. As Tasso manages it anyway, the mutability of the will does not really introduce mixed good and evil. The same opposition that holds for the war between Christian and pagan holds within Rinaldo. He either shines with virtue or is tarnished by vice, one or other but not both. Moreover, the representation of the motions of Rinaldo's will comes over, especially if we have *Paradise Lost* in mind, as strikingly external. Tasso is not concerned with tracing inward motions of volition. Rinaldo is abducted rather than tempted and seduced, and his repentance is left to the ministrations of the Hermit off the human stage.

Perhaps it is not possible for ideal imitation to grasp volition with any degree of inwardness. The nearest that Tasso comes to it is showing how Rinaldo appears to himself in reflections, and still the concern is for appearance, for the figure he cuts. That suits ideal imitation, with its making of images of moral ideas. Heroic images are addressed to our self-image. Their lustre is supposed to draw us to imitate them, to cut a figure like them. This concern for image has something narcissistic in it, or at least self-regarding. It is Rinaldo's self-regard that is appalled by what he sees in the shield. He does not gaze at himself in the shield once he has been restored, but, if one can imagine him at all as a person, one thinks of him as he prays on Olivet fairly tingling with a self-consciousness of restored Christian heroic worth, qualified of course with all proper contrition and humility. How else could a hero feel?

The self-regard to which the rhetorical appeal of ideal imitation is addressed pushes aside regard for other people. It is hard for a hero to stand other heroes, and it is hard for him to be in love without self-immolation. That comes out indirectly in the very curious relationship which erotic self-regard bears to heroic self-regard with Rinaldo and Armida. While heroic self-regard is not only morally respectable but also a prerequisite for the sort of virtue and the sort of ideal imitation Tasso conceives, erotic self-regard is to be deplored. So, when Armida gazes at herself in the crystal while Rinaldo looks on, we are clearly to think of her self-regard as blameworthy.[17] That she is enchanted by herself suggests that her love of Rinaldo is love of being loved by him. Yet, that hardly goes with the rest of her behaviour, which may be possessive and selfish but is too passionately taken up with Rinaldo to deserve the charge of narcissism. Indeed, she is usually more given to languishing over Rinaldo than he over her. The state of affairs once Rinaldo has reformed and has turned his love from her to his heroic self-image, while she pines for him, actually inverts what the mirror-and-eyes conceit tells us. In consequence, it is hard not to feel that the picture of Armida in love with her reflection is inserted to tell us something different from what we are shown in the rest of the poem. It seems inserted to impose the view that, really, her love is not love at all but self-love, or perhaps love of the charms that give her power over a man. It also encourages us to view the charms censoriously.

If this reading of the mirror-and-eyes conceit is right, Rinaldo is not to be charged with erotic self-regard. He is not narcissistically absorbed in his reflection in her eyes but in his reflection as a reflection of her. At this point, the conceit trembles on the edge of the sort of imagery, so habitual with Donne, that looks for love given and returned in the mutual reflections of lovers in the glasses of their eyes. We shall find in Milton a similar interest in mutuality reflected in looks or in the way one finds his image in the other; but in Tasso's conceit, the looks glance away from mutuality. The love which Rinaldo abandons to follow the crusade is not an exchange of persons, for that would involve a betrayal too serious for him to come away with even fairly clean hands. The values of genuine love would challenge the morality of good order. However, Tasso sets things up so that there is no real challenge. Armida's love, he insists, is a fraud; Rinaldo's love, since it is not truly returned, is an empty longing and a longing that involves self-loss. What Rinaldo has to turn away from is not so much Armida as an unruly and self-depleting appetite in himself. Armida, as far as his choices are concerned, is not so much another person as a personification of his own sensuality.

This takes us to the ethic of temperance that is figured in the moral design of the poem. For its rhetorical prompting, the design relies on self-regard; but the egotism of self-regard distorts human relations, and in this it falls in with the self-centredness of temperance as Tasso conceives of it. Temperance for Tasso, as for Erasmus in his *Enchiridion*, takes the form of an inner war of virtue and vice, a war that is enclosed in self-division, in the struggle of a higher, rational self for command over a lower, appetitive self. Real moral choices, however, involve judgements about the world outside oneself and dealings with other people. Tasso does not show Rinaldo's rejection of Armida as such a choice; it is his sensuality that he rejects rather than her. This not only limits the moral interest of Rinaldo's struggle but also confuses it, for, at the end of the poem, Rinaldo feels he may safely make her a gentlemanly offer of marriage. This suggests that Tasso feels obliged by the code of manners to recognise her as someone with a claim on his hero at the same time that his moral ideas compel him to represent her as a demonic force.

It is not, however, simply the self-centredness of temperance that distorts human relations but also its otherworldly drive. The true relation of our higher self in Tasso is with heaven, not any earthly thing. The true heroic calling is to rise toward the spirit by making war on the flesh. Yet *Jerusalem Delivered*, unlike Beaumont's *Psyche*, is not a mystical epic about the soul's intercourse with God. Tasso's heroes are soldiers, not hermits. The values of human love must count for something, but how, without self-contradiction? That was a difficulty which Tasso could not resolve, and his inability to resolve it accounts for the most psychologically resonant part of his epic, his treatment of love as hate.

After he has returned to duty, Rinaldo proves himself fit to hack down an enchanted grove by being ready to plunge his sword into Armida (Book 18, sts 30–5). This Armida is a phantom, but Rinaldo lifts his sword before he could know it. It is because he is ready to murder her image that he becomes the perfect Christian soldier. Unlike him, Tancred kills his love in the flesh: 'His sword into her bosome deepe he driues, / And bath'd in lukewarme blood his iron cold, / Betweene her brests the cruell weapon riues' (Book 12, st. 64). Clorinda was a pagan champion hidden in armour, and so Tancred did not know whom he was killing. Yet he is prostrated by guilt. The official view expressed by Peter the Hermit is that his love is sinful; the grief which he feels is an expression of that sinful love and so at once sin and punishment of sin (Book 12, st. 87). To this Tancred listens and rouses himself as far as is consistent with gallantry and sensibility. However, Peter seems rather to have deflected him than to have brought him to repent the real source of his grief. For what Tancred was lamenting was murder, not the loss of love. His lament is a powerfully-rendered account of despair in which guilt pursues him towards death, 'a wofull monster of vnhappie loue' (Book 12, st. 76): 'Swift from my selfe I ronne, my selfe I feare, / Yet still my hell within my selfe I beare' (st. 77).[18] That, in its succinct though undeveloped way, points forward to the great representations of guilt and self-hate in *Paradise Lost*. There is more in Tancred's despair than the magnanimous self-accusation of a highly-strung temper. One cannot help feeling that his guilt recognises a truth: like every other lover in the poem, he hates what he loves. Noticeably, Tasso insinuates wherever he can that the ferocious combat with Clorinda is a love exchange. As for Erminia, she expresses her love for Tancred as a wish to tear out his heart (Book 3, st. 27). She longs also to tend his mangled body, an office that would equally satisfy cruelty and pity. The notion of being pierced by Tancred's sword also has its attractions as a cure for her own love wound (Book 6, st. 85). In the end, however, it is Tancred's wounds that bring them together. Though an unlucky accident drives her away from the wounds which he receives from Clorinda, she is able to get to work on the new set which he receives from Clorinda's colleague, Argantes:

> And pitie wept for ioy to see that deede
> For with her amber lockes cut off each wound
> She tide: O happie man, so cur'd, so bound!
>
> (Book 19, st. 112)

Tasso is, of course, much more skilful than this bald account suggests at drawing the loves in which Tancred is involved into an echoing figuration. The imagery of cruelty and wounding is a convention of love poetry brought to a certain intensity by Tasso's love of oxymoron, of analysing states of mind in pointed antitheses. However, the pointing of the style and the intensity of the convention are themselves expressive of self-division, of the conflict of body and soul, earthly and heavenly love, which is the theme behind Tasso's holy war.

Tasso's platonising moral ideas make themselves felt most interestingly where they pinch his lovers' humanity. Their otherworldly direction, however, appears in the theme of public order as well, for though the delivery of Jerusalem looks like an earthly goal, the founding of an earthly kingdom, and though the symbolic meaning which Tasso attaches to it in his allegoresis of the poem, 'Ciuill happines', should be a secular concern, earthly politics are in fact absorbed by the supernatural order. The war is a holy war; the kingdom is the Kingdom of God, even if on earth; the city is an earthly image of the heavenly Jerusalem to be attained by Christian warfare. The action of *Jerusalem Delivered* is at heart a pilgrimage, and the desires and the will are bent on a goal beyond the world.

I have been arguing that Tasso's rhetorical design is too simple and his ethical ideas too limited to treat the mixed experience of human life adequately. The whole tenor of his epic, where it represents both public and private ideas of order, is in fact away from human concerns. If we return now to the universal design in which these ideas are cast, we can see immediately how the pull of the supernatural attenuates or distorts the human world. Consider first the way in which the powers of heaven and hell are involved in the poem. Tasso represents the struggle for Jerusalem as an episode in the universal war between God and the devil. Of course, *Paradise Lost* and even *Absalom and Achitophel* are also episodes in that universal war. In all three poems, the human scene opens out on heaven and hell, and behind the human struggle of good and evil we see the conflict of universal powers. *Jerusalem Delivered* is different in that the human struggle is itself a war and, where an epic war is at the same time war between heaven and hell, the peculiar regimentation of virtue and vice and simplifying of moral distinctions so noticeable in *Jerusalem Delivered* seem to follow. The war in heaven in *Paradise*

Lost is another example, a particularly telling one because its simplicities offer so sharp a contrast with the moral subtleties of the temptation and fall of Adam and Eve. A war in which God and the devil take sides leaves no room for the human act of moral judgement or decision that distinguishes the stronger from the weaker reason or the good from where it lies involved with evil. Good and evil wear uniforms, and right is might in the end.

Nor is it only in this respect that the pressure of other worlds squeezes the sphere of earthly action, while seeming to enlarge it. In *Jerusalem Delivered*, the divine interrupts the natural order of things and divinises human action as it turns away from natural towards supernatural ends. Tasso's angelic visitations, as indeed his demonic infestations, suspend the natural order. It is true that Tasso shows God sustaining his creation, but the divine perspective on the world is utterly diminishing. When God looks down on the world, he sees a dim and confused spot (Book 9, sts 55–7). Godfrey, rapt into the heavens in a dream, looks down on a similarly contemptible sphere. The spirit of Hugo appears to him, disclosing how he will shortly take his place among the saints in heaven, though not before he has founded a Christian empire. Hugo goes on:

> But to encrease thy loue and great desire
> To heauen ward, this blessed place behould,
> These shinning lampes, these globes of liuing fire,
> How they are turned, guided, moou'd and rould,
> The Angels singing here and all their quire;
> Then bend thine eies on yonder earth and mould,
>> All in that masse, that globe, and compasse see,
>> Land, sea, spring, fountaine, man, beast, grasse and tree,
>
> How vile, how small, and of how slender price,
> Is there reward of goodness, vertues gaine;
> A narrow roome our glorie vaine vp-ties,
> A little circle doth our pride containe,
> Earth like an Isle amid the water lies,
> Which sea sometime is call'd and sometime the maine,
>> Yet naught therein responds a name so great,
>> Its but a lake, a pond, a marrish streat.
>
> Thus said the one, the other bended downe
> His lookes to ground, and halfe in scorne he smilde,
> He sawe at once earth, sea, floud, castell, towne,
> Strangely deuided, strangely all compilde,
> And wondred follie man so farre should drowne,

To set his hart on things so base and vilde,
  That seruile empire searcheth and dombe fame,
  And scornes heau'ns blisse, yet proffreth heau'n the same.
                                    (Book 14, sts 9–11)

Nothing could make clearer how the involvement of heaven at once raises and reduces the importance of the action. Godfrey is divinised as his heroic action fades from an earthly to a heavenly splendour. His endeavour reaches into the divinely irradiated–dimension of the heroic because he acts in accord with the sphere of grace rather than the sphere of nature. For this reason, he seems more like a churchman than a general. Indeed, the vision brought him by Michael at the final assault, in which heaven opens on the scene and the crusaders struggling below are aided by the blessed spirits of dead crusaders and by the hosts of embattled angels, is in all but name a vision of humanity triumphing in the church triumphant.

It is not just through involving the supernatural powers that neoclassical epic universalises its action; it involves the workings of nature as well. The model here is probably the passage in the *Aeneid*, Book VI, where Aeneas meets Anchises. He sees a crowd of souls hover by a grove overhanging Lethe, and hears from his father how the souls derive from a world soul, how they undergo a cycle of birth into mortal bodies, death, purification and rebirth. Gazing into the swarm, Anchises is able to descry the future of his race and the history of Rome. In this way, Virgil makes us imagine that the destiny of Aeneas's heroic enterprise is written in the bowels of the earth. Milton, in a typically daring appropriation, writes the action of *Paradise Lost* into the bowels of the universe. Raphael tells Adam and Eve that their digestion participates in a universal metabolism refining matter to spirit, and Milton's fancy, as we shall see, everywhere involves the heroic wellbeing of Paradise in the imagery of the world's system. Even the triumph of David in *Absalom and Achitophel* is written in terms of the workings of nature. Tasso could not leave out so significant a motif. The two crusaders sent to rescue Rinaldo from Armida meet a magus, who leads them down to the subterranean fountain of the world's waters and below that to the fountain of metals, for the minerals tempered by the sun's rays undergo a natural alchemy and are transmuted up the scale of nature from base to precious:

There spacious caues they sawe all overflowne,
There all his waters pure great Neptune keepes,
And thence to moisten all the earth, he brings
  Seas, riuers, flouds, lakes, fountaines, wels and springs:
  . . .

> But vnder these a wealthie streame doth goe.
> That Sulphur yeelds and Oare, rich, quicke and new,
>   Which the sunbeames doth polish, purge and fine,
>   And makes it siluer pure and gold diuine.
>   (Book 14, sts 37–8)

Here we have a splendid glimpse of the world's circulation, a process worked out more fully in *Paradise Lost*. It is remarkable, though, how little it has to do with the action of *Jerusalem Delivered*. Tasso does not imagine the crusade as somehow written in the inward parts of the world. The moral ideas to which he attempts to give a universal cast reflect a supernatural rather than a natural order. His picture of the world system is in consequence an epic decoration rather than an unfolding of the universal implications of his epic action. Moreover, the sort of knowledge of nature which the magus professes has been brought into the Christian order of the poem, if not by violence, then at least by a severe chastening. The magus had been a pagan. His sciences are the alchemical and astrological ones of ancient neoplatonism revived so vigorously in the Renaissance, and the impulses behind his science, so far as the implications of the imagery tell the story, remain unregenerate. He studies the bowels of the earth for their prospect of infinite riches, and he studies the heavens to mount in transports above the earth, transports incidentally partly induced by seeing Venus and Mars naked (Book 14, sts 39, 43 – 5).[19] He has repented of his Faustian presumption and brought his learning under the rule of the Church; but though baptised, he has not acquired new impulses, only prudence in indulging the old ones. His idea of forbidden knowledge, far from making those important discriminations we have looked at in Milton, distinguishes merely between pagan pride and submission to Christian authority. Also, his idea of authorised knowledge is exploitative or transcendental; it carries with it no sense of an order of nature of which human nature is part.

The universal design of *Jerusalem Delivered* is Tasso's moral scheme writ large. It reflects the otherworldly tendency of his ideas of order and temperance. In it, the world is so much the theatre of supernatural operations that little room is left for natural ones. Tasso's gaze is not fixed on what things are like in the field of this world, but bends in everything towards heaven or hell. In this, we can detect the impulse of an early phase of humanism which we distinguished in the last chapter, an impulse to the divinising of human ends rather than to the serious criticism of human life. While Tasso is in no sense to be numbered among the neoplatonists, his epic shares with them a transcendental longing to leave the world and the study of human nature in its middle state behind. Yet *Jerusalem Delivered* is not a product of early Italian humanism; Valla had already written and Italian humanism had developed a critical strain. If we are to believe

Toffanin, the precritical strain of humanism, with its cultural ideas of the divinising of humanity in the church triumphant, finally realised itself in the grand project of the Catholic Reformation. That would certainly explain how *Jerusalem Delivered* is at once retrogressive, even primitive, in its humanist ideas and aesthetically advanced in its masterful organisation and painful tensions. In Tasso's hands, the epic becomes a powerful form of admonitory eloquence. The military action and universal design are harnessed to celebrating the heroic attempt to cross the gap between human and divine. But Tasso's remarkable success in giving rhetorical shape to epic fiction according to the ideas of neoclassical humanism was a triumph over the conditions of life, and his design draws everything upwards at the expense of the human world.

Paradise Lost: *Introduction*

I have tried to connect the shortcomings of *Jerusalem Delivered* with its answering too closely to the rhetorical aims of ideal imitation. The rhetorical design of the poem upon us was too simple and too general to take in our moral experience, and the heroic lustre that was supposed to arouse our admiration turned to a self-regard that distorted human relations, especially love. The otherworldliness of Tasso's universal scheme went very well with the rhetorical charge of his poetry. It not merely heightened the splendour of his heroes with a glory more than human, it supplied an infinite goal towards which the epic could be thought of as a prompting. Now *Paradise Lost* can certainly be discussed as a didactic poem inculcating a moral lesson by means of epic eloquence. The moral is, in Johnson's formulation, 'the necessity of obedience to the divine law'.[20] With that in mind, we can easily unpick the poem as a set of images of virtue and vice mounted in a universal scheme. On a superhuman level, the Son exemplifies obedience and Satan disobedience. In between, on the human level, exemplifying the capacity of the will for either obedience or disobedience, stand (or fall) Adam and Eve. It is surely impossible to deny that this is in outline the moral scheme of the poem, an outline that Milton fills in with splendid and subtle figuration. Still, this account leaves out the most interesting feature of *Paradise Lost*: the human action of the poem is not a heroic achievement. Unlike the delivery of Jerusalem or the founding of Rome, the Fall and the expulsion from Paradise are on the face of it a gigantic failure. The human action is closer to tragedy than to the epic triumph celebrated in *Jerusalem Delivered*, and consequently the human heroes of *Paradise Lost* do not strike us as heroic exemplars. Instead of moving our admiration as Godfrey and Rinaldo are supposed to, they touch our human nature and we respond to them more freely than we do to heroic characterisations of moral ideas set in a rhetorical design. Nor is it only the tragic turn of the action that so exceptionally involves us in the humanity of its heroes. The temptation, fall and repentance of Adam and

Eve are worked out with far more understanding of motive than is to be found in other neoclassical epics. Even where Tasso attempts to show the workings of Rinaldo's will, he casts his representation into exemplary images, setting vice against virtue, the fallen amorist against the restored soldier of God. He does not trace the motions of the will connecting Rinaldo's states of mind in the two admonitory set pieces. He is concerned with rhetorical pointing, not with how people work. The contrast with *Paradise Lost* leaps to the eye. Milton develops his action as a connected process of volition, of error, guilt and repentance. The action of his poem is truly a human action, not just a rhetorical scheme disguised as fiction.

Milton's escape from the limitations of ideal imitation has to do with his dismissal of 'Wars, hitherto the only argument / Heroic deemed' (IX, 28–9) as epic subject. Neoclassical epics like *Jerusalem Delivered* tried to moralise hero-worship by making the soldier a pattern of Christian virtue. From that, they gained a tremendous rhetorical charge, but military glory moralised went with simple oppositions of good and evil and with a superficial analysis of the motions of the will. War supplies at best obtuse figures for moral psychology. Milton could not free himself entirely from that obtuseness. The Son is a soldier as well as a martyr, and his divine violence clearly inspires Milton as much as his emptying himself to be taken over by the will of God. Fortunately, however, the action of *Paradise Lost* removed the luggage of epic warfare with all its unwieldiness as an image of moral conflict away from the centre of human interest.

Milton tells us in his invocation to Book IX that he will celebrate 'patience and heroic martyrdom' (line 32). This suggests that he will replace physical warfare with a spiritualised version, and makes a puzzling introduction to the Fall.[21] Milton may be looking beyond that to the vision of human life out of Eden in Books XI and XII. There, the long and depressing vista of human history is punctuated by holocausts (like Samson's) that turn out to be acts of God made possible through human martyrdom. Of this sort of heroic calling, the Son's human life stands as an inspirational paradigm. However, while Adam and Eve may look forward with chastened expectation to patience and heroic martyrdom as the hope of their race, they do not themselves exemplify these things. They do not seize on our regard in the insistent way of heroic exemplars brought inside a rhetorical design.[22] For these, we must go to the visionary edges of the poem, not its centre. So, while *Paradise Lost* has a rhetorical design upon us, this design is a framework for the action rather than the action itself. At the heart of *Paradise Lost* lies a study of volition irreducible to the rhetorical notions of ideal imitation.

The study of the will to be found in Milton's human action is too large a subject for this chapter. Its treatment will be displaced (like an enlarged rendering of a vital part in an anatomical drawing) to the next chapter, while this one will concentrate on the universal design of *Paradise Lost*.

This will make another contrast with *Jerusalem Delivered*. As we have seen, the rhetorical scheme in *Jerusalem Delivered* draws the interest of the poem in an otherworldly direction. At first sight, *Paradise Lost* looks a much more otherworldly epic than *Jerusalem Delivered*. It begins with vast prospects of hell, heaven and the universe, and does not come to rest on earth until the end of the third book. Yet, as I argued in the previous chapter, Milton's universal design centres on the human will. Though we have only brief glimpses of other worlds in *Jerusalem Delivered*, the tendency of the epic is centrifugal, and earthly concerns appear the shadows of supernatural ones in the end. In *Paradise Lost*, by contrast, universal perspectives focus on the human action. Everything turns on the choices of Adam and Eve. Noticeably, it is in the account of the workings of nature, exactly where Tasso's picture of the universe fits most loosely into his poem, that Milton most finely and intricately works his human action into the design of the universe. In *Jerusalem Delivered*, the human action enters into a universal design where it is touched by supernature. In *Paradise Lost*, nature, including human nature, is the most exuberant and imaginative expression of the supernatural energy of God. The world system invests the state of creaturely innocence with universal splendour, and the heroic task is in a sense to live according to nature, not to triumph over it.

The contrast between the universal scheme of *Jerusalem Delivered* that draws us upwards and the universal scheme of *Paradise Lost* that focuses on our earthly condition accords with the shift in neoclassical humanism from the divinising of man to a developed study of humanity in its middle state. *Paradise Lost* sticks out of neoclassical humanism in the way in which its human action represents the motions of the will, but it falls in with the development of neoclassical humanism in the way in which its universal imagery turns to defining what is human. In showing how Milton harnesses his universe to a moral design, this section will at the same time be discussing *Paradise Lost* in terms of ideal imitation. Ideal imitation, with its rhetorical intentions, cannot take in the human action of the poem satisfactorily, but it does account for the way in which Milton works the world system into his poem. The involvement of Adam and Eve in universal processes invests their free standing with the heroic glow of creaturely plenitude. This is a particular development of neoclassical epic elo-quence: a human ideal is being held up through its implication in the universe.

Paradise Lost: *Universal Images*

The moral idea that Milton's universe writes large is freedom. Raphael explains the order of things to Adam and Eve as a monistic system in which everything derives from God 'if not depraved from good' (V, 471). Immediately, that raises a problem, admittedly of a philosophical or theological sort, but nevertheless one with a direct bearing on what happens in Paradise. If everything derives from God, how can anything be depraved from good? How indeed can there be a choice of anything but good? As Satan demands of Eve, 'What can your knowledge hurt him, or this tree / Impart against his will if all be his?' (IX, 727–8). There is no way out of this difficulty unless the will is free to fall out of things and evil is in a sense nothing. The choice facing Adam and Eve is a choice between being in nature and falling out of nature towards unbeing. The notion that evil is a sort of negation was, after all, traditional. Augustine used it against the Manichaean doctrine that evil lies in matter and has a power equal to God's.[23] The Augustinian account became a standard way of absolving an omnipotent God, 'from whom all things proceed', of responsibility for evil, not only among theologians but also among men of letters. The notion of evil as negation was current among English poets: Donne and Herbert make use of it, and Fulke Greville's *Caelica*, CII, is a remarkable exposition of the Fall as an unaccountable seeking-out of privation.[24] The use of this idea here is not only that it will help to explain how Milton conceives of the fall of beings created perfect, but also that it points to the way he images creation. Creation is precarious, not because it is flawed, but because it can lapse into uncreation. While then, as Raphael says, all things derive from God, they may also fall away towards nothing. The images of creation are reversible; the forms of being are capable of turning into unbeing. Milton pictures his hinged universe as an order: things derive their being from God through order, and they are what they are by obeying the laws of their being. However, order can be undone by disorder. Nothing new enters, only the elements of order are set askew. Since creation is order, such a displacement is uncreation, and it is possible to fall out of the system involving all that is into what is not. *Paradise Lost*, accordingly, contains two sets of universal images – a set of images of unfallen creation and a set of the inversion or undoing of creation. The hinge of these alternative sets is free obedience, and so together they represent a world in which there is choice. It is in this way that the action of the poem, the fall and repentance of Adam and Eve, is figured in the universe.

The figuration of Milton's hinged universe falls into two contrasting sets, true version against false version, right way up against wrong way up, figure against disfigurement and so forth, a method of using images familiar at least from Spenser to Pope. Some of my examples will be familiar too, for much work has been done on versions and inversions in *Paradise Lost*. In laying them out, I intend to show how Milton's universal design is articulated and how it hinges on the freedom of creaturely standing.

First, then, the unfallen set, the images of the order of things deriving from God. The obvious place to look for these images is the account of the creation of the world. There are two principles at work here, a dividing and a diffusive one. God creates by setting bounds, severing or separating. At the same time, in creating, He pours Himself forth into creation with divine energy. The process of division seems to contradict the process of diffusion, but in fact they work together.

The first stage of creation is when God takes out the pair of golden compasses to draw a circle in chaos and circumscribe the bounds of the universe (VII, 225–31). Clearly, that is an image of creating by dividing, by appointing bounds. The language of dividing runs throughout the account of the seven days of creation. The elements capable of receiving life are separated from 'the black tartareous cold infernal dregs / Adverse to life' (VII, 238–9), which are purged downwards, while the remaining confused 'embryon atoms' (II, 900) are sorted and disposed into spheres of earth, water, air and fire. After that, there follow the separation of waters from dry land and the creation of species, each in its several kind.

Through this creation by division runs a tremendous diffusion of divine energy. When God has finished with the compasses, the spirit of God impregnates the sphere of chaos that has been marked off for creation with vital virtue (II, 289). Each further stage of creation proceeds, not just in obedience to the divisive principle of God's creating word, but spontaneously as the working of the divine semen in a world pregnancy. That the pregnancy is an Aristotelian affair in which the active force is entirely the All-Father's conveys the diffusion of Milton's masculine God into creation.

> Over all the face of earth
> Main ocean flowed, not idle, but with warm
> Prolific humour softening all her globe,
> Fermented the great mother to conceive,
> Satiate with genial moisture, when God said
> Be gathered now ye waters under heaven
> Into one place and let dry land appear.
>   (VII, 278–84)

At that, the earth heaves and hollows as if impelled as much by a hylozoic force within as by a divine command from without. In the same way, the earth gives birth to the animals when the word is spoken.

Division and diffusion work together. Things emerge in their distinctness through the divine generative force that impels them. We learn from the invocation to Book III that light in some sense flows from God into creation. In flowing, it seems to split into a spectrum, not of colours, but of species; the 'vernal bloom, or summer's rose / Or flocks, or herds, or human face divine' (III, 43–4) are themselves lights or illuminations, both diffusions and refractions of holy light. The sun is the chief physical conductor of that divine diffusion into things, the 'sovereign vital lamp' (III, 23) of holy light in the universe. The stars also, Adam tells Eve, transmit the life-sustaining power of light into the world, shedding vital influences on growing things and preventing the return of total darkness (IV, 66–73). Even the mineral world is quickened by light where the sun grows gems in the bowels of the earth (III, 609–12). As with the creation, so with light: the diffusion of God into the world goes with separation and limits. Light is transmitted through an order of mirrors and prisms. The stars, for instance, draw their light from the sun in an intricate procession (VII, 364–86) that imitates in the physical world the mazy pattern in which the angels revolve around God and draw beatitude past utterance from the light of his countenance (III, 56; V, 619ff.). It is as things stand and move in the order in which they were created that the divine energy passes through them. If they lapse from that order, the mirrors will be set askew and the light will fail.

We may imagine creation working according to the divisive principle on the analogy of a kingdom. Like a king whose power is present wherever his edict runs, God is present in His creation, not pantheistically, but wherever things conform with His laws. Certainly, Milton developed extravagantly the image of heaven, and by extension earth, as the kingdom of God. He lavished on God all the royal display he grudged his earthly monarch. No earthly court could match the dazzle, the music, the bounty that surrounds the ruler of heaven and earth. So opulently royalist an imagination may surprise us in a republican until we reflect that, in transferring royal glory to a spiritual realm, Milton is freeing himself from the attractions and claims of earthly kings.[25]

In this kingdom, Milton sometimes stresses a hierarchical principle as between angel and man or (heavily) between man and woman. Strikingly, though, the gradations of hierarchy do not in practice come between creatures and God. Adam, and equally Eve, confront God's will directly in the command not to eat the apple. The kingdom of God is a kingdom of morally absolute individuals, absolute, that is, in terms of free obedience. Unlike those pictures of the scale of being popular among the Elizabethan and Augustan writers, Milton's universal order is subversive of human order. Nothing can interfere with the direct relation of creature to creator, least of all any human hierarchy.

Even without the paradoxical way in which the image of the universe as the kingdom of God underwrites freedom, the divisive and diffusive principles of creation themselves involve the two sorts of freedom that we saw at work in the thought of Erasmus and Luther, the freedom of self-control (here in the form of free obedience) and freedom from constraint. The divisive principle issues in free obedience. The setting-apart of the fruit of the tree of knowledge is the division that completes the creation and sets it free in the wills of Adam and Eve to obey the command or not through their own acts of rational discrimination between things. The diffusive principle issues in freedom from constraint, the sense of being quickened and sustained in their creatureliness that Adam and Eve enjoy in the state of innocence. That is figured in the enormous curling complexity of the order that Milton imagines.

In their morning prayer in Book V, Adam and Eve call upon the four elements to 'let [their] ceaseless change / Vary to our great maker still new praise' (183–4). The notion of varying yet constant movement, irregular movement finally resolved in a total regularity, comes out wherever Milton describes the order of the unfallen world. In the passage already referred to where Raphael compares the dance of the angels to the movement of the stars, he speaks of 'mazes intricate / Eccentric, intervolved yet regular / Then most when most irregular they seem' (V, 622–4). God's garden also avoids regimentation. Instead of being drawn into the formal geometrical patterning of flower 'beds and curious knots' (IV, 242), it takes the form of a pouring forth, a wantoning of the divine energy in the variety of things. The abounding energy of creation passes through the garden in all sorts of curly movements. The vegetation, the waters, the elephant's 'lithe proboscis', Eve's hair and the unused serpent all go in intricate wreathings and wantonings. Christopher Ricks has suggested that the 'serpent error' of the rivers of the newly-created world must remind us of the serpent's leading Eve into error and that her 'wanton ringlets' (IV, 306) look forward to the wantonness succeeding the Fall.[26] Error and wantonness, these phrases seem to insist, are still innocent, and, in insisting, cast a shadow. One can hardly disagree with this, but at the same time, as so often in *Paradise Lost*, the imagery is indifferent as far as moral value is concerned. There is nothing inherently fallen about error, wandering or wantonness in the poem's scheme, or rather Milton's feeling for mazy movement is such that he uses words 'wanton' and 'error' with a sort of licentiousness, a deliberate violation of their suggestions of blame, as if to say, where nature 'Wantoned as in her prime, and played at will / ... Wild above rule or art' (V, 295–7), all wantoning and erring are blameless, such is the 'enormous bliss' (V, 297) ('enormous' after all means 'inordinate' as well as 'huge') of the freedom of the unfallen order of things. The notion of an order unfolding into individual curly movements informs not only *Paradise Lost* but also Milton's libertarian pamphlets, exuberantly in *The Reason of Church Government*, where he describes the order of heaven as not 'confin'd and cloy'd with repetition of that which is prescribed' but as orbing 'itselfe into a thousand vagancies of glory and delight, and with a kinde of eccentricall equation [being] as it were an invariable Planet of joy and felicity'.[27] 'Eccentrical equation', 'invariable planet' – these oxymorons speak of regular irregularity, variation in constancy. The order makes possible the free play of things, and their free play is the plenitude of the order. In the same spirit as these vagancies of glory and delight, Milton thinks of creation disporting itself in mazy movement. At the same time that his images of the universe, in their stress on boundaries and order, feature the obedience that engages the freedom of human wills, they feature the freedom from constraint that for Milton set the divine order against man–made order.

Raphael speaks, however, not only of how things derive from God but also of how they return to him. According to his account, the workings of the universe make up a sort of metabolic system, a great chain of digestion in which things are refined from gross and base matter up to spirit, spirit in Milton's universe being a refinement of matter, a sort of flame of flame. The basic principle is that 'of elements / The grosser feeds the purer' (V, 415–6). From the earth and water, exhalations rise into the air, and these feed the bodies of fire. The spots on the moon are in fact meals sent up from earth, yet undigested. The moon, in turn, sends up purer exhalations to feed the yet purer fires of the sun, those meals before they are digested appearing as sunspots. The same process is at work in the digestion of angels and humans. The grosser elements of food are concocted into spirits that feed the rational mind. So, even though he is used to ambrosia, manna and nectar, Raphael is still able to transubstantiate an earthly meal to his spiritual substance. To Raphael's analogy of universal digestion, Milton adds the further one of alchemy. The conversion of food to spirit is like the transmutation of base metals to gold. Indeed, the chemistry of the universal metabolism is of an alchemical sort.[28] One recalls that, when Satan landed on the sun, he found that it was a mass of alchemical potencies.

Things ascend, but how do they actually return to God? Spirit is not God. Angels are spirit, and still as separate from God as Adam and Eve. According to Raphael, Adam and Eve may share in the great metabolic return and their 'bodies turn all to spirit' (V, 497) in time. They will still remain creatures; they will not have been assimilated by God. Adam, however, thanks Raphael for having taught him (it must be said with extraordinary obliqueness) how 'in contemplation of created things / By steps we may ascend to God' (V, 511–12). This contemplation sounds perhaps like the sort of unitive knowledge that was supposed to take the human being out of his creatureliness into the godhead; but that would be a good example of the sort of forbidden knowledge that Milton's feeling for human finitude would rule out. Surely the return of things cannot work like that.[29] In fact, Adam's words speak not of the unitive knowledge of contemplating God, but of contemplating created things. Of that sort of contemplation, there is a good example in Adam's first prayer to heaven:

> Thou sun, said I, fair light,
> And thou enlightened earth, so fresh and gay,
> Ye hills and dales, ye rivers, woods, and plains,
> And ye that live and move, fair creatures, tell,
> Tell, if ye saw, how came I thus, how here?

> Not of my self; by some great maker then,
> In goodness and in power pre-eminent;
> Tell me, how may I know him, how adore.
>
> (VIII, 273–8)

Adam's contemplation of created things, of his own being and the world around him, flows out in a longing to know whom to praise. The longing is caught in its Edenic naivety in the repetition 'tell / Tell ... / Tell me ...'. The contemplation of the creatures that are lights and of the 'enlightened earth' prompt Adam's mind, not to a platonising ascent out of his creaturely condition, but to a realisation of his creatureliness and a longing to return thanks. Here, then, is at least one way in which things return to God. The divine energy that sustains Adam and Eve returns to God through prayer and praise for their creaturely being.

There is a striking example of the return of things to God through praise in Book IX that uses the imagery of the universal metabolism. In Milton's description of the morning, the exhalation of the yet unpolluted earth rises up to God in the same way that the exhalations according to Raphael rise from earth to moon to sun, and so to spiritual matter:

> Now when as sacred light began to dawn
> In Eden on the humid flowers, that breathed
> Their morning incense, when all things that breathe,
> From the earth's great altar send up silent praise
> To the creator, and his nostrils fill
> With grateful smell, forth came the human pair
> And joined their vocal worship to the choir
> Of creatures wanting voice.
>
> (IX, 192–9)

The whole process of return is reduced to modes of breath. The plants breathe metaphorically, exhaling scent. That exhalation becomes the inhalation of the animate creatures that draw vital breath, the conversion of breath being pointed up by 'breathed' at the end of one line set off against 'breathe' at the end of the next. Breath then passes through the creatures up to God, who in turn breathes it in like the smell of sacrifice.[30] Finally joining in this process of universal breathing is the prayer of Adam and Eve, the point where breath and the metabolism of creation become vocal, unlike the silent breath of the dumb creation.

The return of the creation in praise does not violate human creatureliness, the terms on which freedom is had in Milton's universe. More positively, the circulation of the world system deriving from God and returning to him completes the way in which the divisive and diffusive principles of Milton's universal imagery issue in freedom. The delightful unravelling maziness in which the divine energy runs into creation is discharged in the transmutation of the praise poetry of Adam and Eve. They participate in the universal circulation, and their participation in its motions of delight is freedom from constraint. However, they can participate only in their innocence. Only by free standing in their creaturely limits can they tap or return the divine current.

In the description of Paradise in Book IV, Milton images his world system most delightfully by conveying a sense sublime of something far more deeply interfused, in the pouring forth of divine opulence and in the transmutation and passing into one another of its processes. Paradise is 'in narrow room nature's whole wealth, yea more, / A heaven on earth' (lines 207–8). There, 'nature boon, / Poured forth profuse on hill and dale and plain' (lines 242–3) and 'the flowery lap / Of some irriguous valley spread her store' (lines 254–5). The form which the opulence takes is variety. This emerges in the composition of the picture of 'the happy rural seat of various view' (line 247). Glades are 'interposed' (line 253) between groves, against 'the irriguous valley' is set a 'palmy hillock' (line 254), and linking these details is the sinuous and intricate progress of the waters of Paradise. Simply as a painterly composition, then, the image of Paradise is the equivalent in landscape of the irregular regularity of the order among stars curling itself into complications of order out of sheer abundance of life.

The energy emerges in other forms of composition. The description breaks down the contours of things so that they can be rendered in the processes of water, light, vegetation and air, and the passage of one into the other conveys the energy flowing from its divine source through the metabolism of nature.[31] The garden is on top of a mountain piled on a river. By a sort of capillary action, the mountain draws the current upwards so that it

> Rose a fresh fountain, and with many a rill
> Watered the garden; thence united fell
> Down the steep glade, and met the nether flood.
>   (IV, 225–31)

The process, later repeated more intricately, is of division and dispersion into things and then of reuniting. The odd use of 'rose' captures the passage of the water from one form into another: the current rose a fountain. Later, a similar use of 'ran' suggests the transformation of water into plants:

> from that sapphire fount the crisped brooks,
> Rolling on orient pearl and sands of gold,
> With mazy error under pendant shades
> Ran nectar, visiting each plant, and fed
> Flowers worthy of Paradise.
>   (IV, 237–41)

The brooks ran nectar: the fountain in its convolutions has insinuated itself into vegetation. Later, this curly, wanton movement glimpsed in the 'irriguous valley' becomes the creeping vine arrested in luxuriance and then is taken up in the wriggling confluence of waters:

> the mantling vine
> Lays forth her purple grape, and gently creeps
> Luxuriant; mean while murmuring waters fall
> Down the slope hills, dispersed, or in a lake,
> That to the fringed bank with myrtle crowned,
> Her crystal mirror holds, unite their streams.
> (IV, 258–63)

Here, the deviousness of the syntax of lines 260–3 captures the meandering of the streams. Not only does the water ramify into vegetation; it also involves light, which is the point of the jewel imagery, of 'the sapphire fount' and brooks 'Rolling on orient pearl and sands of gold', so repellent to modern taste. The water glittering has become a mode of light. Similarly, the trees overhanging the stream are reduced to an effect of light, to 'pendant shades'. Finally, the whole process of water, light and foliage turns into air in a passage which Empson made famous[32]:

> The birds their choir apply; airs, vernal airs,
> Breathing the smell of field and grove, attune
> The trembling leaves, while Universal Pan
> Knit with the graces and the hours in dance
> Led on the eternal Spring.
> (IV, 264–8)

'Airs' is a pun; it means both birdsong and the breath of air into which field and grove have passed as smell. The ambiguity between breeze and music is kept up, for the leaves stirring with the breeze are 'attuned' by the air. The pun transforms one thing to another; indeed, the whole description has depended on a sort of ambiguity. In verbs like 'rose' and 'ran', the water is in transition between forms. It is also in the very nature of water or air or light to be passing from one shape to another. Milton deliberately uses hovering language as he uses fluid or transitional imagery to convey the metabolism of the divine energy through creation. Perhaps the universal Pan is an epiphany of this force running through all things, and the leaves tremble as much with sacred as with musical delight.

In various elusive ways, the physical systems of Adam and Eve belong inside the divine metabolism of nature. When they return to their bower at night, Adam remarks how 'the dew of sleep / Now falling with slumbrous weight inclines / Our eyelids' (IV, 614–16).[33] This suggests how attuned their beings are to the rhythms of the world. Similarly, when Adam awakes the next morning, the light vapours rising from his digestion that have accompanied his sleep are sympathetically dispersed like mists above the fuming rills by the dawn stir of the leaves and birdsong. Above all, however, Adam and Eve join in the divine circulation in their magnificent morning prayer in which the whole universal process 'made vocal by [their] song' (V, 204) passes through their lips and returns to God.

Their participation in the world system in its divinely-impelled free play is a universal image of the freedom from constraint which Adam and Eve enjoy in Paradise. How Milton realises the combination of freedom from constraint with free obedience as a human possibility in their unfallen lives will be discussed in the next chapter. Here, the aim is something more schematic, to note how these two sorts of freedom are implicated in Milton's picture of the universe and in this way given epic lustre. Strikingly, what is being held up is a matter of standing. The heroic task is not to draw away from earth towards heaven, as in *Jerusalem Delivered*, but to enjoy and attend to one's creaturely standing. The prohibition of the fruit of the tree of knowledge makes that clear: it draws a boundary between divine and human. Though in setting up free obedience it delegates a sort of sovereignty to Adam and Eve over their actions, it does so in such a way that the freedom is an expression of creatureliness, of distinguishing what is truly human from what is God's.

Paradise Lost: *Universal Images of Derangement*

Let us turn now from the images of the unfallen universe to the other set, the images of creation inverted. In his *Commentaries on the Book of Genesis*, Calvin develops the idea that since God made everything good, evil must be in some sense nothing, an unthing. One of the peculiar developments which he gives the idea is that since 'fleas, caterpillars and other noxious insects' are bad, God cannot have created them (I, 104); they must have come in with the Fall, cracks in things come to life. Nothing in *Paradise Lost* is as bizarre as that. Still as Milton pictures them, the shapes of evil are not new things but things in reverse. Evil in *Paradise Lost* is the negation of what has been made perfect. However, as even the devils have not actually arrived at nothing, nor even 'at worst / On this side nothing' (II, 100–1), whatever Moloch says, we should think of evil as not so much annihilation as a continuing process of the corruption of good towards total privation of being.

Both Edenic innocence in the unfallen scheme of things and the falling out of the scheme of things towards unbeing may seem perhaps fancies of a theological system with little bearing on human experience. What human experience they do manage to picture will be part of the business of the next chapter to explore. It might be helpful, nevertheless, at this point to glance at a passage in which Satan talks of falling out of creation:

> Me miserable! Which way shall I fly
> Infinite wrath, and infinite despair?
> Which way I fly is hell; myself am hell;
> And in the lowest deep a lower deep
> Still threatening to devour me opens wide,
> To which the hell I suffer seems a heaven.
>
> (IV, 73–8)

This speaks to us directly. The negative imagery of evil takes the form of continuing fall: 'in the lowest deep a lower deep / Still threatening to devour me opens wide' – how tellingly the sense is drawn from line to line so that it is suspended over the delayed verb 'opens'. In this appalling passage, Satan expresses his experience of evil in universal images of falling endlessly out of creation, but clearly what he expresses is an experience, the sort of thing we can recognise as a moral and psychological possibility, not just a myth picture of a theological possibility. We do not feel that a theological system is speaking, but despair, the subjective form of evil as privation. Just as the workings of the universe served to universalise the experience of free standing, so the falling out of the universe or its undoing serves to universalise the experience of guilt and despair. Milton's universal imagery is not so much science or cosmology as figurings of moral conditions.

Very generally, Milton images evil as the negative counterpart of good in terms of abyss and labyrinth. William Bouwsma notes how, for Calvin, the abyss and the labyrinth are contradictory images of evil, the one having to do with a fear of the unbounded, the other with a fear of constriction; and both these images crop up in *Paradise Lost*.[34] Both Satan and Adam speak of falling from abyss to abyss in an endless falling out of creation, and both move through an anguished process of negation into a labyrinthine self–enclosure in their guilty conversations with themselves (see below, pp. 150–2). Strikingly, this picture of evil reverses a heavenly or paradisaical experience of abyss and labyrinth. For the unfallen, God Himself is the abyss, an infinite source who has appointed and sustains the bounds of finite being, while the labyrinth takes the form of the interminable, mazy wandering of the divine energy in which finite forms participate. The evil abyss and labyrinth are the creature's anguished experience of the creator backwards.

Some of the other ways in which Milton pictures evil in the imagery of uncreation are so familiar as to warrant only summary mention. If creation is above all an order of things, evil will take the form of disorder, order turned upside down. The most obvious form of disorder is indeed Satan's rebellion against God. The order of things is God's kingdom; in making war on its monarch, Satan challenges the whole order of things and attempts to set up an anti-order of his own. He himself describes the order of hell as topsy-turvy. In Book II, lines 24–30, he addresses the fallen angels sitting in council and justifies his position as at once liberator and ruler. No-one will envy him, he says, because God makes him as leader suffer most. There is a hierarchy of pain, and no-one will begrudge him his pre-eminence there. Whereas in heaven concord is founded on bliss, in hell it is founded on pain. We can hardly suppose that Satan means in all this to be taken quite literally, since he would be confessing that his leadership is self-defeating. We feel rather that he is speaking with magnanimous extravagance.[35] Yet he is in fact, presumably unknown to himself, speaking what, as he later recognises, is the truth. He is 'only supreme / In misery' (IV, 91–2) and the remarkable concord in hell rests partly on this grotesque inverted principle.

The order of things is an array of mirrors reflecting the light which is ultimately God. Evil turns the mirrors askew, and the radiance of the divine countenance is reflected from them only in glimpses or in perturbed glances. Before the Fall, the order of the heavenly bodies sheds only benign astrological influences (X, 678ff.). However, after the Fall has jangled the system of the world, God has His angels push the order 'askance' (X, 668) into oblique motions, with all the consequent disturbances of earthly life. Creatures as well as heavenly bodies are lights, and they too lose their original radiance with evil. In heaven, Satan's countenance shone 'as the morning star' (V, 708); but, when we see him in hell, his light is obscured and he is compared to the sun peering through mist or in eclipse (I, 591–9). Now that the light of heaven is fading from him, he is associated with another sort of light, the sort of light produced by the minerals of hell, asphalt and naphtha, that illuminates Pandemonium with infernal brilliance (I, 729). Or again, when in Book IV the angels catch Satan in the garden, squat like a toad at the ear of Eve, he starts up at the touch of Ithuriel's spear with a flash like the explosion of gunpowder (IV, 813–19).

This flash of infernal anti-light is caused by an inversion of the alchemical metabolism of creation, first discovered by Satan during the war in heaven.[36] He sees how heaven's rays vitalise the soil so that it shoots forth flowers and gems. His plan is to seize the mineral sources of this shooting forth, separate them from the tempering of heavenly light and point them to destruction instead of growth. So, he has his troops mine for sulphur and nitre and compound them to an anti-creative mixture. In short, he invents gun-powder. In a sentence whose syntax imitates confusion (VI, 584–94), Milton says that Satan's first shot 'embowelled' the air, a metaphor suggesting violent destruction of the living organism of the universe. The same destructive potential of 'The originals of nature in their crude

/ Conception' (VI, 511–2), if not touched by heavenly light, seems to be at work unexplosively in hell in the tormenting fires that burn with darkness visible. The fallen angels take on some of the chemical composition of the place to which they have been consigned, and the prospect that Belial (II, 217–9) and Mammon (II, 274–7) hold out, that the fallen angels will at length adapt to hell and conform to its temper, is in fact the horrible truth about the place.

The divine alchemy of creation was really an organic metaphor for the energy with which God sustained living forms. Fallen creatures undergo a deformation. In the war in heaven, the ethereal forms of the rebels become gross enough to admit pain. In hell, though they retain angelic shapes and 'stature as of gods' (I, 570), Milton prophetically lists the shapes which they will take on as false gods in the course of human history. The shapes are mostly bestial, the image of God 'depraved from good'. While the fallen angels voluntarily defile their original shapes, as Satan adopts animal disguises or imbrutes himself in the serpent, there is still a sinister suggestion of a downward evolution of forms away from God.

The infernal deforming of the living organism comes out curiously in the passage describing the building of Pandemonium. The hill from which the rebels dig minerals has a 'grisly top' (I, 670); it 'Belche[s] fire and rolling smoke' (I, 671) and shines with 'glossy scurf' (I, 672); metallic ore lies hidden in 'his womb' (I, 673); the mining is called wounding and the gold lies in 'ribs of gold' (I, 689–90). The imagery suggests a body hideously misbegotten, an infernal confusion of creation imagined as an organism. The building of Pandemonium itself can hardly be called deforming, since it is in its way a triumph of art. It is better described as a counterfeit of those metabolic processes of creation where light, water and air pass into each other. Instead of returning up to God in exhalations, it raises a pile against him:

> A third [troop] as soon had formed within the ground
> A various mould, and from the boiling cells
> By strange conveyance filled each hollow nook,
> As in an organ from one blast of wind
> To many a row of pipes the sound–board breathes.
> Anon out of the earth a fabric huge
> Rose like an exhalation, with the sound
> Of dulcet symphonies and voices sweet,
> Built like a temple.
>
> (I, 705–12)

Milton begins by comparing the passage of molten metal to the passage of air through an organ. The moulds and sluices are like the flues and pipes of the organ. Then, however, 'by strange conveyance' of style, Milton drops the comparison and allows its two terms to dissolve into one another. The moulds actually turn into a sort of organ, out of which both music and molten metal mingled issue like an 'exhalation', then stand, music turned to architecture, 'the sound ... / Built like a temple'.[37]

In a universe in which everything derives from God, evil can only produce false versions, counterfeits, or parodies of the true versions of things. Along with the alarmingly splendid Pandemonium, we may place other parodies of God's handiwork, the 'sunbright chariot' in which Satan sits, 'idol of majesty divine' (VI, 100–1), for example, parodying the chariot of paternal deity in which the Son rides out to war. Milton has, however, besides inverted, deranged or counterfeit images, a more oblique way of picturing the nega- tivity of evil. The first two books of *Paradise Lost* are particularly thickly studded with epic similes and comparisons. The wealth of small images set within the greater image of hell produces a sort of dislocation, a feeling of having fallen out of the world of true appearances. The most memorable dislocation, the shift of perspective between the second and third books, belongs not to the inset images but to the course of the epic narrative. Up to the end of Book II, the narrative has followed the gigantic figure of Satan in his journey through chaos up to the verge of light, where he sees heaven and the world hanging from it in bigness 'as a star / Of smallest magnitude close by the moon' (II, 1052–3). With Book III, the perspective shifts to heaven. God looks down into the universe and sees Satan diminished to a small, malignant figure on the edge of creation. The effect is not merely to make Satan look small but also to suggest an alarmingly dislocated experience of things.[38] This is the culmination of a series of dislocations and shifts of proportion effected in the epic similes and comparisons of the first two books.

There are no proper comparisons for size in hell, for hell is outside the proportions of creation. This is the point of comparing Satan's shield for size to the moon. How big does the moon look? To compound the uncertainty about size, Milton brings in Galileo's telescope, with a peculiar dilating effect. Galileo's discovery of a world in the moon violates a normal sense of proportion and perspective and suggests a confounding of appearances. In the same way, proportions collapse when Pandemonium is compared to a beehive and the giant angels shrink to fairies. A particularly refined example of this occurs when Satan approaches the gates of hell:

> As when far off at sea a fleet descried
> Hangs in the clouds, by equinoctial winds
> Close sailing from Bengala, or the isles
> Of Ternate and Tidore, whence merchants bring
> Their spicy drugs: they on the trading flood
> Through the wide Ethiopian to the Cape

> Ply stemming nightly toward the pole. So seemed
> Far off the flying fiend.
>
>   (II, 636–43)

Here, obviously, we have a full-blown epic comparison drawn out and expand-
ing into exotic regions, apt enough in that way for Satan's voyage. The logic of
comparison is, however, rather tenuous. The mirage of the fleet hangs in the
sky, and so does Satan. However, the relation of vehicle and tenor is not really
the point. The real work of the image is to bring about a dislocation of
perspective. Until this point, the narrative has followed Satan. Then, as he
approaches the gates of hell, we suddenly see him as a distant object like a fleet
descried in a mirage, and the geographical tract into which the image trails is a
prospect of the vast distance he has covered and has still to cover: 'So seemed /
Far off the flying fiend'. The perspective has shifted, and we are looking at him
from the point of view of Sin and Death sitting at the gates he is approaching
and to which the narrative leaps forward before he arrives. There is more than
a shift of perspective: the gates of hell are in the vault of the infernal sky, from
which we look down on Satan, whereas until that point we had been following
him upwards. It is not so much, perhaps, that he appears upside down as that
his position relative to ours has been inverted and the dislocation is imaged in
the mirage, which inverts the fleet in the clouds.

   In the first two books, Milton images the fall out of the order of things with
baroque virtuosity. By contrast, his treatment of the Fall of Adam and Eve is
sober, more wrapped up in the psychological action, less projected on a universal
screen. It is still involved in the imagery of uncreation, except that, whereas God
allows the rebel angels to fall in endless regress out of things, He stays the falling
of humanity and allows only a limited if severe impairment to human nature
and the human world. Evil in the human world takes the form of distempering
rather than inversion, though it is still the corruption of good and a partial
uncreating of things.

   The original derangement takes place in the wills of Eve and Adam, and a train
of guilt, remorse and hatred follows. However, the fruit of the tree of knowledge
disagrees with their entire creaturely constitutions; it upsets them physically as
well as psychologically. It acts as an intoxicant and aphrodisiac, and leaves them
with a hangover.[39] Since their constitutions are part of the constitution of the world,
the upset poisons not only their metabolisms but also the entire world-metabolism.
Already in Book IV, Satan was pictured at the ear of Eve attempting to taint the
spirits that rose from her purer blood 'like gentle breaths from rivers pure' (IV,
806). On that occasion, he did not manage to infect the exhalations of her
metabolism, though he disturbs them in her dream; but in Book IX he succeeds
in entering Paradise through the underground river rising with the fountain in a

mist. Here, he has succeeded in entering, if not tainting, the exhalations of the unfallen world. When he has succeeded in corrupting Eve, and through her Adam, it is suggested that he has corrupted the atmosphere with them. The sun turns 'as from Thyestean banquet' (X, 688), the tasting of the fruit evidently tainting those exhalations that rise from the earth, and perhaps there is a hint of the same metabolic revulsion in the 'distaste' (IX, 9) of heaven, used as it was to the pure clouds sent up from the unpolluted earth.[40]

Paradise Lost: *The New Creation*

Paradise Lost does not end in universal images of derangement and uncreation, for Adam and Eve repent and move into a new creation. This is supernatural rather than natural; it is the divine plan of history. It involves Adam and Eve in the scheme of things, but not by fashioning universal images.

Milton pictures the undoing of creation as a consequence of sin almost as a natural process, as if the order of things could not endure a discord without the whole system being upset. Yet, it is clear that God does not simply allow things to take their course. He actively wills and assists the derangement of creation. It is not just that the sun turns aside in disgust from the earth; God commands His angels to tilt its axis. Milton could never allow God's sovereign will, which he delights to call 'high' and 'free', to vanish into the operation of mere secondary causes.

The involvement of God's will in destruction raises difficulties. It is hard to understand how Milton could imagine the creator of the world will its uncreation without self-contradiction. It is even harder to understand how God turns evil into good through the divine plan of history. Michael's history of the fallen world does not make the new order of things look good. The grimness of his story may not be grimmer than actual history, but it is not easily imagined as the course of justice, let alone justice tempered by mercy. Perhaps we are meant to have in mind the fate of Satan, who was left to the working-out of his own evil; God's goodness might then seem evident in the way in which Adam and Eve are saved from that self-willed yet helpless total inversion of being. Adam, at any rate, sees in his future and the future of his race the operation of an unaccountable goodness 'more wonderful / Than that by which creation first brought forth / Light out of darkness' (XII, 471–3). He sees in God's shaping of history towards redemption a new creation, a new creation that for him justifies the high and free will of God, which cannot be bound to the workings of nature but can interfere with the process of corruption and make a new beginning. The possibility of a new beginning is indeed the essential point about the new order of things as far as the human action of the poem is concerned. All the beautiful elaborations of the unfallen system of the world turn finally on the human will; the bleak and not-so-fully-realised fallen order looking forward to the Redemption turns on the possibility of a new beginning, the repentance made possible by the divine scheme of forgiveness.

The new creation involves inversions of the original order, but inversions given a twist towards good. In Paradise, Raphael reproved Adam's curiosity about a kind of knowledge which only God could have. After the Fall, Michael shows Adam a prospect of the history of the world that lies in God's mind. Even though this knowledge is tempered to Adam's human capacity, in a sense he has got what he and Eve wanted, that is knowledge of divine secrets and knowledge that will make humanity divine in the end. There is a benevolent irony at work here. In other ways, the order of the fallen world refashions the unfallen order. Raphael spoke of a gradual tempering from earthly to spiritual being if Adam and Eve remained constant inside the metabolism of nature in which they experienced only good. Michael points to a harsher tempering through the experience of good and evil in the fallen world. So Adam and Eve fall out of Paradise, not into the continuing loss of being that the devils suffer, but into history. In Paradise, they had experienced the archetypes or original images of things; in hell, the archetypes are inverted and the devils experience the confounding duplicity of counterfeit appearances; in history, humanity will experience a benevolent duplicity in events, not as archetypes or as inverted types, but as types or promises of the divine events that will fulfil them. Since 'the object of faith is the promise', in history they enter into a new constitution of things through faith rather than innocence.[41]

In tracing the way in which the human action of *Paradise Lost* is involved in the workings of the universe, I have been drawn to give an account of some of the system of ideas on which Milton framed his poem. The images of creation and uncreation unfold a monistic scheme in which everything derives from God and yet the will is free to fall out of the scheme. The images of the fallen world make up a new historical order of things with a promise of deliverance that allows the will to return upon itself free from implication in its own history, the self-bound process of error and guilt. I make no claim for the philosophical or theological coherence of Milton's system; nevertheless, I think it coheres imaginatively. In its images of creation and uncreation, no other epic that I know of works its action into the universe with such intelligent splendour. Systems make sense from within; they are not easily translated out of their own terms. Yet, to speak of the human action of the poem, the task of the next chapter, demands some such translation. Fortunately, whatever its final irreducibleness, Milton's imaginative system has obvious openings, and at this point we can already see how it gives scope to a treatment of the motions of the will. Moreover, it has this advantage for a study of human experience, that as a universal system it centres on the creaturely state of its heroes. A divine and universal splendour is cast on the heroes of the poem in their humanity, not in their attempt to go beyond it. Some of the inadequacy of *Jerusalem Delivered* lay in the way in which its universal scheme divinised the attempt of the heroic will to rise above the earth. From that misdirection, at any rate, *Paradise Lost* is free and indeed marks an intelligent redirecting of humanist attention to the study of human beings in their middle state.

Absalom and Achitophel

Absalom and Achitophel is not exactly an epic: it is no longer than a single book of *Paradise Lost*. It was hastily composed, and lacks the enormously elaborated design of the magnum opus. It is a formidable poem, for all that, densely if not vastly articulated, and it answers with surprising fullness, if rather obliquely, to the rhetorical design of the neoclassical humanist epic. Dryden himself, evidently puzzled about its genre, spoke of it as a Varronian satire, but it is as a short epical poem that I shall discuss it.[42] It shows how neoclassical epic might adapt ideal imitation to the serious criticism of life, not as in *Paradise Lost* by using it as a frame for a human action developed according to the inner forms of volition, but by working entirely within its rhetorical forms, indeed exaggerating them. In the matter of volition, it marks how *Paradise Lost* stands out from the course of neoclassical humanism. In its scheme of universal images investing creaturely humanity with heroic lustre, however, it follows *Paradise Lost* and shows how Milton's poem belongs to the development of neoclassical humanism.

Dryden complicates ideal imitation in a witty way. On the one hand, he shapes his biblical story into an epical ideal imitation, fashioning a set of images of moral ideas.[43] So he represents Achitophel as a type of unscrupulous politician, and in doing so makes an image or example of a vice. Then on the other hand, he shapes the story into a disguised account of contemporary events, the constitutional crisis of the Popish Plot. And so he makes Achitophel into a disguised portrait of Shaftesbury, the fomenter of the crisis. The story, worked up into an ideal imitation, stands at the same time for something other than itself. In representing the idea of wicked politician, Achitophel is just being himself in an exaggerated way; but in looking like Shaftesbury he is stealing into someone else. Achitophel and Shaftesbury are not examples of each other. Their relation is not of example to idea, the relation of ideal imitation, but takes the form, rather, of analogy or allegory, of a correspondence wittily drawn or insinuated between two different things.

The wit of the allegorical double take is what perhaps makes us think we have to do with mock epic.[44] Mock epic, however, works by a disparity between style and subject, and with *Absalom and Achitophel* there is no such disparity. The events of David's reign are quite worthy of epic. The events of Charles's reign that Dryden figured in the biblical events were momentous at the time, and the epic treatment heightens rather than belittles them. The disparity in *Absalom and Achitophel* is not the mock epic disproportion between style and subject treated or glanced at, but an allegorical disparity of the two sets of events and characters.

Even if *Absalom and Achitophel* is not a mock epic, it is still a witty and humorous epic, and wit and humour are out of keeping with the conventional epic gait.

> In pious times, e'r Priest-craft did begin,
> Before Polygamy was made a sin;
> When man, on many, multiply'd his kind,
> E'r one to one was, cursedly, confind:
> When Nature prompted ...
>   (lines 1–5)[45]

The tone of that introduction sounds libertine. Unrestrained sexuality, it suggests, was the primitive piety of mankind, their living according to nature. The guild or mystery of priests has made a sin of it, as later they are said to make gods of every shape and size. So, through a startling compression of wit, Dryden represents patriarchal times as the golden age of the contemporary fashionable set. The tone is ambivalent, of course. At the very least, to compliment the king on his promiscuity is raillery. Even a word like *'Polygamy'* faces both ways, looking backwards with nostalgia to a world in which unrefined patriarchal energy held sway, and at the same time through the grotesqueness of the word drawing a line between the rude manners of the early world and modern decency and law. The tone is urbane and manages its poise by a play of wit backwards and forwards between the biblical story and the London scene, the heroic and the familiar world. Urbanity is not characteristic of the conventional epic voice, and the play of wit makes ideal imitation work differently from the way in which it conventionally does in, for example, *Jerusalem Delivered.* Tasso sets out to impress the imagination in order to shape desires and articulate them into a universal frame of moral ideas. Dryden's way of fashioning his images is far less expansive: he sets them so as to glance not just at universal ideas of good and evil but also at events and personalities in everybody's mind. His wit plays on the recognition of local fact. So, while his biblical story suggests, as we shall see, a universal design, at the same time it is brought to bear on the contemporary human scene. Conventional epic images such as Tasso's Rinaldo, representing the warfaring Christian, or for that matter Milton's Abdiel, representing zeal, disengaged as they are from contemporary manners, apply to life in a far more general way than Dryden's. While theirs may be more inspiring images, Dryden's reflect upon the conditions in which real virtues and vices engage and real social admiration is won more keenly. The witty indirectness which he gives to neoclassical epic may limit its scope, but it sharpens its didactic edge to the point where we may take the rhetorical designs of ideal imitation seriously. At the same time, this new sophistication is capable of grandeur. The generous mingling of greatness with absurdity in the portrait of Achitophel, the magisterial judgement behind the ridicule of Zimri – these modulations of voice convey an achieved humanity as grand in its way as the more elevated and ceremonious character of the conventional epic speaker.

To do justice to that achieved humanity requires an examination of how Dryden brings neoclassical epic to bear on the human scene. Although truncated, *Absalom and Achitophel* contains a surprisingly complete array of images of moral ideas set in a universal design, and Dryden's design, like Milton's, turns on creaturely human nature, at once focusing the poem on 'this scene of man' and investing it with a heroic largeness of spirit.

The schematic simplicity of the narrative of *Absalom and Achitophel* illustrates with exceptional obviousness the way in which ideal imitation presents an array of images of virtues and vices. The action is the corruption of part of the nation and the successful meeting of the corrupted part by the part that remains true. Clearly, such an action should dispose the characters into representatives of virtue and vice, and in fact the poem opposes two sets of portraits, one of vicious types and one of worthy. On the one hand, Zadock stands for true piety combined with humility and learning; on the other, the ignorant, conceited and visionary Corah stands for the perversion of religion to private and factional interest. Jotham, representing true wit, constant in the king's service, confronts no doubt the 'Kind Husbands and meer Nobles' (line 572) but also Zimri, the wit-would, the man of freakish extremes. In Hushai's disinterested political economy, there is perhaps the true version of the disfiguring avarice and business interest of Shimei. In the portrait of Barzillai, patriotism, which is simulated by Achitophel, is ideally depicted. His son's filial piety contrasts with Absalom's filial impiety. Finally, Amiel's art of politics, put to defending the state, contrasts with Achitophel's politics of private ambition.

The distinction between the two sets of portraits is not simply an antithesis of true and false. Throughout the poem, words like 'moderate' (line 75), 'sober' (line 69) and 'mild' (line 77) characterise the 'honest' party,[46] 'extreme' (line 110), 'warm' (line 459) and 'mad' (line 336) the popular one. The virtuous characters show the mean of their political attributes, while the vicious show the excess or defect. Apart from the king, the characters of the virtuous are not individualised and indeed not interesting. The sharply individualised portraits are of the vicious characters, degenerations from the true or generic type and singular aberrations from the mean. The excellence of Zadok and Jotham comes out in the generality of their portraits; the peculiar viciousness of Corah's composition comes out in the grotesquely particular:

> Sunk were his Eyes, his Voyce was harsh and loud,
> Sure signs he neither Cholerick was, nor Proud:
> His long Chin prov'd his Wit; his Saintlike Grace
> A Church Vermillion, and a *Moses's* face.
>
> (lines 646–9)

Behind Dryden's characterisation lies a traditional theory of humours. The justly-tempered man is exceptional only in his balance or soundness.[47] An excess or deficiency of temperament will express itself in some singular excrescency or deformity. So it is that an ill-compounded nature, such as Zimri's, lacking any principle or cohesion, runs out in freaks and unstable forms; and a lumpish and dull one, such as Shimei's, is sullen and resentful of whatever is sovereign and disinterested in government, the tempering of the body politic, and its un-generosity contracts into municipal politics, the sphere of hot brains and cool kitchens. In Zimri and Shimei, Vanity and Dullness respectively, there is a sinister suggestion, surely, of human nature returning to chaos like the shapeless lump that was born to Achitophel.

Yet, at first sight, it does not look as if Dryden's array of images of virtue and vice belongs to a universal scheme, except as moral ideas. Heaven is glimpsed, but there are no scenes in hell. Indeed, the scene is restricted to the earth more than is common in epic. Yet in fact, Dryden's scheme of virtues and vices does involve the world's system and heaven and hell, not through their being mounted in a described universe, but through the implications of imagery.

First, the imagery that involves heaven and hell. The plot itself is inspired by hell, for 'when to Sin our byast Nature leans, / The carefull Devil is still at hand with means' (lines 79–80). The temptation and seduction of Absalom continually recalls the Fall and indeed Milton's treatment of it.[48] Achitophel's role is satanic: Dryden calls him 'Hells dire Agent' (line 373). His lengthy temptation of Absalom is in its way as splendid a display of fallacious argument as Satan's of Eve in *Paradise Lost*, and, lest the comparison with the serpent should go unnoticed, Dryden says that he 'sheds his Venome' (line 229) into Absalom's ear. Moreover, Achitophel pictures the fortune with which he tempts Absalom as fruit that 'must be, / Or gather'd Ripe, or rot upon the Tree' (lines 250–1). His temptation of Absalom, like Satan's of Eve, is to aspire beyond himself until Absalom says to himself:

> My Soul Disclaims the Kindred of her Earth:
> And made for Empire, Whispers me within;
> Desire of Greatness is a Godlike Sin.
>
> (lines 370–2)

Even the greatness of Achitophel and the ambition that corrupts his greatness are in character with Milton's Satan. These images, of course, in no sense make *Absalom and Achitophel* into a coherent recapitulation of *Paradise Lost.* They point the action, rather, and involve it with universal forces of good and evil.

There is a more latent resemblance, however, with the universal scheme of *Paradise Lost.* In *Paradise Lost,* evil is a principle of negation, and Satan is in league with chaos to undo creation. The vices in *Absalom and Achitophel* are involved in the same way, not only with hell but also with an uncreating force. I have shown how images of vice are set against images of virtue in the relation of excess or defect to a mean, and I have suggested that the excesses or defects are involved with images of reversion to chaos. The notion of the mean is involved with a notion of the universe. Like creaturely standing in Paradise Lost, the mean is the fullness of being. To depart from the mean through excess or defect is to fall into the grotesque or absurd shapes of unbeing. However, whereas in *Paradise Lost* the creation at issue is the whole universe, in *Absalom and Achitophel* the images of creation and uncreation are mostly bodily. The mean is the fullness of the human body in its creaturely powers; the departure from the mean is the distempering of the body.

The crisis of the plot is imaged as if it were a crisis in the physical as well as political constitution. 'If the Body Politique', Dryden concludes his Preface, 'have any Analogy to the Natural, in my weak judgement, an Act of *Oblivion* were as necessary in a Hot, Distemper'd State, as an *Opiate* would be in a Raging Fever'.[49] The image of the body politic runs through the poem. In the crisis, the moderate party,

> looking backward with a wise afright,
> Saw Seames of wounds, dishonest to the sight;
> In contemplation of whose ugly Scars,
> They Curst the memory of Civil Wars.
> (lines 71–4)

The plot itself is imagined as the progress of a fever, imagined in turn as a curious boiling-over of a stagnant lake:

> For, as when raging Fevers boyl the Blood,
> The standing Lake soon floats into a Flood;
> And every hostile Humour, which before
> Slept quiet in its Channels, bubbles o'r:
> So, several Factions from this first Ferment,
> Work up to Foam, and threat the Government.
> (lines 136–41)

One of the causes of this fermenting of idle humours in the body politic is indigestion, for the allegations of a plot were 'swallow'd in the Mass, unchew'd and Crude' (line 113). Other causes are suggested. The civil madness is ascribed to the moon (lines 216–7) and to the heat of the dog star, astrological influences disordering the complexion of the mind through their influence on the body. The extremes of the state are pictured, then, as a distempering of the body politic from its natural mean.

The imagery of the distempered body works also in the individual extremes, most notably in the portrait of Achitophel. He is an example of a grander sort of excess than discussed so far. In Corah, the aspiring mind is likened to mephitic exhalations, which rise from the earth and shine as meteors with a visionary and disastrous light: 'What tho his Birth were base, yet Comets rise / From Earthy Vapours ere they shine in Skies' (lines 636–7). The grand astronomical image has a peculiarly diminishing effect. However, with Achitophel, whose ambition is allowed to be the consequence of great parts, the apparently diminishing physical imagery peculiarly magnifies the character. The disproportion between the angel-ically aspiring 'fiery Soul' and the creaturely inadequacy of 'the Pigmy Body' invests the character with pathos. His human nature is a miscarried hyperbole and the designs of his spirit and the child of his body are equally misbegotten. That the son is not merely 'born a shapeless Lump, like Anarchy' (line 172) but is an 'unfeather'd, two Leg'd thing' (line 169) conveys with Swiftian animus the physical absurdity of the human creature attempting to breed wings. Both his designs and his son are set against Barzillai's justly-tempered politics and issue. However, though Achitophel is played off against the mean, clearly he is a grand defect. The disproportion of body and soul suggests the greatness of the soul, its defiance of its creaturely condition in the tenement of clay. Even in appealing to a just standard of human creatureliness, the portrait suggests something terrible in the precarious con-dition of wit or reason in the human creature. Admittedly, in Achitophel, the disproportion of mind and body goes with a sort of madness, a kind of human monstrosity; but it is the greatness of the portrait that it goes beyond mere satire or imaging of vice through its feeling for the general condition of humanity on 'this isthmus of a middle state'. One is made to feel that Achitophel's disproportion is a tragic version of a disproportion more or less innate in 'the glory, jest and riddle of the world' and of an entirely different order from the merely ridiculous and pinched, uncreaturely disproportion of his fellow plotters.

We have in *Absalom and Achitophel* a scheme of images of virtue and vice, of creation and uncreation analogous, though on a smaller scale, to what we found in *Paradise Lost*. Nor does the analogy stop there. The position of Absalom in this scheme is analogous to the position of Adam and Eve. What draws Absalom into the plot is not deficiency or disproportion but an excess of humanity, 'a Spark too much of Heavenly Fire' (line 308). He has no natural affinity for the defective creatures of whom Achitophel is first, no leaning to run 'Popularly Mad' (line 336); he is corrupted, rather, through what is innately good and generous in him. When he has been corrupted, however, the good is inverted or displaced in a remarkable way, receiving what one might call a negative sign. Achitophel's most inspired subversion of good, of God and monarchy is to hail Absalom as the Messiah, anticipating the fulfilment of a prophecy (yet to be made of David's line) by many centuries. The identification is false and there-fore blasphemous, and consequently Absalom, as he journeys like the sun from east to west and is received everywhere as a Guardian God, takes his place in the masquerade of vices as a grand counterfeit.

At first sight, the position of the king in this scheme of virtues and vices seems anomalous. Clearly, he is a figure of excess, and yet he is not an image of a vice. On the contrary, if it is debatable whether he is the hero of the poem, it is certain that the virtues of the poem are most fully expressed in him. He is the sovereign image of creaturely man in a poem about the body politic. Like Adam and Eve, he is godlike because the divine energy expresses itself in the primitive vigour of his frame. Adam's heroic redundancy, naturally, does not make 'Promiscuous use of Concubine and Bride' (line 6) to scatter 'his Maker's Image through the Land' (line 10). Nor does Dryden model David on Milton's Adam, nor indeed does he ascribe godlike virtues to the king's promiscuity without irony. In Dryden's poem, however, as in Milton's, heroic humanity is godlike through the fullness of its creaturely powers. Accordingly, the king's excesses are creative, or at least procreative, unlike Achitophel's, which are uncreating. Whereas the huddle of Achitophel's spirit issued in a misbegotten progeny, it is suggested that the king's generous warmth, 'inspir'd by some diviner lust' (line 19), begot Absalom, beautiful and brave. It is not merely a libertine suggestion that moderation goes with the king's vigour. The suggestion is also that his excesses are the overflow of a generous, I might say Brobdingnagian, nature, and that means a basically well-tempered and moderate nature. At any rate, the king is as blameless of extremities of mind and spirit as he is of undue exertion, to judge from the half-amused and self-deprecating speech that extinguishes the plot. He is a good-tempered man, and that is part of being a well-tempered man; the poem makes a serious case for being good-tempered. Good temper prescribes a sense of human proportion in the body politic, and, combined with political astuteness, is the necessary virtue to moderate the extremities of the crisis and restore the state to a temperate course.

Dryden makes more of the King's patriarchal vigour. The king is a godlike heroic image, not just in the generosity of his creaturely proportions, but because he is the father of his people. Sovereignty is lodged in his patriarchal sway, and the vigour of the king's constitution is the vigour of the political constitution. To undermine the king's authority, Achitophel suggests to Absolom that the bond of father and son is humbug: "'Tis Natures trick to Propagate her Kind. / Our fond Begetters, who woud never dye, / Love but themselves in their Posterity' (lines 424–6). At the same time, he makes out that the king's vigour is already much depleted, and, with it, his authority. He speaks of *'Old David'* (line 262) and suggests that the king's 'Goodness' (line 386) is greater than his wit, and so implies that his clemency is impotence lacking in 'Manly Force' (line 382). His suggestion that Absalom should assume that 'Manly force' and 'Commit a pleasing Rape upon the Crown' (line 474) is his final insult to patriarchal authority.

It is a short step from imagining the king's authority as a father's to imagining it as God's. So, Dryden makes the constitutional party religiously as well as politically subversive and connects the deformation of political authority with the deformation of God at the hands of idolatrous priests and godsmiths. Whoring after strange gods becomes a metaphor for innovation in forms of government. When, however, the divine form of government asserts its authority over the subversive powers at the end of the poem, the 'Godlike David' is again restored and God makes His authority felt with approving thunder.

The investing of the king with divinity is ambiguous, and necessarily so, since the vigorous warmth that begot Absalom is partly responsible for the heat that infects the people and the idle humours that ferment into a rising. Yet as the crisis draws to a head, a sort of separation occurs, for the excesses of the constitutional party and those of the king become clearly of a different order. More importantly, the plot goes to such extremes as to sanction the office of king as guarantor of the nation's liberties and laws against the tyranny of the people. No doubt there is some irony in the stage management of David's speech and in the machinery of God's thunderclap, which ratifies it. Yet the epic does involve universal issues, and its action naturally moves into the heroic element of the divine and marvellous. We are made to feel that the king's is the voice of a moderation which holds the poise of government, maintains the true spirit of the laws, sustains the human proportion of civility, and hence is in the image of the celestial and universal sway from which it derives its authority. Dryden is therefore being serious as well as witty when he adapts the epic fiction of the god-filled hero who carries everything before him to the picture of a king on whom the power of heaven devolves to dispel anarchic and demonic powers.

In design, at least, *Absalom and Achitophel* exemplifies the method of the neoclassical epic. It contains an array of virtues and vices involved in an implicit universal scheme. It suggests that its action is involved with the divine government of the universe and that its heroic man is the godlike agent of the divine government. Such epic schemes can feature the heroic human vocation in two different ways. In *Jerusalem Delivered*, the heroic vocation is the pursuit of a more than human glory, and humanity is divinised in its infinite striving. In *Paradise Lost*, on the other hand, and in *Absalom and Achitophel*, the heroic vocation is to remain fully human. Both *Paradise Lost* and *Absalom and Achitophel* are concerned with the creaturely human scope. However, whereas in *Paradise Lost* human standing depends on a poise of will, in *Absalom and Achitophel* it depends on a balance of temper. In consequence, the action of *Paradise Lost* is more interesting. A temper is more or less fixed; it may perhaps be improved through the imitation of good models or corrupted through the attraction of bad; but the moral possibilities in the shaping of a moral temper, the fashioning of a character or inner statue, seem to me less interesting than what a study of the will and its motions has to offer.

Absalom perhaps looks like an exception to the rule that Dryden's characters represent moral tempers, not motions of the will. Achitophel tempts him and he falls. However, though the temptation of Absalom is worked up, like Eve's, in a number of ways, as a study of volition it is attenuated. Its real interest lies in Dryden's rhetorical manipulation. It alludes to the fall to make rhetorical points: Achitophel and his constitutional arguments are typed as satanic; Absalom's rebellion is both a serious crime and the fall of a noble nature worthy of forgiveness; and the King's clemency is like God's. As for Absalom's attempt to consider Achitophel's arguments, the point there is not so much to represent vacillation as to voice the orthodox defence of monarchical authority, and in putting it in Absalom's mouth, to insinuate that the rebels act perversely and against their better knowledge. *Absalom and Achitophel* shares with *Paradise Lost* a sense of the precariousness of being, of the ease with which one falls into nonsense and absurdity. However, in *Absalom and Achitophel* humanity is not particularly at stake in the will of Absalom. It is rather that Dryden's voice in the poem, his urbanity, observation and balance, make us feel that humanity is a feat of intellectual and imaginative control.

That may seem hard to maintain, given the way in which *Absalom and Achitophel* converts the rhetorical drive of ideal imitation into propaganda. Neoclassical epic is an immensely affirmative form, and the moral and universal scheme extracted from *Absalom and Achitophel* may seem at odds with the fine distinctions of good and evil that apply to the mixed conditions of human life. To make the king divine and the plotters diabolical is, we might suppose, to make as gross distinctions as any in *Jerusalem Delivered*. Of course, *Absalom and Achitophel* is a discreetly epical poem. Unlike *Paradise Lost* or even *Jerusalem Delivered*, with their overt cosmic designs, it has only one fleeting appearance of a supernatural power, and otherwise the universal imagery of the poem is secondary, glancing from metaphors, similes, allusions, and not part of the primary narrative. Besides, Dryden's wit makes us take the epical design with a pinch of salt. We think in very different ways of Achitophel as 'Hells dire Agent' and of Milton's Satan. Yet, the question of how the rhetorical and universal design of neoclassical epic, however discreet, can avoid enormous simplicity remains unanswered.

The best answer can be found in the rhetorical nature of ideal imitation. *Absalom and Achitophel* applies ideas to life with finesse and judgement, not because it escapes the terms of rhetoric or even propaganda, but because it fulfils the requirements of rhetoric; it is very good rhetoric or propaganda. Here we might hark back to the point, made in the previous chapter, that rhetoric claims to be the art of discourse of incorporated minds. It cultivates the sort of reason that applies to the mixed condition of humanity, the sort of reason that Milton says 'also is choice', bent as it is on extricating the stronger reason in a case from the weaker one and making it prevail. It is in the very nature of such a reason that it is engaged in debate with other reasons and that its conclusions are rhetorically provisional and not theoretically final. What is admirable about *Absalom and Achitophel* lies in its giving supple yet natural and vigorous intelligence to the rhetorical impulse of ideal imitation and neoclassical humanism.

It is through adroitness that Dryden is able to get at the reality of the political issue. The mixed condition of human life, where good and evil are inextricably confused, requires such a suppleness of reason if its issues are to be grasped. Behind the conflict of royal prerogative and popular will, the issue of which Dryden lays hold is authority. Though he attaches authority to the king and God, he nevertheless deals with the temporal condition of any authority. He brings out its precariousness through the ambiguously respectful treatment of the king at the beginning. The tone arouses mixed feelings about majesty. The apparently libertine suggestions of the opening seem half in league with the subversive wit and blasphemy of the republican party. It is only as the unrest develops to a crisis and the sound elements range themselves against the destructive that the poet's wit is seen to disengage itself from subversion and assert a human authority. At this point, wit aligns itself with clemency, and clemency shows itself as manly vigour. The explicit assertion of the king's authority is finely qualified. In lines 753 to 810, the poet makes out a case for the sovereign power of the king. His case is moderate; indeed, it is based on the need for a moderating power. It does not rest explicitly on absolute principles of right, but on expediency, the judgement that civil war and revolution are the worst of political evils. Nevertheless, the rhetorical tendency of his argument is to assert the sovereignty of the king; kings are 'the Godhead's images' (line 792); and even when he supposes (with some sarcasm) that monarchy might finally depend on the grant of 'our Lords the People' (line 795), he does so only to insist that the common interest should hold sacred the king's prerogative, 'our Ark' (line 804), which cannot be touched without common disaster. When, however, the king himself asserts his authority at the end of the poem, he speaks of a limited affair tempered to the conditions in which he has to exercise power:

> What then is left but with a Jealous Eye
> To guard the Small remains of Royalty?
> The Law shall still direct my peacefull Sway,
> And the same Law teach Rebels to Obey.
>   (lines 989–92)

This, quite apart from vindicating Dryden's claim for the moderating power of kingship, shows moderation as an adroitness of judgement necessary in dealing with the confusion of human affairs – how skilfully the king turns his acting within the law into a threat against those who plead law in order to subject him to the popular will. Of course, for Dryden to show the king outdoing Dryden in moderation is the final coup of rhetorical adroitness. Dryden's art of poetry and the art of authority which he shows are in fact akin; both temper reason to the mixed condition of human experience. It goes with such arts of tempering that they aim to assuage, to charm rather than force, to draw their power from ease, naturalness and amenity. In the same spirit, Dryden speaks in his Preface of how sweet verse will make its way in the minds even of hostile readers, and in his poem of how the good nature of the king is irresistible.[50] We may indeed feel that the king's nature as Dryden draws it is too melting for real political force.

One of the impulses of neoclassical humanism was to urbane observation of human nature, urbanity implying that the human nature was cultivated socially. Dryden represents the mature development of this impulse in English humanism. In *Absalom and Achitophel*, he adapts neoclassical epic so that it is in command of social experience. Here, he at once narrows and focuses the possibilities of ideal imitation. Rhetorically-charged images of moral ideas treat morality externally. Tasso, as we saw, was unable to get hold of the process of volition with any inwardness. Dryden makes a virtue of the external glance. He treats the world of social appearances, the stage on which people's worth is made known by the figure they can maintain. In this, he has taken the neoclassical epic in the opposite direction from Milton. For if the excellence of *Absalom and Achitophel* lies in its command of the social and political scene, what distinguishes *Paradise Lost*, not only among neoclassical epics but also among the writings of neoclassical humanists generally, is its treatment of the private world of volition. Milton's study of the will, however, is the subject of the next chapter.

Notes

1 Aristotle, *De Poetica*, ch. 26, 1461b–1462b. Torquato Tasso, *Discourses on the Heroic Poem*, tr. Mariella Cavalchini and Irene Samuel (Oxford, 1973), p. 18, speaks of epic as 'this noblest

kind of poem'; René Le Bossu, *Treatise of the Epick Poem*, tr. 'W. J.' (London, 1695), in *Le Bossu and Voltaire on the Epic*, ed. Stuart Curran (Gainesville, Florida, 1970), p. 5, concludes that if in some respects epic is inferior to tragedy, it arouses passions more conducive to instruction. Dryden's opinion in 'Dedication of *The Aeneis*', *Essays of John Dryden*, ed. W. P. Ker (Oxford, 1900) 2, 154, sums up the tradition.

2   *Pro Archia*, II, 3, ed. James S. Reid (Cambridge, 1928), p. 27.

3   *Pro Archia*, VI, 14, p. 26.

4   See Eckhard Kessler, *Das Problem des Frühen Humanismus: Seine Philosophische Bedeutung bei Coluccio Salutati* (Munich, 1968), pp. 152–200, for the place of the exemplum in humanist thought about literature; also Donald Lemen Clark, *Rhetoric and Poetry in the Renaissance: A Study of English Rhetorical Terms in the Renaissance* (New York, 1922), p. 136ff. Bernard Weinberg, *A History of Literary Criticism in the Italian Renaissance* (Chicago, 1961), I, p. 350, makes it clear that Renaissance critics were unable to take in the newly-discovered *Poetics* of Aristotle because of their rhetorical theory of poetry.

5   *A Defence of Poetry*, ed. Katherine Duncan-Jones and Jan van Dorsten, *Miscellaneous Prose of Sir Philip Sidney* (Oxford, 1973), p. 85; cf. Salutati on the exemplum, Kessler, p. 183.

6   'Ideal imitation' is used by J. E. Spingarn, *Literary Criticism of the Renaissance*, ed. Bernard Weinberg (New York, 1963), p. 19, to cover a theory which he thinks Aristotle and the Renaissance critics held in common. I use the term for the imitation of moral ideas, as distinct from Aristotle's 'imitation of an action'. This is more or less how John M. Steadman speaks of ideal imitation in *The Lamb and the Elephant: Ideal Imitation and the Context of Renaissance Allegory* (San Marino, California, 1974).

7   *Of Education*, ed. Donald C. Dorian, *CP*, 2, 403.

8   For decorum and verisimilitude, see Horace, *Ars Poetica*, lines 119–78, Boileau, *L'Art Poétique*, 3, *Œuvres Complètes de Boileau*, ed. Antoine Adam and Françoise Escal (Paris, 1966), p. 173, and Weinberg, I, pp. 182–3, 436–7. For verisimilitude and the marvellous reconciled by tradition, see Tasso, *Discourses*, pp. 37–8. For paralogism, see Aristotle, *De Poetica*, ch. 24, 1460a, and Spingarn on Robortelli, p. 20. See also Weinberg, I, p. 122, on mingling truth with falsehood. A. D. Nuttal, *A New Mimesis: Shakespeare and the Representation of Reality* (London, 1983), p. 58ff., makes the philosophical point against Roland Barthes that neoclassical critics did not mean decorum or convention by the *vraisemblable*. My point is that their ideas of the *vraisemblable* were conventional and unexacting as far as the representation of reality was concerned.

9   Le Bossu, p. 6.

10   *Lives of the Poets* (London, 1906), I, p. 117.

11   All citations of Edward Fairfax's translation of *Jerusalem Delivered* are to Torquato Tasso, *Godfrey of Bulloigne*, ed. Kathleen M. Lea and T. M. Gang (Oxford, 1981). Citations of *Gerusalemme Liberata* are to Luigi Bonfigli's edition (Bari, 1930).

12   Cf. Tasso, *Discourses*, pp. 77–8; S. K. Henninger, 'Sidney and Milton: The Poet as Maker' in *Milton and the Line of Vision*, ed. Joseph A. Wittreich (Madison, 1975), p. 69ff.

13   Cf. Thomas Greene, *The Descent from Heaven* (New Haven, 1963), p. 189ff.

14   Milton, *Areopagitica*, ed. Ernest Sirluck, *CP*, 2, 514.

15   Greene, pp. 217–19, however, thinks Tasso sympathetic in a melancholy way with the pagan champions. See also Judith A. Kates, 'The Revaluation of the Classical Hero in Tasso and Milton', *Comparative Literature*, 26 (1974), pp. 293–317.

16   A contrast drawn by A. Bartlett Giamatti, *The Earthly Paradise and the Renaissance Epic* (Princeton, 1966), p. 206.

17   Giamatti, p. 199ff., remarks on the narcissism of the scene. Tasso compares Armida to Narcissus Book 14, st. 66.

18   Tasso has '*Temero me medesmo, e, da me stesso / Sempre fuggendo, avro me sempre apresso*', which, like Fairfax's splendid embroidery, looks forward to 'Which way shall I fly / Infinite wrath and infinite despair? / Which way I fly is hell; myself am hell' (IV, 73–5).

19   'As bare as erst when Vulcan took them short', st. 43, is Fairfax's interpretation of Tasso's '*ivi spiegansi a me senz' alcun velo / … Venere e Marte in ogni lor sembianza*'. See also Tasso's allegoresis of the poem, *Godfrey of Bulloigne*, p. 91, for an account of how science has been baptised.

20   *Lives of the Poets*, I, p. 118.

21   Michael Cavanagh, 'A Meeting of Epic and History: Books XI and XII of *Paradise Lost*', *ELH*, 38 (1971), p. 215, argues that Adam's acceptance of the history which Michael shows is

heroic. However, the education of Adam at Michael's hands, though well integrated into the design of the poem, is not worked out as a human action as his fall and repentance are in Books IX and X. It is, in consequence, a strain to see Adam's acceptance of history as the heroic theme of the last four books. Richard S. Ide, 'On the Uses of Elizabethan Drama: The Revaluation of Epic in *Paradise Lost*', *Milton Studies*, 17 (1983), pp. 121–40, holds that the repentance of Adam and Eve is heroic, but neither 'patience' nor 'heroic martyrdom' seems quite appropriate to the case.

22   John M. Steadman's distinction in 'Heroic Virtue and the Divine Image in *Paradise Lost*', *Journal of the Warburg and Courtauld Institutes*, 22 (1959), 89, between heroes as chief actors and as exemplars of heroic virtues is relevant here.

23   Augustine, *Confessions*, Book 7, ch. 12. As a theologian, Milton did not make use of the theory of evil as privation. A. S. P. Woodhouse, 'Notes on Milton's views on the Creation: the Initial Phase', *PQ*, 28 (1949), p. 231, deduces from the monism of Milton's ideas about creation and the goodness of matter in *Christian Doctrine* that he could not have shared Augustine's views, but concedes in a footnote that in *Paradise Lost*, mere matter or chaos appears as a principle of disorder, which, if not evil in itself, has at least some affinity with evil, a point developed by Regina Schwarz, 'Milton's Hostile Chaos ... "And the Sea was No More" ', *ELH*, 52 (1985), pp. 337–74.

24   See e.g. Herbert's 'Sinne' and Donne's 'The Bracelet', lines 71–5; cf. Calvin, *Commentaries on the Book of Genesis*, tr. John King (Edinburgh, 1848), I, p. 142: 'We must conclude that the principle of evil with which Satan was endued was not from nature, but from defection'.

25   Hester Lynch Thrale, *Thraliana*, ed. Katharine C. Balderston (Oxford, 1951), I, p. 12: 'Doctor Collier used to say that although Milton was so violent a Whig himself, he was obliged to write his poem upon the purest Tory principles'. Malcolm Mackenzie Ross, *Milton's Royalism: A Study of the Conflict of Symbol and Idea in the Poems* (Ithaca, New York, 1943), and J. B. Broadbent, *Some Graver Subject* (London, 1961), p. 225ff., develop what they take to be an imaginative self-contradiction. However, it seems to me that the imaginative transference works quite coherently in *Paradise Lost*, as it did for instance among the Scottish Presbyterians.

26   Christopher Ricks, *Milton's Grand Style* (Oxford, 1963), pp. 110, 112.

27   Ed. Ralph A. Haug, *CP*, 1, 752.

28   See Edgar Hill Duncan, 'The Natural History of Metals and Minerals in the Universe of Milton's *Paradise Lost*', *Osiris*, 9 (1954), p. 386–421.

29   William G. Madsen, 'The Idea of Nature in Milton's Poetry', *Three Studies in the Renaissance* (New Haven, 1958), p. 234ff. and *From Shadowy Types to Truth* (New Haven, 1968), pp. 85–144, points to the oddity of Milton's having Adam and Eve ascend to spirit in an essentially anti-Platonic system.

30   'In Reformation commentary, "sacrifice" becomes a verbal action, though not entirely an inward one; "sacrifice" becomes praise': Georgia B. Christopher, *Milton and the Science of the Saints* (Princeton, NJ, 1982), p. 81.

31   Ricks, *Milton's Grand Style* (Oxford, 1963), pp. 82–3, makes the point about flow. See also G. Stanley Koehler, 'Milton and the Art of Landscape', *Milton Studies* 8 (1975), p. 17ff., on water as 'the key to Milton's landscapes'.

32   *Some Versions of Pastoral: A Study in the Pastoral Form in Literature* (London, 1935), p. 157.

33   I owe this point to Mr Roy Henderson.

34   William J. Bouwsma, *John Calvin: A Sixteenth-Century Portrait* (New York, 1988), pp. 45–7.

35   See William Empson, *Milton's God* (London, 1965), p. 48.

36   Duncan, p. 388ff.

37   See John Onians, 'On How to Listen to High Renaissance Art', *Art History*, 7 (1984), pp. 412–9, for Renaissance theory about music and architecture.

38   Cf. Isabel Gamble MacCaffery, *'Paradise Lost' as Myth* (Cambridge, Mass., 1959), p. 60.

39   Intoxicant: IX, 793–4, 1003; aphrodisiac: IX, 1011ff.; poison: IX, 1044–54.

40   Fowler's note to IX, 9, draws the connection with X, 688. Ricks, pp. 69–72 explains the force of 'distaste'.

41   *Christian Doctrine*, Book 1, ch. 20, *CP*, 6, 476.

42   'Discourse Concerning the Original and Progress of Satire', *Essays of John Dryden*, 2, 67.

43   See Bernard Schilling's distinction between the portrait and the character in *Dryden and the*

Conservative Myth: A Reading of 'Absalom and Achitophel' (New Haven, 1961), pp. 199–202.

44   See e. g. Reuben Arthur Brower, 'Dryden's Epic Manner and Virgil', *Essential Articles for the Study of John Dryden*, ed. H. T. Swedenberg (Hamilton, Conn., 1966), pp. 482–3. Ian Jack, *Augustan Satire: Intention and Idiom in English Poetry*, 1660–1750 (Oxford, 1952), pp. 53–76, discusses how *Absalom and Achitophel* manages to be at once witty and heroic.

45   All citations of *Absalom and Achitophel* are to James Kinsley, ed., *The Poems of John Dryden* (Oxford, 1958), I, pp. 215–43.

46   'If I happen to please the more Moderate sort, I shall be sure of an honest Party', 'To the Reader', Kinsley, I, p. 215.

47   For the balancing of opposites in later seventeenth-century verse, see Brendan O'Hehir, *Expans'd Hieroglyphicks: A Critical Edition of Sir John Denham's 'Cooper's Hill'* (Berkeley, 1969), pp. 165–76.

48   For Milton parallels, see Leonora Leet Broadwin, 'Miltonic Allusion in *Absalom and Achitophel*: Its Function in the Political Satire', *JEGP*, 68 (1969), pp. 24–44; see also Morris Freedman, 'Dryden's Miniature Epic', *JEGP*, 57 (1958), pp. 211–19; Anne Davidson Ferry, *Milton and the Miltonic Dryden* (Cambridge, Mass., 1968), pp. 21–40.

49   'To the Reader', Kinsley, I, p. 216.

50   'There's a sweetness in good Verse, which Tickles even while it Hurts: And no man can be heartily angry with him, who pleases him against his will' (To the Reader, Kinsley, I, p. 215).

Chapter 4

The Motions of the Will in *Paradise Lost*

Theology

Milton's representation of the motions of the will makes *Paradise Lost* truly remarkable among neoclassical epics. However, as I observed in the first chapter his theological ideas are not at all remarkable or interesting in the same way. They are at best pegs on which he can hang the moral preoccupations of the poem. At worst they supply a rigid structure, vigorously and redoubtably argued, but indifferent or even hostile to intelligence about human experience. I shall discuss them briefly only in order to put them in their place before turning to what is of value in Milton's study of the will.

Milton encases his ideas about the will in God's providential scheme of countering the fall and condemnation of the human race with the atonement and redemption, a casing hard to understand, let alone swallow, whether it is to be thought a scheme of justice or of mercy:

> man disobeying,
> Disloyal breaks his fealty, and sins
> Against the high supremacy of heaven,
> Affecting Godhead, and so losing all,
> To expiate his treason hath nought left,
> But to destruction sacred and devote,
> He with his whole posterity must die,
> Die he or justice must; unless for him
> Some other able, and as willing, pay
> The rigid satisfaction, death for death.
>
> (III, 204–12)

This is a passage which Matthew Arnold singled out to illustrate the sterility and legalism of seventeenth-century Puritan theology,[1] the legalism here being couched in feudal terms archaic even in Milton's day. It is true that the Father's speech is something of a front. He has already intimated that it is His will that 'man … shall find grace' (III, 130–1). He speaks with the severity of legalistic theology only to elicit the fullness of divine love in the Son's response. Yet if God's mercy is to make sense, His justice must make sense first, and unfortunately no amount of rhetorical mastery can get round the difficulty of understanding how it is just to condemn the whole human race for the sin of Adam and Eve or how the sacrifice of an innocent victim can help.

Into this grand, orthodox, yet mystifying scheme of God's justice and mercy, Milton sets his unorthodox Arminian views concerning grace and free will. Orthodox Protestants held that the entire fallen human race could do nothing to redeem itself in God's eyes. Only grace could do that, but grace was extended only to some, and to them irresistibly. They could neither redeem themselves nor cast themselves away. Their will was of no account. God's will was everything. Those to whom he did not extend grace were lost helplessly. Milton's unorthodox view, as he explains it in the *Christian Doctrine* or has the Father declare it in *Paradise Lost*, is that grace, 'what may suffice' (III, 189) to stand again, is extended to all, but some, 'when they may, accept not grace' (III, 302). In other words, God gives humanity another chance, continually renewed, to stand or fall. So, while in a sense it owes everything to God, fallen humanity has it in its power at least to reject grace. It may not be able to pick itself up again, but its effort is necessary if only to accept another chance to stand and not to let go of or swerve away from God.[2]

The place which Milton found for free will did something to vindicate God's justice. The responsibility for sin was human, and God could not be said to punish or reward what only He could help or effect; but the vindication is very limited and does nothing to explain the overarching scheme of original sin and atonement. Our concern, however, is with *Paradise Lost* as a study of the will, not as a theodicy, and here the point is that Milton's Arminianism makes the human action of his poem possible. The continual renewal of mankind after the Fall means that fallen moral experience is not utterly different from Adam and Eve's. Fallen humanity may have it harder, but it is to regain Paradise on terms of free obedience, the terms on which Adam and Eve were to have kept it. It is renewed to stand or fall. So, in imagining life in Paradise, Milton was able to represent not an alien existence but what he took to be the essence of human experience. In Milton's theology, we have only the possibility of his human action. No actual insights are given into how people work. It is when Milton is doing his job as poet, representing his characters' actions or thoughts, that his insights are to be found.

The Son

A complete account of Milton's study of the will in *Paradise Lost* would have to take in the Son. The Son's entire submission to the will of the Father not only represents Milton's ideas of free obedience in ideal form, but also has a powerful hold on his imagination. Milton was quite clearly not forcing himself to celebrate something to which he could not really respond. He was caught up in the Son's emptying himself to be filled with a tremendous infusion of the Father's might.

Blake's idea that the sources of Milton's imaginative energy were infernal will not stand up to the power poetry of the Creation or of the Son's going out to war against the rebels in the chariot of paternal deity, each an event in which the Son takes on the power of the omnipotent Father and becomes His 'effectual might' (III, 170). Even in Michael's survey of history, a part of the poem which few unchartered readers feel engaged Milton deeply, an austere energy makes itself felt in the narrative of the duel with Satan, where the Son puts forth the power of the godhead through voluntary humiliation and perfect attention to the Father's will:

> so he dies,
> But soon revives, Death over him no power
> Shall long usurp; ere the third dawning light
> Return, the stars of morn shall see him rise
> Out of his grave, fresh as the dawning light.
>   (XII, 419–23)

Some of this is merely summary, but the discreet association of the Son with the dawning light and the pregnancy of 'fresh', appropriate at once to dawn and Christ's rising untainted from the grave, make their points as memorably as the sublimely grotesque details of the Son's chariot studded with eyes and powered by whirling cherubim. Again, Milton is imagining a triumph through submission. The complaint, if any, about such passages is not that Milton wrote in chains, but that the energy in which he delights is omnipotent and can do anything; to ally oneself with such power may be humanly damaging. It is not for that reason, however, that the Son is not a suitable subject for this chapter, but rather because the operations of the will which he transcendentally represents are not realised in the central human action of the poem. For these, we would have to go to *Paradise Regained* or *Samson Agonistes*. In *Paradise Lost* they are supernatural, not human, motions.

Satan

Satan is a supernatural being too, but he speaks to us as the Son does not, because he is up against circumstances over which he has no supernatural power. He suffers, and we can recognise a fellow creature. Moreover, his anguish takes the form of the will enthralled to itself, and on a grand or mythic scale shows how Milton imagines evil as loss of freedom. The motions of Satan's will, unlike the Son's, help us to understand Adam and Eve's.

God's part in Satan's continuing fall is chilling. While He is prepared to give humanity a second chance, He will leave the fallen angels to go on falling for ever. No grace will be extended to them, so they will not repent, so no grace will be extended to them. Satan can only will to do evil. And yet, though he is given no opportunity and cannot help himself, the Father puts him in the position of those humans who, since they freely do not accept the opportunity to turn from evil, shall 'hard be hardened, blind be blinded more, / That they may stumble on, and deeper fall' (III, 200–1). In extenuation of the Father's malice, we might say that what provokes Satan's rancour is the Father's goodness, and this is not only how Milton explains God's hardening of sinners' hearts in the *Christian Doctrine*, but also what he shows happening in Satan's soliloquies.[3] However, such hardening only makes the Father's malice more exquisite, for Satan has no power to respond to the Father's goodness except by rejection. The Father's argument for denying the angels the grace which He extends to humanity is as follows:

> The first sort by their own suggestion fell,
> Self-tempted, self-depraved: man falls deceived
> By the other first: man therefore shall find grace,
> The other none.
>
> (III, 129–32)

This is baffling. The angels, like Eve, were tempted by Satan, not by their own suggestions. Even if the Father means that the angels were tempted by one of themselves, not by another sort of creature, that sheds no light on why they should be the more damnable.[4] It must be said that the rebel angels do seem more malignant from the start, more determined and more formidable enemies of God than Adam and Eve, and they defy Abdiel's warning. However, even these considerations do not make it easy to accept God's eternal complaisance in the rebel angels' course of destruction, let alone His relish of it.

The scheme of justice in which Satan is caught appals. We may wonder indeed if it is possible to discuss his case in terms of the moral psychology of the will without muddle, ordinary notions of good and evil being so distorted by Milton's theology. To probe into Satan's psychology, one might think, would simply be to turn a blind eye to his wrongs, to displace them and find their origin within him. Yet, what Milton pictures in Satan is not just a figment of his theological system. Satan's anguish is simply more general than that; we can recognise his trouble and malignancy apart from the specific scheme on which he is drawn.

Without our conceding anything to Milton's God-centred universe, Satan still appears as someone who irrevocably breaks with the order of things in which he finds himself, but is not strong enough to make a new beginning or a new world (hell after all turns out to be hell), and whose defiance in consequence takes the form of negation. Although he has broken with the system, he cannot break away from it and indeed falls into orbit as the adversary. It is remarkable that *Paradise Lost* can allow so uncommitted a view of Satan, even if only at the edges of the picture, for it is as if Milton could conceive of the order of things in which he placed himself, from the outside. Partly, the uncommitted view is encouraged in us by Milton's insisting on God's will and power, partly by the way that Satan's subversive utterances show us how things might look the other way round. At any rate, Milton manages to make us feel what it is like to be the enemy of God and rebel against the order of things, instead of simply presenting a figure of execration, like Dante's Satan, whose three mouths chew Judas, Brutus and Cassius, or indeed like Tasso's complicated monster.

However, Milton also draws us into feeling that Satan on his malign course is a tragic figure. This is partly because, as he suffers the ruin to which his own choice committed him, Satan gives expression to the anguish implied in the freedom of the will. His case has a general significance, and he has a power of utterance that speaks of someone anguished to the depths of his being. His being, incidentally, is what, for lack of a better word, I shall call cosmic. Where Shakespeare's tragic heroes typically express their anguish in terms of the sexuality that ties them to the world, Satan's tragic consciousness has to do with his place in things and universal height and depth. He is tragic, however, not just through the resonance of his anguish, but because he makes a choice that destroys him. Macbeth, in choosing to murder Duncan, and Othello, in yielding to Iago's suggestions, make choices that not only bring them to grief and death but also involve their integrity as human beings in ruin. In the same way, Satan confounds himself by an original choice of error. We see this when Satan is alone soliloquising after the event. Unfortunately, Raphael's account of the rebellion in heaven cannot make us feel that Satan's original crime was of the same order of wickedness or folly as Macbeth's or Othello's. Satan disobeys the Father's command to accept the Son as their ruler. However, the obedience which the Father demands does not sound like a principle of life in as intimate or as vital a sense as Macbeth's loyalty to Duncan or Othello's love of Desdemona, though the explicit theology of the poem tells us it must be far more so. Indeed, the whole account of Satan's breaking with the communion of the blessed, in spite of the feasting and dancing in heaven, in spite of God's being God, fails to engage our deepest intuitions of good and evil. Given that Satan has violated the law by which he lives, his ensuing career is a tragic study in the negative will bound in its own error, but the given has to be taken on trust.

Raphael fails not only to persuade us that Satan has chosen a course that damns him as a moral being, but also to show in detail how Satan fell. He tells us of feelings of pride and envy, which make Satan unable to bear the Son's exaltation, but he does not explain how such evil feelings could enter the heart of an unfallen creature. Indeed, he leaves blank the whole process of self-suggested temptation and fall. The first thing we hear about it from him is Satan's tempting Beelzebub to revolt, but by that time Satan must already have made up his own mind, though confusingly elsewhere we learn that Sin springs from his head only the next day in the Council in the North. Raphael is interested in the politics, not the moral psychology, of the fall.

Although Raphael gives us Satan only as he might appear to the other camp as conspirator and rebel, Satan himself on Niphates brings to mind at least something of what was involved in the deflecting of his will from obedience. His fall was instantaneous:

> lifted up so high
> I sdeigned subjection, and thought one step higher
> Would set me highest, and in a moment quit
> The debt immense of endless gratitude,
> So burdensome still paying, still to owe;
> Forgetful what from him I still received,
> And understood not that a grateful mind
> By owing owes not, but still pays, at once
> Indebted and discharged; what burden then?
>
> (IV, 49–57)

To this account of mounting and falling, Satan's physical position as he soliloquises on the top of Niphates lends a peculiar vividness. Lifted up high, he wished to take a step higher, and yet to try to step higher from his bright eminence in heaven was, as it would be from Niphates, to quit his perch and step into nothing. The lines, with their strategic placing of 'high', 'higher'and 'quit', catch a precarious balance and sudden tumbling out of it. The fall has to be instantaneous, since beings created perfect cannot be sinful before they fall. In heaven or paradise, they cannot have flaws that would somehow explain their fall. It is the fall that flaws the nature, not the flawed nature that somehow brings about the fall. This perhaps sounds too paradoxical to be imagined, though it is little more than to say that God makes His angels and humans free to stand or fall. Yet, while Satan does not analyse his choice of evil, he speaks of gratitude and resentment in a way that makes the instantaneous succession of innocence by evil comprehensible. For he draws out the universal figuring of his case, the falling in space, which so memorably suggests free fall in inner space, into a moral understanding of what has happened. In ordinary human experience, gratitude and resentment are alternative responses to obligation, and we have no trouble in imagining the one changing into the other. In the unfallen world, the rule is that creation returns in thanks to the creator, and this return is made freely by good will 'at once indebted and discharged', as Satan, borrowing from Cicero with Milton's extraordinary boldness, beautifully puts it.[5] To bad will, however, debt becomes extortion, and the return of gratitude sticks in Satan's throat. In his loss, Satan speaks with a moral understanding of both the freedom of gratitude and the unfreedom of resentment that makes us understand him and brings before us the experience of which the apparently paradoxical notion of an instantaneous free fall out of things into self-enclosed unfreedom has a grasp.

The motion of the will here is one of negation. The theological idea of evil as nothing informed Milton's scheme of universal images, as we saw in the last chapter; but equally it informs his study of volition. To choose evil is not just to fall into an anti-world; it is also to will oneself out of creation into the abyss of the self. So Satan converts what is a source of gratitude and freedom into a source of resentment and constraint. That is how he enters into the negative process of evil, the process of all his soliloquies. On Niphates, he is initially moved by the sun towards God, but immediately that reminds him of the state he has lost and draws hate out of him instead of wonder. A motion of remorse follows, and confession of his freedom to have stood, but this too turns to cursing. The good and freedom he enjoyed turns to blame and so to a transference of blame upon what blames him:

> whom hast thou then or what to accuse,
> But heaven's free love dealt equally to all?
> Be then his love accursed.
>
> (IV, 67–9)

Whatever we think of heaven's free love when Milton or Raphael describes it, through Satan's eyes its goodness seems compelling, even in the way in which it compels him to hatred and recognition of his hatred and so more hatred. The same process, a coiling regress out of reality into an inner world of negation, is at work elsewhere. The sight of Adam and Eve in love moves Satan. His words, 'these two / Imparadised in one another's arms / The happier Eden' (IV, 505–7), speak overwhelmingly of that. However, his feeling for their happiness torments him with the realisation of his own loss of love and provokes him to his envious and destructive plan. In Book IX, he sees the earth, rather than the sun, as like God, because it is the fertile and productive centre of things, and he speaks with appreciation of the play of life in variety, the 'sweet interchange / Of hill, and valley, rivers, woods and plains' (IX, 115–16) that distinguishes creation. Then, realising how he has no place there, all the goodness of creation 'becomes / Bane' (lines 122–3) to him and the 'sweet interchange', a 'hateful siege / Of contraries' (lines 121–2) tormenting him with the pleasures that are lost to him and bringing out the will to destroy, 'For only in destroying find I ease' (line 129). Finally, in his last soliloquy, on the point of corrupting Eve, more than ever he is carried away towards good by loveliness, only to take vengeance on the awe and delight which he feels before her by willing to hate.

The motion of negation is a motion of despair. That may seem to contradict the heroic energy that Satan's actions as well as words display in the first two books and even in the war in heaven. When Satan on Niphates tells us that in hell his legions have no idea 'under what torment inwardly I groan; / While they adore me on the throne of hell' (IV, 88–9), he does not sound like the orator and leader of the first books 'whom transcendent glory raised / Above his fellows' (lines 427–8). In those books, Milton presents him from the outside making as much as he can of the contrast between the wretchedness of his situation and the high spirit with which he meets it. Yet even there, Milton comments on one of Satan's most defiant harangues that he was 'vaunting aloud but wracked with deep despair' (I, 126). It might be of course that Milton was clumsily trying to correct too attractive a picture of the devil, lying about his fiction for our moral good.[6] However, a feeling of doomed splendour invests all of Satan's heroic energy in hell. Besides, neither despair nor even pain need be inert. The soliloquies show entirely convincingly the fierce appetite for destruction which pain and grief may cause. The sense of being lost, far from causing him to slump, propels him with furious energy. Something of the same conversion of motive is at work when he is making war in heaven. When the rebel angels see the chariot of paternal deity, they should know that it is all up, but instead they stand 'obdured / And to rebellious fight rallied their powers / Insensate, hope conceiving from despair' (VI, 785–7). To that sort of transmutation of despair into resistance, Moloch later gives wild expression. However, the transmutation can take a calmer form of defiance. When the fallen angels file before Satan on the bank of the burning lake,

> anon they move
> In perfect Phalanx to the Dorian mood
> Of flutes and soft recorders; such as raised
> To highth of noblest temper heroes old
> Arming to battle, and in stead of rage
> Deliberate valour breathed, firm and unmoved
> With dread of death to flight or foul retreat,
> Nor wanting power to mitigate and swage,
> With solemn touches, troubled thoughts, and chase
> Anguish and doubt and fear and sorrow and pain
> From mortal or immortal minds.
>
>   (I, 549–59)

Milton is a master of the effects of music. While he speaks of how the music raises and calms the mind, the music of his own verse here suggests how fear and despair are turned into courage. The polysyndeton in line 558 – 'Anguish and doubt and fear and sorrow and pain' – together with the anapaest or elision in the last foot, not only converts anguish, doubt, fear, sorrow, pain to music, but also, by passing over them glidingly, seems to convert them into a spirit of overcoming. Clearly, such a turning of hell to fortitude is admirable. Milton even encourages us to admire it for what it is worth, despite his ideas about the direction which heroism should take. It is no cheapening of the heroism to say that it consists in making energetic resistance out of despair. Much heroism is of that sort, nor the less heroic for being so. Nor even in Satan is it somehow unheroic because it falls in with the demonic negation of things to which he is bound.

The usual means by which Satan converts despair into heroic energy is the rhetoric of negation. Psychologically, the most revealing examples are to be found in the soliloquies, where we shall find the clue to what he is doing in his more obviously heroic public speeches. A tattered yet fascinating specimen of how Satan's rhetoric is addressed to himself occurs in his first soliloquy on viewing Adam and Eve. He is moved first to admiration and love and then to pity:

> Ah gentle pair, ye little think how nigh
> Your change approaches, when all these delights
> Will vanish and deliver ye to woe,
> More woe, the more your taste is now of joy;
> Happy, but for so happy ill secured
> Long to continue, and this high seat your heaven
> Ill fenced for heaven to keep out such a foe
> As now is entered; yet no purposed foe.
>
> (IV, 366–73)

His pity is hypocritical since he is the destroyer; but his crocodile tears are deeply felt. By keeping himself out of the picture as long as possible and talking of the results of his actions as 'your change', he can savour a noble emotion. The curious, halting repetitions of 'woe', 'happy', 'heaven' and 'foe' hold up the movement and draw out the feeling, which then modulates into something obscene:

> league with you I seek,
> And mutual amity so strait, so close,
> That I with you must dwell, or you with me
> Henceforth; my dwelling haply may not please
> Like this fair Paradise, your sense, yet such
> Accept your maker's work; he gave it me,
> Which I as freely give; hell shall unfold,
> To entertain you two, her widest gates,
> And send forth all her kings.
>
> (IV, 375–83)

'The cuddling movement of *mutual amity*, with the flat mouth of the worm, in *am-* opening to feed on them, the insinuating hiss of *so streight, so close*, full of the delicious softness of the tormentor belong to the Satan who will have his guests tortured by incongruous furies (II, 596).' So Empson comments in *Some Versions of Pastoral*, and very justly calls attention to Satan's gloating accents, but imports an interest in torture foreign to the character which Milton draws.[7] Satan quite clearly is not thinking of torturing Adam and Eve; he wants them to share his torture. That longing is repulsive in itself and is the more so for Satan's language of love and regret, but the cuddling and insinuating which Empson heard in fact come from bitter self-pity, not sadism. In turn, this passes into a self-fascinated gesture in which the language, free from sarcastic accents, presents a malignant and sordid action to Satan's imagination in the self-enhancing rhetoric of melancholy generosity. Originally Empson, whose feeling for the music of the verse seems to me faultless, considered that this offer to make Adam and Eve free of his dwelling could not come from the same character as did the sinister lust to be united with them in hell.[8] He retracted this in *Milton's God*, arguing that Satan had not yet quite grasped how hellish God would make hell and so could sincerely play the part of host and patron in throwing open hell to Adam and Eve, though 'even as he speaks his lips are twisted by the new suspicion that God is only waiting to turn all he does to torture'.[9] Here, Empson seems to have forgotten the force of his earlier observation on the lines on 'mutual amity'. These would not sound so ugly if they did not express a lively sense of the hell which he suffers, and so the generosity of his offer can only be self-bamboozling. The whole soliloquy hangs together convincingly as a study of evil as the corruption of good. It shows Satan in the process of making himself worse, and traces the extraordinarily live, anguished play of his mind as he does so. The original impulse of love runs throughout; but this is an impulse which he has to deny, and, in denying, distorts to pity, lust and generosity. All the while, he is telling himself a story about what he is doing that not only represents his negative movement as something grand but also helps him to turn wretchedness to a kind of negative energy.

In its negations, Satan's rhetoric does not always express such intense personal feeling. Where it is directed at others as well as himself, it is more successfully engaged in putting a good face on his actions. Indeed, his negative will is at its most vigorous, one might say its most creative, in representing him publicly. Here he comes close to imposing a subversive view on Milton's God-centred universe. A good example occurs at the beginning of his rebellion in Book V, where he stands as republican and atheist in heaven.

The Father has declared that His Son will reign from now on as vicegerent of heaven. Against this declaration, Satan incites his followers: surely they will not submit to their new king,

> if ye know yourselves
> Natives and sons of heaven possessed before
> By none, and if not equal all, yet free,
> Equally free; for orders and degrees
> Jar not with liberty, but well consist.
>
> (V, 789–93)

It is usually supposed that Satan, in his eagerness to justify his position as leader, has ineptly undermined his stand as libertarian: if, as he says, you can be free in subordination, why quarrel with the Son's promotion?[10] Empson's explanation of these lines, however, seems to me the right one. Satan is appealing to an aristocratic notion of established status and constitutional rights.[11] These are the liberties for which Satan is contending and which the Father's imposing of a new king threatens, not least by his implying that all dignities and titles are owed to the sovereign and so may be resumed or altered by him at will. Even Abdiel does not try to catch Satan out in a contradiction here. Given his assumptions, then, Satan's republicanism is coherent. It appeals, moreover, not to what is low in the angels but to what is high – their consciousness of worth and intolerance of servitude. Like Adam and Eve, they fall for sublime reasons.[12] Even the atheism with which Satan scoffs at Abdiel's argument for their owing everything to God is 'sublime'. With a flash of intellectual brilliance, Satan overturns customary opinion and completes his case for rebellion. In doing so, he appeals to the angels' consciousness of heavenly worth:

> We know no time when we were not as now;
> Know none before us, self-begot, self-raised
> By our own quickening power.
>
> (V, 859–64)

To this, Abdiel can only reply that God's power to uncreate them will teach the rebels who created them.

However sublime the arguments which Milton gave to Satan, obviously he thought him wrong. He was indeed committed to thinking him wrong politically as well as religiously. His own earthly republicanism was suspended from divine absolutism: what was wrong with earthly orders, particularly monarchies, was their encroaching on the Kingdom of God, in which individual conscience was absolutely bound to the divine will. But as Boswell observes, heaven is 'a place where there is no room for Whiggism'.[13] In heaven, where Satan challenges God, there is no transcending kingdom. Whereas, on earth, religious loyalty appeals beyond political loyalty, in heaven Satan can make no such appeal. There, political loyalty is religious loyalty, and Satan's republicanism violates both. It can only appeal to personal dignity and native vigour, but even these in their true form Milton attaches elsewhere in *Paradise Lost* to an integrity dependent on God. Because of the curious way in which the heavenly order may turn ordinary earthly judgements upside down, Milton can even talk of Satan as a tyrant: what looks like republicanism in him is in fact a claim to equality with God, for Milton the essence of tyranny and the crime of such usurpers of God's rule over men as Nimrod.[14]

Milton, therefore, held a theory that implies that Satan has violated the conditions for true liberty. How then should we take Satan's 'sublime' arguments for rebellion? We may feel that Satan voices some inner protest of Milton's against his theory of true liberty. At some level, no doubt, Milton was in two minds about Satan. It is humanly improbable that so compelling a figure as Satan was not drawn from deeply self-contradictory stuff in his author, and the strain of calling the rebel a tyrant suggests some sort of suppression. Against the subversive appeal of Satan, though, we have to set the subversiveness of God's authority, which in lived principle liberated Milton from the claims of earthly authority. It is by no means clear that Satan's is the truly subversive voice; and, even if we feel that subversiveness is the mark of authenticity, it does not follow that Milton most deeply wanted to say what Satan was saying. There is in any case a very simple way in which Satan can at once voice and contradict Milton's beliefs, or at least utter good arguments, though he is in the wrong: he is fabricating; he has chosen to rebel, and finds arguments to justify his course. Raphael does not tell us how he came to make his original error; but, if it was anything like the Fall of Adam and Eve, it was the turning of the will against God that made the arguments seem plausible to Satan and required further arguments to explain himself and his defection. The arguments are good; they have to be – but they are misplaced, and Satan's formidable intellectual powers are engaged in what is self-deception before it turns to deception of others.

The idea that Satan's most subversive rhetoric is a kind of self-deception is consistent with Milton's stated beliefs. It is also consistent with the way in which Satan's story falls apart in his soliloquies. On Niphates, the beauty of creation strikes him so forcibly after hell that the case which he made in heaven against God vanishes. He allows that God made him and that His rule was benevolent. However, the soliloquy involves more than an implicit confession of having deluded himself. As we have seen, he is driven by being undeceived to further denial, though it means turning himself upside down. The process of negation takes him from heroic denial of the order of heaven to a perverse and mean form of resistance, and ruses of concealment and self-deception re-enter in ignoble, self-corrupting forms. The interest of Satan's character lies then in what always concentrated Milton's best understanding, the motions of the will. We may admire not only the coherence on a grand, bold scale of Milton's working-out of the process of negation from height to depth in Satan, but also his insights into how great powers of mind may be employed in the service of delusion and self-delusion. I stress this interest, because the idea that Satan is deceiving himself may seem to make him absurd, and, according to Empson, we cannot be deeply interested in such a character.[15] However, the absurdity which Milton draws is not ridiculous. To fall, as Satan does, out of reality is a dreadful thing, and his absurdity is of the tragic sort. God may be in a position to laugh, but humans, for whom error and justification of error are familiar painful experience, are in no position to jeer, not even at what in Satan's case is wilful error. Satan's self-deception in fact represents a frightening possibility. In some respects, he resembles Othello, who, when once he entertains his absurd notion of Desdemona's falsity, finds evidence for it in the truth itself: if she is kind and loving, she is the more accomplished a hypocrite. Similarly, it strikes Satan that the way in which God has made heaven mostly a matter of feasting and singing shows that he wants to keep his angels servile, 'the minstrelsy of heaven', 'Ministering spirits, trained up in feast and song' (VI, 167–8).

We cannot doubt, however, that Othello is deceived, whereas with Satan's rhetoric we are always conscious of fabrication, a continual concealing from himself and his followers of his original error. It turns defeat into victory by sheer energy of negation. Only a poor reading could fail to respond to the moral appeal of Satan's heroic reaction to ruin. Yet, the triumph of 'the unconquerable will' (I, 206) and of 'A mind not to be changed by place or time' (I, 253) has as self-destructive implications as less noble forms of resistance to the despotism of fact have. The grand assertion that 'The mind is its own place, and in itself / Can make a heaven of hell, a hell of heaven' (I, 254–5) turns out to be all too accurate about Satan's displacement from things, the journey into the self that discovers 'myself am hell' (IV, 75).

It is not that the heroism of Satan's defiance is bogus. It is genuinely heroic to defy circumstances as he does. That Milton has another pattern of heroism in the Son, a pattern of self-surrender instead of self-assertion, makes no difference. The Son too has to turn defeat into victory. Even if he goes about it in what Milton thinks the right way, and successfully, what makes him heroic, as distinct from good, is his triumphing in spirit over the circumstances of his life. However, the heroic denial of what confronts it can take a lethal turn. That is Milton's insight into Satan: his negation of things runs to heroism, and heroism energetically pushes him out of the order of things he defies. This is not to show up a particular sort of heroism as false or satanic, but to understand the psychology of heroism and to see how it can go with Satan's self-corrupting negative will.

Although Milton's study of the will focuses on the inner world of temptation, guilt and repentance, he treats these things not just as they bear on one's relation to oneself or to God, but to others also. Satan's fall corrupts others as well as himself. Again, this is something worked out more fully in the human fall, Satan's course representing it with grand figurative simplicity.

Satan's fall carries with him 'Millions of spirits for his fault amerced / Of heaven, and from eternal splendours flung' (I, 609–10). His legions obey him with strange docility. Though Milton calls him a tyrant and a sultan (I, 348) and hints that his legions fear him (I, 333), they cannot plead compulsion. They have been seduced and serve him of their own free will. They have been persuaded by his 'transcendent glory' (II, 427), by his superior courage and abilities and above all by his rhetoric, a rhetoric evidently so persuasive that none but Abdiel protests against its wrongness; the others respond to him as one man. But at the same time that his rhetoric sways them, their being swayed confirms him in his own mind. Satan was inspired to ask Abdiel how he knows God created the angels, his most daring denial of the order of things, when he saw that his legions were firmly persuaded by his earlier arguments for rebellion. He needs others to harangue so that he may carry himself along. His conversations with himself, by contrast, take an unhappy turn.

The complicity of the rebel angels in Satan's fall is reflexive. Here, we touch on what, given Milton's predilection for solitary heroes, is a surprising insight into people, the reflexiveness of the self in others. This he brings out particularly in the way in which looks reflect each other. The face is a mirror, which at once sees and reflects what it sees; a 'look' means both a gaze and an appearance, both a looking and the expression on the face as it looks. In heaven, Satan's countenance shines as the morning star, a particularly brilliant reflection of his creator's glory, compelling enough to draw after it 'the third part of heaven's host' (V, 710).[16] In hell, however, the reflection is clouded. His troops come flocking,

> but with looks
> Down cast and damp, yet such wherein appeared
> Obscure some glimpse of joy, to have found their chief
> Not in despair, to have found themselves not lost
> In loss itself; which on his countenance cast
> Like doubtful hue.
>
> (I, 522–7)

Here we have looks and glimpses that are both the seeing glance and the reflection in the face of what the eye takes in. As the looks of others brighten when they find Satan, so his look brightens as he finds them brightening. Even in utter hopelessness, the complicity of looks holds them up, and they discover what they are to themselves by looking at each other. Something of the same play on looks is going on when, a little later, Satan, looking on his troops, feels an access of pride as he views the image of his power in them,

> their order due,
> Their visages and stature as of gods,
> Their number last he sums. And now, his heart
> Distends with pride, and hardening in his strength
> Glories.
>
> (I, 569–73)

Still later, the dubious half-light of those looks is magnificently reflected in the similes comparing Satan's looks to the sun peering through mist or, in eclipse, shedding disastrous twilight.

This viewing of himself in his followers is not mere narcissism. The sight of the 'fellows of his crime' moves him to 'Tears such as angels weep' (I, 606–20), tears of pity as much as self-pity. In any case, Milton draws almost all the relationships in the poem at some point as viewings of one self in the other. The Father views Himself in the Son, and indeed all of creation reflects His glory back to Him. The mutuality of Adam and Eve expresses itself continually as an exchange of looks, as a finding of one self in the other.[17] Such mutuality, though not expressed in looks, holds apparently between Satan and Beelzebub in Heaven:

> Thou to me thy thoughts
> Was wont, I mine to thee was wont to impart;
> Both waking we were one; how then can now
> Thy sleep dissent?
>
> (V, 676–9)

This speaks, though Satan is abusing it, of the union of souls that reigns in heaven, and the syntax suggests an interchange of 'thou' and 'I'. The reflexive-ness of the self in the other comes out more explicitly in Satan's affair with Sin, which began, Sin reminds Satan, when he 'full oft / Thyself in me thy perfect image viewing / Becamest enamoured' (II, 763–5). No doubt this parodies the love of the Father and the Son, but equally it imitates in a sinister way the love of Adam and Eve, who sprang from Adam's side (rather than his head) in answer to his deepest longings for another self. Sin, however, is an allegory and consequently not really other; but the unhappy self-enthralment of Satan's love for Sin is clear enough without labouring the point.

There is nothing wrong in itself with Satan's viewing himself in others. It is true that, as an attempt at self-authentication, it is doomed in the eye of eternity. It is true that the way that Satan magnifies himself in others' eyes and ears is vain. Like the summons to his prostrate legions, which was so 'loud that all the hollow deep / Of hell resounded' (I, 314–15), both his glory and his rhetoric come back to him charged with infernal echoes. However, it is not hollow of him to look for himself in the response of others, for Milton shows that as the rule of all creatures that live in conversation with each other. It is rather that, with Satan's fall, the reflexiveness of the self in others has been corrupted. It is tempting to supply a theoretical account of this corruption. The true reflection of oneself would be the image of God; a true viewing of oneself in the other would then be a mutual beholding of the image of God; and, since Satan has turned away from God, the image which he finds of himself in others must also involve a denial of God's image and an engrossing of all reflections of himself for the purpose of self-enhancement. If that is Milton's idea, he only touches on it occasionally. Satan is indeed moved first to love and then to hate by the likeness of God in the human form divine (IV, 362ff.). He sees Adam and Eve not as possessions of an enemy, which he might fairly destroy in war, but as fellows because they bear the image of God. We have already seen how he corrupts that recognition. His love for Sin, on the other hand, involves a viewing of himself that excludes the image of God, and that must in turn involve a disfiguring of himself. The copy of himself which he propagates on Sin is Death. The reflection of that allegory on Satan's relation to himself emerges in his first encounter with Death at hell's gate. Satan runs towards Death, and Death meets him as fast (II, 674–5). Satan meets him with scorn and anger; Death answers in kind. Death grows in fury as Satan faces him with equal terrors. In short, Death, 'the meagre shadow', confronts Satan with an image of himself, unrecognisably deformed, an abstract of all those deformations of self which Satan will undergo as he pursues the course of error that binds him to his own unmaking.

Tasso wrote *Jerusalem Delivered* to a theory of ideal imitation that harnessed self-regard to moral ends, with unfortunate results for his treatment of human relations. In Rinaldo's shufflings with Armida, the demands of heroic narcissism, as we saw, distorted the reflection of one self in the other. Milton takes that reflexiveness far more seriously than Tasso and makes something much more intelligent of it. His poem cuts below the stiff figuring of ideal imitation and frees itself from the values of heroic self-regard to show Satan manipulating himself and others through heroic appearances. This does not mean, though, that Satan's heroism is false; it is genuine heroism wrongly used in relation to himself and others. Far less does it mean that Satan personifies a false heroic idea; that would be to reduce him to the terms of ideal imitation. We are interested not so much in what Milton's character represents as in what he does and suffers, in how he destroys himself through willed corruption of his own innate goodness. We see this corruption as the effects of a will whose negative motions have been drawn with understanding. That is above all why his 'absurdity' strikes us as tragic.

In Satan, Milton's study of the will draws only the process of error fully. It shows how the fall means for him a continuing negation of the good in himself, and shows how the process, though intensely isolating and self-centred, implicates other centres of self. It also suggests sketchily how the fall of beings created perfect may be instantaneous. These are all mattters that receive further treatment in the fall of Adam and Eve; but with them, the chief persons of the poem, Milton is concerned with not merely the process but also the choice of error, and with repentance.

Adam and Eve: The State of Innocence

Milton's treatment of free choice in Paradise can sound very paradoxical. Adam and Eve were made sinless and naturally good. The fall of such unflawed creatures makes everything turn on the freedom of the will. The choice of evil cannot go back to flaws in their nature, or their creator would be to blame. So, evil must originate in the wills that choose. What Milton shows, therefore, lies at the furthest extreme from what Strindberg shows in *Miss Julie*, where the characters are compelled (are fascinated, one might say, since they watch themselves as in a dream) by murky motives. In *Paradise Lost*, the motives are the arguments that are put to Adam and Eve, first by Satan and then by themselves. They can be chosen or rejected rationally. The courses of action which Adam and Eve take lie within their own powers. If in the end there is something unaccountable about their choices of error, that is perhaps because error is a lapse of mind and, like nonsense, cannot be understood. Nevertheless, the lapse of mind hides behind a show of rational deliberation, and the irrationality that is let in with it does not implicate the unfallen natures of Adam and Eve; it runs forwards into their future, not back into their past.

Yet, however paradoxical an action caused by choice rather than motive may sound, it makes good human sense, if we get close to what Milton shows. First, though, we should consider the moral framework in which the choice of error is made. I shall not attempt a philosophical unravelling of the paradoxes involved, since I am not a philosopher and have not found that philosophical criticism unfolds the poem sensitively. I shall aim simply at some descriptive observations to show how Milton's treatment of free fall comes within the scope of moral understanding.

Milton has set up things morally so that Adam and Eve are faced with an absolute choice, by which they stand or fall. Perhaps even more than with Satan, it is hard to feel with them that the choice turns on an issue of life and death. God's prohibition stamps the fruit of the tree of knowledge as a symbol of obedience. To take the fruit is to violate the symbol and throw off the obedience. So much is clear; but, because the command bears the stamp of arbitrariness, we cannot feel that the issues of good and evil depend on it absolutely. It is not the absoluteness of the command that puts it outside natural moral comprehension. We feel immediately that the murders of Duncan and Desdemona are absolutely wrong. God's prohibition of the fruit, however, does not externalise a natural abhorrence. On the contrary, the prohibition sets up a duty entirely separate from human nature. By nature, Adam and Eve are neither inclined nor disinclined to what it orders. That leaves them free to obey without either natural compulsion or unnatural abstinence. They obey, rationally conscious that the fruit is a 'pledge of [their] obedience' (III, 95). It clearly matters to Milton that they should understand what is involved. He does not set out to show tragic choice stirring up emotional depths as Shakespeare does. He aims at a clear representation of the rational will in its choice of irrationality and evil; but what he gains in clarity he loses in the command of an instinctive sense of good and evil.

The clarity of Milton's picture depends on a final arbitrariness, as he himself recognised in his *Christian Doctrine*. A command with moral reasons behind it would not serve. Adam and Eve do not need to be told, for instance, to love each other. They do so according to the free play of their natures. If, however, they enjoyed only that freedom from constraint, they would differ only in degree from the other animals; they would be God's toys. To bring about the freedom of free obedience, God has to make an arbitrary cut in things with the prohibition of the fruit, and in doing so makes Adam and Eve accountable beings. None of this, however, circumvents the arbitrariness of the prohibition, which we have to take as given. Once we do, we are free to see the Fall as a human action. Breakings of a divine and of a moral law involve the same motions of the will. The error, guilt and repentance of Adam and Eve take a human course, and Milton's peculiar grasp of volition is as good moral psychology as religious psychology.

The other part of the moral framework to be clarified is freedom of choice. Milton's scheme of images, as we saw in the last chapter, makes up a hinged universe which turns on the freedom of the will. That points us in a useful direction. When thinking about free choice, it is better to look for alternative possibilities, a forking of ways in the situation itself, than to think only of some inherently indeterminate faculty within the characters themselves. The hinged universe, however, which leaves open the possibility of falling out of creation, is more of an epic metaphor for free choice than an actual moral situation that faces the characters with alternatives. What really sets up the terms of freedom is the prohibition itself, the final command or setting of limits to things that completes creation by conferring the reason that is also choice on human beings.

It seems highly puzzling that a prohibition should set free, that the blocking of a course of action with a command should somehow open up the world morally. I cannot satisfactorily unriddle all that is implied by the paradox, but certain things are clear. The prohibition makes a mark in the undifferentiated goodness of unfallen creation, the enormous bliss of the garden, in such a way that evil becomes a possibility. Adam and Eve consequently know what evil is as a possibility; they have an innocent knowledge, unlike the guilty knowledge of good and evil which they obtain by eating the fruit. Until the possibility is realised, it resolves itself without constraint simply as part of the freedom of innocence. It is a sort of shadow of the goodness of Paradise assuring us that the goodness stands in a three-dimensional moral world. Again, the prohibition implies freedom because it binds Adam and Eve in words. It is in the nature of power, however arbitrary, that where it imposes itself in words, in a command, it leaves one free to obey or disobey according to the discourse of one's reason. Finally, the prohibition determines innocence and guilt: innocence is obedience, guilt transgression. This explains the instantaneous fall. Formally, Adam and Eve are innocent until they decide to infringe the prohibition.

The way in which the prohibition distinguishes innocence and guilt should discourage us from looking at the passage from one state to the other metaphysically. It may perhaps substitute a legal fiction for a metaphysical puzzle, but it works in ways that make human sense. It clears up at least two unnecessary puzzles. First, since innocence means honouring the prohibition, we need not imagine something somehow sinful before the Fall about the paradisaical strayings of Adam and Eve, which indeed, if they were sinful, 'were to make Sinne of being a man'.[18] Just because the prohibition lays down right and wrong so categorically, for 'the rest', as Eve says (IX, 653–4), they 'live / Law to ourselves', free of guilt and conscientious fears. Second, there is no need to be mystified by the corruption of the will immediately succeeding the eating of the fruit. Eve and Adam know what they have done, and their guilty knowledge of transgression fills them with crooked desires and fears. What corrupts them is a bad conscience.

In distinguishing innocence and guilt, the prohibition also divides freedom and unfreedom. Milton makes clear how guilt is unfree or 'self-enthralled' in Satan's soliloquies, where, as we have seen, Satan's will is bound helplessly to his guilty knowledge of having fallen foul of God's command, and with Adam, as we shall see, he shows the same process. As for the freedom of innocence, that means not just the opposite of the unfreedom of guilt, the freedom from constraint of a good conscience, but also the freedom of choice to obey or disobey the prohibition. So conceived, the freedom might seem intolerably narrow: morally, only the possibility of abstaining or not; psychologically, the consciousness of abstaining while being free to do otherwise. In fact, Milton gives the freedom of innocence considerable scope, quite enough to make it a morally interesting condition. I shall try to explain this aspect of the moral framework quite circumstantially, for unless we think that the life at stake is worth living, we cannot take the choice that forfeits it very seriously.

The freedom of innocence emerges crucially in the lack of constraint in the relationship with God. Of this, Milton draws a truly remarkable picture in the colloquy in which Adam asks God for a companion. Adam has to persist. At first, God tells him to amuse himself with the animals 'and seemed / So ordering' (VIII, 376–7). In the face of what looks like a command, Adam has the boldness to argue that what he requires is the companionship of an equal, and that unlike God, who is 'alone / From all eternity' (lines 405–6), no-one is human by himself; one becomes human in conversation with other humans. Adam has to advance this argument in the face not only of seeming peremptoriness, but also of what is perhaps more unnerving – ironic amusement. Yet, after a gruelling stretch, God not only accepts Adam's request but also says that in fact He had only been testing him; He had been planning to give him a companion all along. When Adam, 'strained to the highth / In that celestial colloquy sublime' (lines 454–5), sinks exhausted, God makes Eve from his side, 'Thy wish, exactly to thy heart's desire' (line 451). Adam's freedom here comes out as inner sovereignty, a confidence in what he knows to be just and reasonable. In his dealings with Eve, Adam often strikes us as patronising and immature; but in his talk with God, he shows the admirable poise and dignity of the Miltonic free conscience. This delights God, who recognises in Adam's rational firmness 'the spirit within thee free / My image not imparted to the brute' (lines 440–1). It is in Adam's freedom towards God that God recognises His image in Adam and in turn gives Adam his image, his likeness, his other self in Eve.[19] The Son in Book III perhaps acts with the same freedom when he dares the Father's apparent anger to bring out what is to be seen as the mercy behind it. Milton found in the Genesis story little more than a hint for what he made of Adam's conversation with God.[20] The episode, conceived in the innerness of Milton's religious imagination, is a remarkable attempt to realise what human freedom might be like in dealing with God. Against all that in *Paradise Lost* seems to dwell on God's 'uncontrollable intent', His absolute power and will, we must set the openness to sound reasons which He shows in this scene and His delight in Adam's trust that He will be open to them, and we must bear these things in mind when judging Adam's behaviour at the Fall.

In the colloquy with God, Adam has displayed not merely freedom from constraint of 'the upright heart and pure' but also freedom of choice in conceiving of Eve and arguing for her. Rational discrimination is called into play in other scenes before the crucial test in Book IX. The state of innocence is not a retreat from moral existence. This has led to misunderstanding, and, in particular, three incidents have often been interpreted as showing that Adam and Eve are fallen before the Fall, as if their sorting things out rationally between themselves involved them in evil.[21] What in fact these incidents show is that, in their innocence, Adam and Eve are in charge of their experience and that they can cope.

About the first of these incidents, Eve's bemusement with her reflection in the lake, I can be summary. It seems absurd to me to make this enchanting scene, full of Eve's wonder at her as yet unfixed being, into an exhibition of sinful vanity. No doubt Eve's grasp of what makes her human is less sublime than Adam's.[22] Still, she feels the same hunger for another self that inspires Adam's colloquy with God,[23] and she does in the end choose Adam, whose image she is and to whom she will bear 'Multitudes like [herself]' (IV, 474) in preference to her image in the pool. So far from tending to sin, her motives here are the longing for a like being without which she would not be human, and her eventual choice of Adam, made in conversation with his 'pleaded reason' (VIII, 510), shows that she can put behind her what has become, beside the man who woos her, a recessive object of desire. From this scene, she emerges creditably as well as delightfully.

About Eve's dream, again little need be said. The source of evil is Satan, not Eve. The dream shows how evil, if it should enter an unfallen mind, will appear as a disordering of the real arrangement of things, rather than anything intrinsically base. It rearranges Eve's life in Paradise. So, sauntering out in the dream by night picks up her innocent question to Adam about why they should spend the night in bed. The nightingale that is singing as she walks back to the bower with Adam is still singing in her dream, except that it has now become masculine (V, 41). It is as if, in this dream derangement, the nightingale that sings the marriage song of Adam and Eve has become the amorist of Milton's hymn to married love (IV, 769–70) and curiously duplicates Satan's role as serenader and seducer. Finally, the tree, which Adam and Eve had discussed over supper, crops up, and the prohibition which they had talked of honouring in real life is violated in the dream. The dream is like 'a tangled chain / Nothing impaired but all disordered', a piece of nonsense, which disappears when things are straightened out. And that is something that Adam and Eve can manage for themselves. In their discrimination between the thought and the reality of evil, Adam and Eve actually overcome the evil that Satan's suggestion might have worked if it had issued into the world in the form of choice and act.[24] They manage a sort of human goodness while remaining innocent. I can see no evidence at all that Eve actually starts incubating 'discontented thoughts / Vain hopes, vain aims, inordinate desires / Blown up with high conceits engendering pride' (IV, 808–9) as a result of the dream. When Satan tries again eight days later, he has to start from scratch.

Milton, Raphael and Adam are clear that Eve is an inferior being. Obviously, someone in that position would tend to behave 'irrationally', but she is supposed to be closer to the irrational by nature than Adam anyway. Her self-bemusement at the pool and her dream no doubt bear out Milton's feeling that she is an uncertain quantity. However, Milton shows her to be magnanimous, and there is no evidence of ill-will before the Fall. Moreover, in the argument about working apart, she shows that she has a good mind, perfectly capable of judging rightly and perfectly capable of keeping that part of her 'tending to wild' in its place.

Adam seems more in charge of his feelings than Eve. It comes as a surprise to learn from what he says to Raphael that his love for her disturbs his cool judgement – one sees little evidence of that until the Fall. It is unpleasing that he tells Raphael rather than Eve about it. Indeed, the whole tone of the gentlemen left to themselves over their 'inoffensive must' (V, 345) as they discuss Eve makes one uncomfortable, in spite of Adam's half-hearted attempts to stand up to Raphael's angelic ideas about how to manage one's wife and emotions. Yet whatever one's unease with this conversation, there is no reason to doubt Adam, when, 'half-abashed' (VIII, 595) by Raphael's crushing rebuke of his confession, he points out that he has said only that he is tempted to adore Eve, not that he cannot resist the temptation. Until the Fall, Adam appears to have his feelings of adoration remarkably well under control.

That Eve and Adam together are in rational control of their lives comes out clearly in the third incident that has been thought to show that they are fallen before the Fall, the conversation about working apart.[25] Its going before the Fall does not mean that it implies the Fall. From its allowing Eve to go off by herself, which gives Satan his opportunity, it does not follow that the fall is already under way. We know the story – we know that Eve will succumb – and so we see the Fall coming through their talk, which, though it is shot through with grim and pathetic ironies, is still innocent and free. On parting, they have done nothing that could not be made up on their return to each other. Technically, their conversation is innocent because, in Paradise, only touching the fruit is transgression. More seriously, there is nothing to condemn by sensible standards in what they say. It is easy to imagine that, in view of the Fall, everything must be weighed with anxious scrupulosity; but Milton's notion of innocence is robust and allows free play to harmless wishes.

There is certainly no harm in Eve's suggestion that they would get more done if they worked separately. Milton himself tells us that 'their work outgrew / The hand's dispatch of two' (IX, 202–3). Eve's eagerness to do something about it is commendable, nor does Adam fail to commend it with Edenic sententiousness: 'nothing lovelier can be found / In woman, than to study household good, / And good works in her husband to promote' (lines 232–4). As it turns out, Adam has a more relaxed, perhaps better, idea of work in Paradise: it should go with apt and cheerful conversation, and they need keep trim only the parts of the garden they use. However, that does not make Eve's idea bad, far less demonically-inspired.

As for separating, which becomes the point at issue in the debate that follows, the argument between Adam and Eve leaves the choice morally open. It might seem sensible to stick together in view of the threat from Satan, as Adam would have them do, but Eve has perfectly good reasons for not thinking so: to huddle together in fear would not be Paradise; they are each in themselves capable of withstanding the sort of assault which Satan will make; and above all – and this comes straight from the heart of Milton the moralist – their innocence has moral worth only if it can withstand assault. They should therefore go about in Paradise with some confidence in themselves and in each other. Nothing that Adam says against separating can circumvent these arguments. Indeed, he repeats the one about being sufficient to stand alone, though with a fervour ('O, Woman ...') that sounds as if he were correcting her. After that, he cannot demand that she should stay. He even suggests a positive reason for going: they may be more on their guard alone than absorbed in each other's company. That undermines his previous arguments for their giving each other moral support, and Eve takes hold of it, sure that she is equal to any temptation that may come her way.

Adam is not weakly indulgent in letting Eve go, nor does he wobble over the authority which he should exert, nor is Eve rebellious. Adam agrees to parting because argument has convinced him that he has no valid objection, and Eve goes because on balance she thinks she has quite a good reason for doing so. The argument has clarified to themselves and us what free standing in Paradise means. It has incidentally given us a good example of the sinewy process of human reason on which Milton thought right action depended. People who can argue like that are well equipped to deal with Satan.

The focus of the scene of parting is on the play of discursive reason and judgement, and yet it is not the argument of merely rational beings. Character comes into play as well. Milton catches Eve very sharply – her eager plans, the 'sweet, austere composure' (a phrase wonderfully expressive of how Adam has nettled her) with which she replies to his objections, the coolness with which she knows her own mind and has the last word ('but Eve / Persisted, yet submiss, though last, replied' (lines 376–9). The sharpness owes something to a rueful masculine perplexity about her independence, about her wayward quick-wittedness and her resistance to Adam's covert appeal for company – surely Adam wants her to deny that she feels constrained by him and to show it when he says, 'Go; for thy stay, not free, absents thee more' (line 372). However, waywardness need not be a fallen characteristic, let alone a vice. Adam and Milton probably find it an accentuation of 'coy, reluctant, amorous delay', and most readers must find Eve's unsettling of Adam pleasing. The innocence of Milton's Paradise takes in such wanton motions and equally allows a certain clumsiness in Adam. His protectiveness is rather bumbling, his arguments are uncharacteristically maladroit. The heat with which he replies to Eve's supposing that he must suppose God had made them insufficient to stand is comic; but his heaviness is well-meaning, and his consciousness that solitude is sometimes best society and that he cannot place constraints on Eve's free will is sensible and considerate. Though he may not be at his best in this exchange, he is sound enough. Because he is the authority figure, he is the butt of the touches of domestic comedy. Milton's Paradise, however, can take that without disintegrating. Adam and Eve cannot even be said to have quarrelled. When Eve goes off to her roses, she works 'mindless the while' (line 431). No doubt 'mindless' is charged with warning, but first of all it speaks of blithe absorption in her task. She is entirely free of the thoughts that would be coursing through her mind if they had quarrelled.

The play of character in this exchange does not expose subversive motives. We may suspect in Adam and Milton an anxiety about Adam's independence expressing itself as an anxiety about Eve's. Adam has exchanged his garden solitude with God for human society with Eve. Raphael warned him not to allow his tie to her to interfere with his lonely obligation to God; she must not be given too much independence in case that gets in the way of his. Also it may be that, at some level, Adam is confused about standing alone and standing with Eve.[26] That he at once asks her to stay and finds reasons for her leaving may point in that direction; but this confusion or anxiety, if it is there, he has under control. If there seem to be diabolic face-pullings round the edges of the picture, they vanish as Adam at this point judges and acts rationally in letting her go.

Though the scene of parting makes the Fall possible, it does not show it already happening. No side of the natures of Adam and Eve has come out that cannot be accommodated in the liberal dispensation of Paradise. No transgression has taken place that would alter their lives. What has come out there and in those other incidents that bring choice into play is that Adam and Eve not only know they have the freedom that makes rational discrimination possible but also use it to direct their lives.

The moral discriminations and choices which Adam and Eve make before the Fall do not mean that they know good and evil in the same way as they do after the Fall. While they are constant to the prohibition, evil can only present itself as a possibility; the only reality they know is good. However eccentric or irregular their revolutions round the possibility of evil, their obedience to the command resolves them in goodness; but, although it seems that good and evil are tied up in Paradise in an unproblematic way, the unfallen experience of Adam and Eve allows real tests of their moral judgement. Although the prohibition draws the line between innocence and guilt and the only possibility of evil is transgression, other things besides honouring the prohibition are good or may look good. That is how good, or evil camouflaged in the serpent as good, may call the prohibition into question. So, while Adam and Eve are not called on to discern what is right in the mixed experience of good and evil, as they will be after the Fall, nevertheless even in Paradise their choices are not simple. They are, indeed, far less simple than the choices confronting the heroes in the fallen world of *Jerusalem Delivered* and more like the complex choices which people actually have to make.

Adam and Eve: The Fall

As we have seen, the state of innocence is not a moral cocoon, and still the choice of error implies a radical discontinuity. With Adam and Eve, as with Satan, the fall is an instantaneous passing of the will from innocence to guilt, from freedom to unfreedom. This radical discontinuity takes for them the form of an impossibility. From the point of view of innocence, the possibility of evil seems an impossibility, an inconceivable actuality. How then does the free choice of evil come about? How can Eve, entirely enfolded in an innocent world, be brought to approve of a course that undoes her?

Here, Satan's master move is to fake an impossibility, something that negates everything which Eve has experienced or known so far. In doing so, he overturns her world, or rather brings it to a point where only staunchness of trust in God could have steadied her and kept it from overturning. First, Satan comes before her as the impossibility of a talking snake: 'What may this mean? Language of man pronounced / By tongue of brute, and human sense expressed?' (IX, 553–4). She calls it a 'miracle' (line 562) and it leaves her 'not unamazed' (line 552), a phrase suggestive of both her wonder and her disorientation. Having contradicted the natural order so, Satan can go on, when he has led her to the tree, to suggest that in other ways the world Eve takes for granted is an imposture. The world which she knows is a system descending from its creator and returning to Him in praise. So, Satan insinuates the possibility that the earth is itself the source of life and 'warmed by the sun, [produces] every kind' (line 721) and that the gods (rather than God) have taken advantage of their earlier origin to tell humans that everything is owed to them. He slides away so quickly from the suggestion that God and His angels have been attempting an imposture that it stays only as one of the many questionings of what Eve has taken for granted. On such issues, he aims to bewilder rather than challenge, to open up a chasm in reality rather than anything definite for Eve's mind to grasp firmly.

The central issue is the prohibition. Satan's other contradictions of what Eve had taken for reality are all accessory to making it look as if God must be lying here. Eve tells the serpent that God has said of the fruit of the tree of knowledge: 'Ye shall not eat / Thereof, nor shall ye touch it, lest ye die' (lines 662–3). In their simplicity, her words express a mind that takes the prohibition and the penalty of death to itself as its own principle; Satan has to undermine that simplicity and firmness. There is first the 'evidence' that the serpent has not died. Or if he has, then, as he ingeniously suggests later, he has died to his snaky nature only to put on 'internal man' (line 711) capable of rational discourse, this to encourage Eve to follow suit: if snakes become human, humans should become gods. The serpent produces other reasons, not only for thinking God's threat of punishment idle, but also for not believing that His command is binding. With peculiar insidiousness, he casts the reasons for disobeying God in the form of a dilemma. Either God is good and so must wish his creatures to enjoy the benefit of godhead, in which case He cannot mean what He says, and must be testing Eve and, by threatening her with death, really want to see whether her 'dauntless virtue' (line 694) is prepared to take the risk for higher being; or God is not good and does not wish humans to enjoy a higher state of being, in which case He means what He says because He wants to keep divine knowledge to Himself. But then, if he is not good, he is not God and his threats are idle. In either case, it is Eve's duty to seize the promise of the fruit. The dilemma is false because it rests on the assumption that the prohibition really does keep something good, valuable knowledge, out of human reach. It is also insidious because working out its forked alternatives draws the mind away from looking at the assumption on which they rest. It uses her reason against her as a decoy.

In other ways, too, Satan tempts Eve through what is best in her. Her rational desire for knowledge, even the desire to ascend towards God, which Raphael has encouraged, her highest promptings, are turned against her. He cannot appeal to inherent baseness in an unfallen creature. He can only get at her through her goodness.

Satan's temptation presents Eve with an impossibility in the form of a lie, which, entertained, turns all she knows and all her virtues upside down. And she does entertain it. Milton gives both Eve and Adam speeches of self-communion, which convey with peculiar inwardness the process of taking in, getting used to, approving the temptations that have been put to them.[27] In her musing, Eve swallows the 'evidence' of the speaking serpent, which seems to tell her not only that the fruit has divine benefits but also that there is something improbable about the death penalty. Having swallowed that, she produces arguments of her own for thinking that the prohibition cannot bind and that indeed only an access of knowledge from the fruit will clear up the mysteries surrounding it.

In comparison with the serpent's 'surging maze', Eve's arguments are straightforward and entirely free from diabolical sneering. Her style is her own, direct and spirited. Given her assumptions, her argument makes a fair show of sense. There is something innocent too about the desire for knowledge as she expresses it. She wants forbidden knowledge for Adam as well as herself: her talk is all of 'us'. That may not quite amount to her having sought godhead chiefly for

Adam's sake, as she tells him when she goes to him, fruit in hand (IX, 877–8), but still her wish at this point is unselfish. It is only once she has eaten that she thinks it might be nice sometimes to know more than Adam. She falls for sublime reasons.

Far from bringing to the surface a badness latent in her from the start, Eve's choice of error brings out instead qualities that are in themselves admirable. Also, she is deceived: she tells Adam she was 'unweeting' (X, 916) when she took the fruit, and Milton himself says she was 'unweeting' (X, 335) when she gave it to Adam. She falls for a lie that stands all she knows in Paradise on its head. That the serpent's story is so improbable, that it inverts things so completely, is paradoxically one of the strongest reasons for the lie taking hold. Only a total overturning could have overcome the reasons which Eve has for not eating the fruit. If, however, she is deceived and if the deception takes hold of what is good in her, how can she be blamed?

At the very least, she is guilty of unthinking, and unthinking about an issue which she knows to be of the utmost moment. To say she is 'unweeting' absolves her from deliberate malice, but to say she does not fully realise what she is doing does not mean that she was so cleverly tricked that she could not have seen through the deception. She should have known better. Raphael's conversation was full of instructions that one cannot be too suspicious about whether the sort of knowledge that the serpent holds out is suitable for human consumption. Eve should not have been 'unweeting' about an offer of knowledge of 'the ways / Of highest agents' (IX, 682–3). The slipperiness of the serpent's reasons for eating the fruit should, in any case, have aroused her suspicion. She should have been able to catch him out in self-contradiction, as Gabriel did when Satan was discovered as a toad at her ear. The scheme of faculties which Milton makes use of brings out her failure very clearly. According to it, Eve falls through a lapse of right reason 'whose function it was to discern the chief good'.[28] The scheme puts reason in charge of will and appetite, not as a faculty of abstinence from well-known vices, but as a faculty of discernment. The serpent's lie holds out a seemingly good thing that calls the obedience to the prohibition in question. There, Eve's discernment fails. A momentary failure of attention is no great matter in itself, nor is a mistake that involves a mere failure of cleverness; but the discernment that fails Eve is a more vital matter: what fails her is the human judgement that directs her life. The issue which it judges is momentous, for it involves believing a story that gives the lie to all that she knows or has experienced up to that point. All that she has known or experienced so far are reasons for believing God. To believe the serpent is to allow herself to be swayed to an extraordinary inversion of Edenic reality. However unhinging the serpent's tale, whatever virtue we allow to her boldness in believing him, her 'unweetingness' and her misjudgement are the sort of errors for which we hold people seriously to blame, and they open an abyss in Paradise that cannot be closed up again.

Behind the failure of rational attention lurks a less distinct failure in which will and reason run together. In lending belief to the serpent's story and rehearsing it to herself, Eve has in fact let herself be swayed against God and has broken trust with Him. She may not sneer at God, as the serpent does, but still she has been brought to assume that God 'Forbids us good, forbids us to be wise' (line 759). Eve herself earlier, when she was indignant with Adam for fearing that Satan could overcome her by fraud, tells us how to be deceived might be culpable. Adam's fear, she said, showed that he doubted 'her firm faith and love' (line 286). In choosing to believe the serpent's lie, she is in fact letting go of the firm faith and love about which she has been so sure.

If Eve falls through an instantaneous deflection of the will and judgement from their mark, what do we make of the rival stories that she fell through vanity, intemperance or curiosity? The serpent begins his temptation by flattering Eve that her beauty is the focus of creation, and this overture, we are told, 'made way' into her heart (line 550). He adds later that the speculative knowledge that he has attained turns to her as cynosure of the universe. However, Eve seems quite capable of handling those metaphysical compliments. Her reply is tart: 'Serpent, thy overpraising leaves in doubt / The virtue of that fruit, in thee first proved' (lines 615–16). Vanity, then, is certainly not a compelling motive. As for intemperance, we are told that it was noon, and Eve had 'An eager appetite, raised by the smell / So savory of that fruit' (lines 740–1). Michael later speaks of Eve's 'inabstinence' (XI, 476) and suggests that it is somehow responsible for the ungoverned appetite of the unfallen world. However, Michael is aggravating the guilt of the Fall in order to explain the history of the world. There is, in any case, nothing wrong with Eve's appetite, and indeed it enters into Eve's choice only in a very secondary way; it helps to make the act feel natural. Greed comes in only once she has let go. Intemperance, then, is simply a name applied not very exactly after the event to the form that the displacement or inversion of good takes in her, the shape of the crack made by the defection of her will and judgement. The same may be said of her curiosity. Her appetite for knowledge is not merely innocent but also admirable. It is only because she fails to discern that the serpent's knowledge does not fit her human standing that we call it curiosity. What is wrong is not the desire but the misjudgement and swerving aside of the will.

The process of corruption sets in immediately Eve has made her choice; but let us first examine Adam's fall. With him, the pattern is much the same. When Eve comes back to him with the fruit and the story of what she has done, he too is faced with an impossibility, not a lie this time, but the unaccountable fact that the 'fairest of Creation, last and best / Of all God's works' (lines 896–7) has fallen: 'How art thou lost, how on a sudden lost, /

Defaced, deflowered, and now to death devote?' (lines 900–1). For Adam, the impossibility does not arouse wonder; he is 'amazed', but by 'horror' (line 889). Nevertheless, for him too, a chasm opens up in reality. He too is tempted through what is good in him, his love for Eve, and he is faced with a dilemma, either to obey the prohibition and desert Eve, or share Eve's fall and break his tie with God. This dilemma, like the one that faced Eve, is bogus. For one thing, the 'completing of the mortal sin / Original' (lines 1003–4) is his eating of the fruit. Until he has eaten, 'man', which includes both Adam and Eve, has not fallen and so has not incurred the penalty of death. For another, Adam has no good grounds for thinking that obeying the prohibition means deserting Eve. To fall with Eve makes no sense as a way of helping her or meeting the situation. It is curious that he does not see that he would be in a much better position to stand by her and face God, unfallen. In Book X, he boasts that he would be the first to importune God with prayers that all the punishment might fall on him. Now, while he is still innocent, the idea of sacrificing himself (like the Son) does not occur to him. He simply assumes that the situation is 'remediless' (line 919) and that God and fate are bound by what has happened. In doing so, he has let go of the trust which he had in God's good will and openness to rational pleading that he had shown earlier when he stuck to his request for Eve in the face of what looked like God's prohibition. The way things turn out later is surely meant to emphasise how unaccountable Adam's failure of trust is in his crisis. When Adam and Eve repent after the Fall, Adam is given a vision of what is supposed not only to vindicate God's justice but also to show His power to overcome evil with good. On the point of falling, however, Adam leaps, or perhaps slumps, to the conclusion that he is faced with an ineluctable choice between his human duty to Eve and his religious duty to God. Here, as in Eve's case, is an unaccountable swerving of judgement and will.

Milton encourages us to contrast Adam's fall with Eve's. Eve was deceived; Adam was 'not deceived / But fondly overcome by female charm' (lines 998–9). However, this is a very rough distinction, and, though Adam is tempted through his heart and Eve through her mind, nevertheless both falls consist essentially in misjudgement and mistrust. The sense in which Adam is 'overcome by female charm' is that he lets Eve sway his judgement and will against God and at the same time surrenders the inner poise and authority that might have helped her. As with Eve's error, once he has let himself swerve, from the perspective of that lapse out of reality, the issue presents itself askew. Adam is not really deceived into thinking he is doing right, but his failure of nerve or trust or independent judgement makes him take the point of view of Eve's bound or guilty self. He sees God threatening and Paradise a forlorn wilderness, and can think of no way out but to die with her.

Adam's first speech expressing this resolve is moving. It is also short. There is none of the vacillation between passion and reason which we might expect of a hero of Restoration tragedy. The mind, though falling, remains certain of its choice. Adam's certainty is one of the finest things about his speech, and shows as clearly as the love which he expresses the nobility of the unfallen nature that his choice of error is at that instant undoing. His next speech, once he has sided with Eve, is less admirable. It sounds as if he were trying to justify a choice he knew to be wrong. He insists that the situation is remediless and entertains Eve's story about rising to divinity. Even his renewed declaration of love (lines 952–9) has perhaps an air of excusing himself by insisting too much on the bond of nature:

> if death
> Consort with thee, death is to me as life;
> So forcible within my heart I feel
> The bond of nature draw me to my own,
> My own in thee, for what thou art is mine;
> Our state cannot be severed, we are one,
> One flesh; to lose thee were to lose my self.
> (lines 953–9)

To say 'to lose thee were to lose my self' is very fine. Yet selflessness and an objective care for the situation and for Eve would be a truer expression of love for his 'other self' (VIII, 450).[29] At this point, a certain falsity has crept into his love, the very generosity of its expression concealing from himself what he is doing.

Adam and Eve have made those choices that increasingly entangle them in error. The issue on which they have fallen is symbolic. Not to eat the fruit is a symbolic duty arbitrarily imposed so that Adam and Eve's obedience may be tested. However, though there are no particular reasons for the prohibition, there are good general ones for honouring God's symbol. It is a pledge of trust between them and God, and honouring it is the one stipulated way in which they can make return for their being in Paradise. Whether such a symbolic duty could have stood up against the demands of another duty with real reasons behind it is another matter. To bring in a slight comparison, Portia in *The Merchant of Venice* was no doubt right to make trouble about the way in which Bassanio gave away her ring to reward the lawyer who had saved his friend's life: Bassanio takes the symbol of his being pledged to her too lightly, but it would have been unreasonable of Portia if she had been angry with him for giving away the ring in order to save his friend's life. The urgency of that claim on him would have suspended the claim of the symbol; but a clash between symbolic observance and human claim never truly arises in *Paradise Lost*, though Adam and Eve think it does. The reasons which Eve thinks tell against the prohibition are bogus, and Adam too is deluded in thinking that the crunch has come between his duty to God and his duty to Eve. In these circumstances, though the pledge is symbolic, Adam and Eve can violate it only in bad faith.

The moral scheme in which he has drawn paradisaic existence allows Milton to present the free choice of error with paradigmatic simplicity. I have perhaps too often invoked *Macbeth* and *Othello* as analogies for what is at stake in Milton's poem. Milton's picture is much clearer than Shakespeare's, partly no doubt because of his interest in moral deliberation, the *proairesis* of Aristotle.[30] It is notoriously difficult to say whether Macbeth and Othello are free agents, or where exactly the choices that undo them are made. Their soliloquies are not so much deliberations as upwellings of obscure passions. Macbeth does not really deliberate over murdering Duncan; rather, he trembles over the direness that the thought of the crime causes in him. Positive reasons for murdering Duncan never reach utterance. Similarly, Othello is apparently incapable of rational deliberation in the face of Iago's insinuations. We are moved in each case by the hero's passions rather than his thoughts. In the Fall in *Paradise Lost*, however, the action and passion are gathered into the movement of thought, and we are shown with great clarity the deliberative mind missing its mark and the collusion of mind and will in the choice of error, in which there remains something unaccountable. It is indeed one of the great strengths of Milton's picture of innocence and fall that he does not attempt to rationalise this unaccountableness, for example by making the Fall the simple outcome of character and motive. The origin of error is the wrong choice itself. That accords with the theoretical demands of Milton's fable for an instantaneous lapse of the will from a state of freedom to a state of guilt and bondage. However, Milton's representation of the Fall shows the actual process of volition as well as representing a theological idea. In it, we can recognise the shape of a universal, not merely Edenic, experience. If intellectually, as distinct from experientially, there remains something unsatisfactory about referring the Fall finally to an unaccountable or irrational lapse of mind and will, it is surely preferable to the endless recession of error before the event, such as is caught with morose pleasure in Larkin's 'As Bad as a Mile':

> Watching the shied core
> Striking the basket, sliding across the floor,
> Shows less and less of luck, and more and more
>
> Of failure spreading back up the arm
> Earlier and earlier, the upraised hand calm,
> The apple unbitten in the palm.[30]

Adam and Eve: Guilt

Both Adam and Eve fall instantaneously: the prohibition marks the instant on one side of which lies innocence, on the other side guilt. In both, the actual commission of error is in a sense unaccountable: nothing in the state of innocence can explain the choices of error. In both, the swerving-aside corrupts good motives: displaced from their mark, Eve's noble intellectual aspirations become a rather desperate greed, and similarly, once he has lost his inner command, Adam's love for Eve becomes a rather desperate huddle. The quality of desperation and passionate urgency in both has to do with a consciousness of having violated the prohibition. Guilt, the consciousness of having fallen foul of God, which is, however covered up, at the same time a consciousness of having done wrong, drives them to corrupt themselves further. That seems to me the innermost impulse of the process of evil in them. In outline, it follows the same negative course of the bound will that we traced in Satan. Some of the consequences of the Fall are magical: Eve's fall sets off a series of sympathetic janglings in the universe, beginning with the sigh which nature gives when she first seizes the fruit. The fruit damages the human system with a series of physical distemperings that prepares the way for the entrance of death; but the disastrous effects of the Fall on human nature take a psychological or moral course. The physcial or magical effects accentuate rather than determine the chain of human volition.

The heady state of intoxication that comes over Eve by herself and later together with Adam arises as much from elation at having broken a law as from the properties of the fruit. The law sets a limit to their being, and to break it is to break out of their finite state. Satan was merely making up a story when he said that the knowledge of good and evil was a taste that would make them as gods. Still, both Eve and Adam feel themselves becoming divine as they eat. They are drunk, but they also feel that breaking the law that sets a bound to their human scope makes them more than human. Eve's gorging herself with a greed that is as much for knowledge as for fruit itself expresses in a gross way her violation of limit. The serpent tells Eve that God forbade the fruit in order to keep humans in subjection, and this Eve chooses to believe once she has eaten (IX, 805). The law in fact makes Adam and Eve fully human, but they fall to thinking of it as a restriction on their scope imposed by God's jealousy. So, while there is nothing in Satan's story, they can still feel miraculously enlarged from what they now grudge as a limit that grudges them completeness.

Adam and Eve enhance themselves by negation, by denying the limit that makes them what they are. In this, they follow Satan, though they are not propelled to such lengths. Aso as with Satan, the enhancement of self corrupts the relation to the other, though again there is a distinction: Satan's course shows essentially the twisting of self-love, whereas Adam and Eve are not so far gone; it is in their love for each other that we see the process of corruption at work. In his colloquy with God, Adam, as we have seen, divines that to be human is a social condition, and asks for fellowship 'fit to participate / All rational delight' (VIII, 390–1). He dwells on the reflexiveness of one self in another, instancing how the human need for others will express itself in propagating 'Like of his like, his image multiplied' (VIII, 424). With this, God agrees, and as a start gives Adam 'thy likeness ... thy other self' (line 450) in Eve, meanwhile remarking that He sees His own image in Adam since he can express his understanding of his own nature so freely. It is perhaps not stretching the point to think that the loving conversation of Adam and Eve, their participation in all rational delight, is not merely the reflection of one self in the other (what Adam woos Eve to from her image in the pool), but also, while it expresses the free spirit of humanity in conversation, the best expression of the divine image. While love in Paradise can express that, it remains 'the happier Eden' (IV, 507). This human fellowship is the first thing to be corrupted by the Fall.

Once Eve has eaten the fruit, self-seeking becomes possible. She has truly gone off on her own. Having broken the terms of her humanity, she has left her fellow human behind and can wonder to herself whether she should admit him to a new fellowship in the godhead which she thinks she has acquired. She toys with the idea of taking advantage of Adam, but in the end plumps for love and fellowship with him. By now, however, a new and sinister motive has come in, corrupted the love and made it desirable to self-seeking. The fear of death that goes with her new state makes her afraid that Adam will have a dreadful advantage over her: he will live on and be given a new wife. With that, the mortal taste of death enters into her love along with the passions of fear and jealousy. In all this, Eve's motives are understandable, not to say human, but they are also confused and self-deceiving. She conceals from herself her discreditable intention of seeing to it that, if she dies, Adam will have to share her fate, by telling herself that she loves him so dearly that she would gladly share the fate with him. She is using talk of love to represent base intentions to herself nobly in the same way that Satan concealed his intention of bringing Adam and Eve down to his own wretchedness by imagining it as a magnificent gesture.

So far, she has been talking only to herself; but then she returns to Adam, and the infected talk enters into their conversation with each other. Having deceived herself, she must somehow take in her likeness, and Adam's love, once he decides to fall with her, answers to hers, like to like. His fall, as we have seen, is a failure in responsibility to his 'likeness ... his other self'. The 'agony of love' (IX, 858) that, like Eve, he feels, the dread that he feels of losing himself in losing her, is a form of self-seeking. He is taking the fallen humanity of Eve as the 'best image' of himself (V, 95) in place of the freedom of spirit that, in expressing the image of God, might truly have stood up for her. This sounds perhaps a rather cold-blooded analysis – Adam's declaration, is after all, passionate and moving – but the issues have been set up too sharply for us to let it go at that. Adam is seduced into complicity with something which his free judgement knows to be false. The falsity infects his talk of love, for he uses it to hide from himself how he is opting for a fallen humanity in himself and Eve. At the same time death has entered into his love: 'for with thee / Certain my resolution is to die' (IX, 906–7). This is a noble declaration, and, if it were truly called for by the situation, we could only applaud. However, the sort of love sacrifice which Adam is making of himself, 'the illustrious evidence, example high' (line 962) that Eve praises, is not the sort of sacrifice that is needed at this point. The passion with which it is charged displaces attention from what ought to be done. There is something wilful here in making a tragedy and asserting the supreme value of love in death. There is also a parallel with Satan, whose heroic nay-saying helped to drive him inwards into self-undoing. The tragic assertion of love turns Adam and Eve towards annihilation, not just as the future they dare, but as a consummation of their love. That at least is the feeling which lines such as 'if death / Consort with thee, death is to me as life' (lines 953–4) distinctly utter.

The taste of corruption that enters their love with the consciousness of death and the assertion of love as a concealment of what they are doing go some way to explain why Milton talks of lust in describing the love-making that follows eating the fruit. Above all, however, their love is corrupted because of their guilty knowledge of each other. That, rather than some aphrodisiac property in the fruit, is probably what excites them. At any rate, whether the scene is particularly voluptuous or not is irrelevant. It is the consummation of a mutuality that has become guilty: it is 'of their mutual guilt the seal, / The solace of their sin' (lines 1043–4) because it is the enjoyment of their fallen selves. For Adam, indeed, Eve takes on the relish of forbidden fruit:

> For never did thy beauty since the day
> I saw thee first and wedded thee, adorned
> With all perfections, so enflame my sense
> With ardour to enjoy thee, fairer now
> Than ever, bounty of this virtuous tree.
>
> (lines 1029–33)

What is the bounty of the tree? Eve, enhancement of her beauty, Adam's desire? Whichever way the ambiguity glances at us, Adam is saying that his love of Eve has taken on the taste of his sin. Eve, after stealing the fruit, wanted to steal Adam for herself, and now Adam dwells on the thought of enjoying her like the fruit which he has just taken part in stealing. It is an easy step from his libertine remark, 'if such pleasure be / In things to us forbidden, it might be wished, / For this one tree had been forbidden ten' (lines 1024–6), to the discovery that the tree has further fruit to be seized. Milton's treatment of the scene of fallen love-making is sober. C. S. Lewis, who felt that Eve was a murderess when she turned from the tree in search of Adam, evidently found it disappointing.[32] Milton, though, had much too firm a grasp of his human material to write it up sensationally. His restraint is telling because it is sympathetic. Though he calls it 'lust', he knows that it is still love and still Paradise:

> Flowers were the couch,
> Pansies, and violets and asphodel,
> And hyacinth, earth's freshest softest lap.
> There they their fill of love and love's disport
> Took largely.
>
> (lines 1039–43)

Above all, his restraint is telling because it is understanding. Even though he is dealing with so portentous an event as the Fall, he has worked it out plainly as a human action. Even with so heavily charged a term as 'lust', he has followed through the human motivation that turns the mutuality of love into a dishonouring of one self in the other.

After love-making, they fall asleep, and again the effects of the fruit, this time a hangover, are subordinate to the moral or psychological development. What they wake to is their naked selves, their selves as they appear to shame or guilt:

> up they rose
> As from unrest, and each other viewing,
> Soon found their eyes how opened, and their minds
> How darkened; innocence, that as a veil
> Had shadowed them from knowing ill, was gone,
> Just confidence, and native righteousness
> And honour from about them, naked left
> To guilty shame he covered, but his robe
> Uncovered more.
>
> (lines 1051–9)

It perhaps sounds magical that the creatures of Book IV, in whose 'looks divine / The image of their glorious maker shone' (lines 291–2), should suddenly lose the divine image. The loss of the faintly metaphorised moral qualities, 'innocence', 'just confidence', 'native righteousness', 'honour', does little more than say they felt ashamed. Nor does Milton's account in the *Christian Doctrine* of how guiltiness, as the first degree of death, is a state of mind as well as a loss of divine effulgence, explain what is happening very fully:

> Guiltiness is either accompanied or followed by terrors of conscience: Gen. III. 8: *they heard the voice of God, and Adam hid himself: he said, I was afraid;* ... also by the loss of divine protection and favor, which results in the lessening of the majesty of the human countenance, and the degradation of the mind: Gen. III. 7: *they knew that they were naked.* Thus the whole man is defiled. ... Hence comes shame: Gen. III. 7: *they sewed leaves together and made themselves aprons;* Rom. VI. 21: *for which you are now ashamed, for the end of those things is death.*[33]

This supplies only the bare bones of a human action, but it is enough at least to suggest how the shame they feel at their nakedness arises from a guilty knowledge of themselves. From that follow their making of fig-leaf aprons and their mutual recrimination. Both are coverings-up of guilt from themselves. The fig leaves follow the shame that 'covered', though 'his robe / Uncovered more' (lines 1058–9); and mutual accusation evades the unpleasant knowledge of self-condemnation (lines 1187–8).[34]

What particularly distinguishes Milton's treatment of the regress into the consciousness of the guilty self, 'this partial death ... by which we are fettered to condemnation and punishment as by some actual bond', is the way in which he shows it working not just in individual volition but also in the love and mutual consciousness of Adam and Eve.[35] It is on seeing each other that they become conscious of their guilt: 'each the other viewing, / ... silent, and in face / Confounded long they sat' (lines 1052, 1063–4). The sight of each other, one the other's image, makes it clear to them how they have dishonoured each other, and each becomes the image of the other's guilt. In drawing the process, Milton makes a lot of the looks on their faces. The unfallen way in which one face reflects another emerges when Adam, answering Eve's suggestion that they work apart, reminds her of

> this sweet intercourse
> Of looks and smiles, for smiles from reason flow,
> To brute denied, and are of love the food,
> Love not the lowest end of human life.
> (lines 238–43)

Their one-anothering before the Fall is expressed in the rational and delightful conversation of looks, the smiling glimpse of oneself in the smile of another. Adam can even say later that he receives 'Access in every virtue' 'from the influence of [Eve's] looks' (lines 309–10). So much for the unfallen mutuality of looks. However, the look may reflect askance: when Eve denies that to be tempted is an affront to their honour, she says that

> only our foe
> Tempting affronts us with his foul esteem
> Of our integrity: his foul esteem
> Sticks no dishonour on our front, but turns
> Foul on himself.
>
> (lines 327–31)

She is punning on 'affront', which means not only 'insult' but also 'set face to face'.[36] The tempter's crooked mind then cannot cast its dishonourable reflection upon the 'human face divine' while they remain blameless – it reflects rather on himself. Eve was, of course, speaking metaphorically. Nevertheless, when she returns to Adam after the Fall, she does in fact wear a false face: 'in her face excuse / Came prologue, and apology to prompt' (lines 853–4). The odd theatrical image, with its implications of acting and self-division, conveys how her look has become a pretence. Once she 'with countenance blithe her story told' (line 886), the assumed expression gives way and 'in her cheek distemper flushing glowed' (line 887). Her story, with its subtle untruths and distortions of what she has done, shows a confused consciousness of guilt, and it is that moral distemper as much as any physical disturbance produced by the fruit that now invades her face. Finally, after their love making, they find 'in [their] faces evident the signs / Of foul concupiscence' (lines 1077–8). Adam does not mean simply that he and Eve look a little debauched. 'Concupiscence', even 'foul concupiscence', means not merely lust but all the other crooked desires that are part of the guilty will. So, to draw out Milton's figuration, the human face divine is no longer a clear mirror of the other but is turned askew by guilt. Nor is it able to reflect the image of God. It not only cannot face itself in another, it cannot face God either. In the *Christian Doctrine*, Milton talks of a loss of the divine image particularly visible in the human face. This occurs partly because God withdraws it, but, like all the operations of God's will on the human pair, it works through human volition.[37] Losing God's countenance in both senses of the word, their guilty minds cannot meet the divine regard, and their faces show it. That, humanly, is how their glory, like Satan's, is in eclipse.

From this sustained picturing of the mutuality of looks, it is clear that Milton did not think of the Fall as the fall of two isolated individuals. Humanity consists in the rational conversation of looks and talk. That makes it particularly hard for Adam to stand alone for Eve and himself; and still when Eve faces him with a corrupt version of humanity, he need not take that as the best image of himself, and, until he has fallen, humanity has not fallen. Although the prohibition lays down a symbolic duty to God, in Milton's poem its honouring and violation involve relations between people, and in this the Fall is most clearly a moral fall. Here again, an invidious comparison with *Jerusalem Delivered* comes to mind.

The seduction of Rinaldo by Armida and his restoration sound like more centrally moral subjects than the myth of the Fall, but in fact Milton's treatment of his subject is morally and humanly much more developed than Tasso's. We need look no further than the reflection of one self in the other. For Rinaldo, the viewing of the image of himself in another is the sophistical mirror-and-eyes conceit. The true image of himself is what the military shield gives back to him; and that, we saw, reduces temperance to a matter rather of self-direction than of choice made by someone whose life is led with others. Milton's grasp of the reflexiveness of the self is much sounder than Tasso's, and his understanding of the field of moral action takes in other humans. It is one of the contradictions of *Paradise Lost* that, though Milton insists on the inferiority of Eve, he should nevertheless draw the fellowship of Adam and Eve as that which makes them human.[38] At least in Book IX, Milton succeeds in showing Adam and Eve participating in each other rationally and irrationally, and the doctrine of sexual inequality gives way to a lively, open and complex understanding of how in the society of marriage man and wife are implicated in each other.

Adam and Eve: The Return Upon Themselves

What we have followed so far of the negative process of evil is chiefly the corruption of love and its involvement with death and guilt. In Book X, the process works itself to a crisis. When the Son comes down to judge them, Adam accuses Eve, and, once the Son has passed judgement, he is left to accuse himself. In his wretched conversation with himself, he finds himself bound to death. To him in this state of despair, Eve comes insisting on reconciliation, and wins him round. If the Fall was the first turning point, or peripety, this is the second.[39] Eve repents of having brought Adam down with her, and Adam forgives her. This cuts into the chain of recrimination and guilt to which they are bound, and makes a new beginning possible between them. They can return upon themselves. No longer bound to guilt and death between themselves, they can now turn to making up matters between humanity and God through repentance and forgiveness. This second turning point then takes the form of a double repentance and forgiveness worked out first between Adam and Eve and then between them and God.

In his self-accusation, Adam follows in many ways the same course as Satan does on Niphates. Unlike Satan's defiant despair, Adam's is all prostration, guilt, self-hate, self-reproach. However, the way in which he finds himself bound to death resembles Satan's unhappy course into the abyss of the self, which leads to the discovery that 'myself am hell': 'O conscience! into what abyss of fears / And horrors hast thou driven me; out of which / I find no way, from deep to deeper plunged!' (X, 842–4). That, though distressed and dispirited, recalls Satan's tormented 'And in the lowest deep a lower deep / Still threatening to devour me opens wide, / To which the hell I suffer seems a heaven' (IV, 76–8). Even in the mazy, self-involved movement of the bound will, Adam's thoughts imitate Satan's. The serpentine coiling of his thoughts, the recoil, the redounding, the reflux of guilty self-knowledge upon himself lead only to further self-condemnation and despair. It is not necessary to follow Adam through this gloomy labyrinth in which he keeps returning to the realisation that he has brought death into the world, only in each self-enclosed circling to find himself more wretchedly to blame, until he comes to see himself 'To Satan only like both crime and doom' (line 841). It will be enough to observe how his thoughts turn on himself in execration and pursue him towards death.

In the following passage, Adam laments the transformation of the world 'all summed up in man' (IX, 113) to a world of woe of which he is the centre.

> O voice once heard
> Delightfully, *Increase and multiply,*
> Now death to hear! For what can I increase
> Or multiply but curses on my head?
> Who of all ages to succeed, but feeling
> The evil on him brought by me, will curse
> My head, Ill fare our ancestor impure,
> For this we may thank Adam; but his thanks
> Shall be the execration; so besides
> Mine own that bide upon me, all from me
> Shall with a fierce reflux on me redound,
> On me as on their natural centre light
> Heavy, though in their place.
>
> (X, 729–41)

The passage, like the whole soliloquy, follows the course of the incurved will turning everything against Adam in self-condemnation. The self-dramatisation of 'me' here expresses the guilty consciousness of the self as object of blame and self-hate. He blames himself above all for having become the source of death. In Paradise, Adam had a joyful intuition of how 'man by number is to manifest / His single imperfection, and beget / Like of his like, his image multiplied' (VIII, 422–4). The multiplication of his image now turns to a curse, for, bringing children into the world, 'what can I increase / Or multiply but curses on my head?' In the consciousness that he has become the origin of a death-bound humanity, Adam comes to see himself as a centre of execration, all the evil that issues from him recoiling upon his own head. Just how extremely he imagines himself as the centre of universal execration comes out in the simile where he talks of all that proceeds from him returning in curses upon him 'as on their natural centre'. He thinks of himself as at the centre of a universe of hate towards which all things gravitate; but whereas in nature, so it was held, things rest at the centre weightless, the curses, though they have found their aim, weigh terribly on Adam.[40] The cosmic imagery conveys the hell within, where everything is involved in the self-centredness of guilt.

Self-execration so intense is really a pursuit of the self toward death. Adam has turned in on himself away from the happy conversation of self and likeness with Eve, and, in twisting argument with himself, finds only disfiguring of self until he arrives at the discovery that 'both death and I / Am found eternal, and incorporate both' (lines 815–6).[41] He has by now spiritualised or metaphorised the idea of death to mean something like 'the body of this death' of which Paul speaks, the process not just of physical corruption, which he has already begun to feel in the world about him, but also of evil in his own mind and will. With that, a new abyss of guilty realisation opens to receive him:

> from me what can proceed,
> But all corrupt, both mind and will depraved,
> Not to do only, but to will the same
> With me?
>
> (lines 824–7)

He sees himself as the centre of guilt, not just because he is the progenitor of children who will suffer misery and death, but also now because he is the progenitor of the continuing process of corruption in his own actions and his children's: 'On me, me only, as the source and spring / Of all corruption, all the blame lights due; / So might the wrath' (lines 832–4). Here, the movement from him as origin and the redounding and lighting upon himself in blame dismally repeat the experience of the abyss from which he has just fallen. It is at this point, seeing himself as the parent of sin as well as death, that he compares himself to Satan (lines 839–41).

The turnings of Adam's thought are often hard to follow, sometimes even abstruse, for Milton seems to have tried to work in points that were important to him as a theologian, and I have not attempted a thorough explication. In its outline, however, the soliloquy is a gloomy masterpiece, comparable in its representation of guilty self-centredness to Fulke Greville's 'Down in the depths' (*Caelica* XCIX), and like it also in bringing Christian ideas of hell, sin and death to life as figures of a state of mind. The earlier part of Book X deals with the Son's descent to earth to pass sentence on Adam and Eve, the entry of Sin and Death into the world, Satan's return to hell and his transformation along with the other devils into snakes involved in a universal hiss and the deranging of the world into the fallen order of things. Some of these events seize the imagination more than others, but the imaginative focus of Book X is the action of these supernatural events in the human mind. Pictures of the universe serve many purposes. One of their uses, the one most relevant here, is as figures by which one takes hold of one's relation to oneself. In his soliloquy, Adam represents his guilty consciousness of himself through the cosmic imagery of the dead centre of the universe and of a world deranged by sin and death. The magnificent cosmic array of *Paradise Lost* has come to revolve inside Adam's head in corrupted or inverted forms as figures of his crooked relation to himself.

What rescues Adam from his self-imprisoned consciousness is the intervention of Eve. His first reaction is to turn his self-hatred against her:

> Out of my sight, thou serpent, that name best
> Befits thee with him leagued, thyself as false
> And hateful; nothing wants but that thy shape,
> Like his, and colour serpentine may show
> Thy inward fraud.
>
> (lines 867–71)

Earlier, Adam had seen himself incorporate with death. Here, he pictures her who had been the best image of himself in the shape of sin, snaky, like Sin herself in whom Satan had once viewed his perfect image. He follows that up with a distressing anti-feminist tirade full of such topics as crooked ribs and women's longing to be seen 'Though by the devil himself' (line 878). This is what the conversation of like with like in Paradise has fallen to, accusation full of self-hate in soliloquy or hate in conversation with the other. In the face of this outburst, Eve's pleading shows magnanimity and firmness of mind about what matters: 'While yet we live, scarce one short hour perhaps, / Between us two let there be peace' (lines 923–4). She sees that humanity can be restored, at least between them, by her contrition and Adam's forgiveness. It is a pity that Milton did not give Eve a soliloquy, but, if we may suppose that like Adam she has been going through a hell of self- accusation, then somehow she has been able to die to the self that was bound to death and turn to that 'Whereon I live, thy gentle looks, thy aid, / Thy counsel in this uttermost distress' (lines 919–20). In turning to him as to her living self, she turns him from hate of her, 'his life so late and sole delight' (line 941), and to that extent has turned him away from the self that was 'incorporate with death'.[42] At the same time, she suggests another object for his hate than himself or herself, namely the serpent (lines 925–7). This enmity is to play an important part in the ensuing conversation between them. By thinking about the promise that Eve's seed shall bruise the serpent's head, they grope towards an intuition of the acts that will deliver them from sin and death. The initial movement is not in itself an attempt to understand God's purpose but a deflection of hate away from the self, a movement rather like the one which Harapha provokes in Samson. Still, the movement is part of that chain of volition and deliberation that leads to repentance and the understanding of their human possibilities in the fallen world. At the very least, Eve, in restoring love between herself and Adam, has restored the possibility of rational conversation or 'counsel'; and the mind, instead of pursuing itself in circles of guilt, turns now in talking with someone else to the situation and what can be done between them.

In what follows this act of courage, one has an uneasy feeling that Milton misses how Eve's generosity in bringing about a reconciliation is beyond Adam. As so often in *Paradise Lost*, where the hierarchical principle operates, the inferior comes over as the more mature person. After the reconciliation, Adam and Eve turn to practical matters, and the inner movements of volition, the master theme of Book X, recede into the background. We see Eve making proposals and Adam not very agreeably correcting her. Nevertheless, we can trace even here, as Jun Harada has shown, the reflexive operation of one self in the other.[43] Eve's suggestions bring up matters which we have already seen Adam turning over despairingly. He could do nothing while locked in conversation with himself, but now when Eve, his other self, puts them to him, he can correct himself in correcting her and so 'To better hopes his more attentive mind / Labouring ... raised' (lines 1011–14). Eve's suggestion, for example, that suicide would free 'both ourselves and seed at once' (line 999) recalls Adam's earlier cry for extinction: 'Why comes not death, / Said he, with one thrice acceptable stroke / To end me?' (lines 854-6). However, when Eve suggests death as a solution, Adam now argues that, though her proposal sounds like self-sacrifice, the vehement despair behind it comes from self-love. Seeing this in Eve, he is able to go back on his own earlier despair and think how the situation might be remedied. Perhaps even in refusing to let himself be swayed by Eve's proposal that they kill themselves, Adam overcomes his earlier desire to die with Eve and puts the death-seeking of his fall behind him. This also would be part of his turning from despair, from 'Submitting to what seemed remediless' (IX, 919), to thinking objectively about their situation, and implies a movement out of the 'abyss of conscientious fears' to hope and trust – hope that the humanity to spring from them might overcome the serpent, trust that this is in fact God's will, to which despair had blinded him. With this, their situation becomes clearer; it is the world as we know it more or less. The more Adam thinks precisely about the sentence which God passed on them, the more his confidence rises that there is another way out than death. He sees that the curse which he thought in his despair was aimed at him in fact 'aslope / Glanced on the ground' (lines 1053–4). With astonishing resourcefulness, he sees immediately how primitive technology might make the fallen world habitable. Now, reconciled to Eve, to himself and the life ahead of them, he is ready to complete with her the movement from the bound self through repenting. Here, the return upon the self, set in motion by Eve's refusal to be repulsed, meets the counter-action of divine forgiveness, which makes a new beginning for humanity in history.

Repentance is completed in what Milton calls in the *Christian Doctrine* 'saving faith'. This is not to be confused with the 'awareness of divine mercy which results in repentance'. That awareness they have already arrived at, as Adam comes to take a hopeful and trusting view of the Son's sentence on them. 'Saving faith', on the other hand, is 'the firm persuasion implanted in us by the gift of God, by virtue of which we believe, on authority of God's promise, that all these things which God has promised us in Christ are ours, and especially the grace of eternal life'.[44] This second effect of regeneration is the subject of Books XI and XII. It begins with Adam's conviction, after they have prayed repenting, that they have been heard (XI, 152–5). It is completed in Adam's rejoicing in the promises of God contained in Michael's account of the plan of salvation. In the overall theological design of the poem, this completion is of the first importance. Even in terms of the human action, it is important since, without a belief in the final restoration of the human race, the repentance that goes hand in hand with forgiveness and being restored to good will could not be truly gone through, nor the passage from the bound to the delivered self completed. Yet, as a human action, Adam's instruction by Michael in the history of his race is not particularly interesting. Michael corrects some of Adam's all-too-human motions, and Adam learns to rejoice in the coming of a redeemer, the overcoming of death and the elevation of his race to God at the end of time. However, the machinery of this reconcilation with God belongs more to a course of instruction in Christian faith than to the representation of the motions of Adam's spirit, and, in comparison with Books IX and X, Books XI and XII work meagrely as a human action. We may therefore stop at this point, since to follow the restoration of humanity further in Adam would not add much of interest about Milton's study of the will.

Conclusion

What Milton has worked out most fully as a human action in Book X is the idea of the self bound to death. In the process of guilt that involves the wills of Adam and Eve, he has rendered the Pauline concept of the body of this death as a chain of volition, and to the Pauline concern with the individual will he has added an understanding of how the process of guilt corrupts the relation of individuals bound to each other. Milton's treatment of the deliverance from the self-enthralment of guilt is, by contrast, limited to the first motions of repentance. However, for our purposes these will do.

As with the process of guilt, Milton shows the return upon the self as a matter of human mutuality, not merely of the individual will. This grasp of mutuality may owe something to the exchange of persons which Paul speaks of between believer and Christ. What sets Adam free from the intwisted mirror of the guilty self is the self-sacrificing motion of Eve, who in spite of his hate turns to him insisting on his love and, repenting, offers to take the blame on herself. To forgive here is to restore humanity between them at least on the level of human relations, and the subsequent transaction with God follows from that. The reconciliation of Adam and Eve cannot follow with any exactness the exchange of persons which Paul and Luther describe taking place between the sinner and Christ, but it seems likely that the Pauline text pointed Milton towards thinking of the return upon the self in terms of the reflexiveness of one self in the other. Classical texts may also have entered into his understanding. Plato's *Alcibiades* talks of how one self is reflected in the other in love, and Cicero's *Laelius* develops lofty ideas of the true friend as another self; but these books talk of an ideal state. They do not analyse the interdependence of selves in their innermost motions as Milton does. There, probably, Milton owes more to Christian than to classical thought.

Christian thought, however, analysed the motions of the will in terms such as sin, grace and atonement. The remarkable thing about *Paradise Lost* is that it represents Christian ideas about the will as a human action. To that extent, it is a humanist interpretation of Christianity. This is not to say that, like Feuerbach in the Nineteenth century or even Winstanley in the seventeenth, Milton has reduced Christian ideas to human truths. The supernatural mysteries of grace and atonement are clearly operative, but Milton has shown them working with human motions and with sufficient grasp of human experience to make one wonder how Johnson could have complained of deficient human interest. Milton's grasp of volition, indeed, is what our own humanism might point to as his most serious claim on our attention. At the same time, though, it goes beyond the humanism of his own age. It certainly cuts below the simple didacticism called for in neoclassical humanist literary theory and in those epics that completely answer to the theory. The way in which *The Lusiad*, for example, or on a higher level *Jerusalem Delivered*, engage the will through investing their heroes with epic glory goes with a rather primitive idea of the will. *Paradise Lost*, by contrast, offers a study of the will rather than a firing of it, and its concern with choice belongs with more sophisticated concerns than epic efforts to instil magnanimous desires. Besides, Milton's treatment of the images presented by the characters in his poem makes the heroic self-regard to which neoclassical epics typically appealed for moral ends look superficial. Especially in the way in which Adam and Eve reflect each other, the images cast by Milton's characters involve more complicated moral relations than are easily accounted for in the contemporary literary theory of ideal imitation. Just as *Paradise Lost* is a study of the will rather than a harnessing of it, so it is a study of the image of the self rather than a glorifying of it. *Paradise Lost* stands apart from other neoclassical epics in going behind the externality of ideal imitation. Behind the playing-off of the heroic figure against his disfigurement, Milton grasps the inner processes of wrong choice and guilt. Behind the lustre of the hero, his exemplary posing, his self-preoccupied concern with the image he bears to himself and others, Milton lays hold of moral and psychological insights into the way in which one self is reflected in other selves.

The previous chapter showed how *Paradise Lost* developed both in bold outline and in delightful intricacy a universal scheme of moral images. To say now that in his study of the will Milton goes beyond the scope of ideal imitation does not mean that either intellectually or artistically his poem falls apart. However subtle and unexpected his representation of the will, it fits inside the universal scheme which enjoins 'the necessity of obedience to the Divine Law'.[45] The one respect in which *Paradise Lost* seems to break radically with conventional ideal imitation is that it has put by the mechanical ethical appeal of glorifying its human heroes with epic splendour. The repentance of Adam and Eve, so crucial in the action of the epic, is an act of unassuming human goodness. Milton gives it none of the epic pointing of Rinaldo's repentance on Olivet. Epic decoration of the event would indeed be out of place, and Milton writes the crisis of his poem with grave simplicity. The restraint carries its own moral appeal. No-one would wish to say that Milton's treatment had somehow broken loose from his design; and for some more strongly than for others, the unassuming action may even pick up a reflection of the divine works of Book XII, where God's method 'by small accomplishing great things' is shown at work in the human life of the Son. The repentance of Adam and Eve opens out into that historical prospect, and in some primitive way may even foreshadow that pattern of voluntary humiliation. Certainly, Milton's epic design upon his readers aims at some such transvaluation of heroic values. Moreover, the universal images of Milton's grand design enter as metaphors into the representation of volition. The further we push our analysis of Adam's soliloquy in Book X, for instance, the harder we come up against the universal images of Sin, Death and the Serpent, now absorbed into his consciousness of guilt. It is through such metaphorising of these figures that Adam can grasp his own experience.

Having said that Milton involves his study of the will thoroughly in his universal and ideal scheme, I return to what is obvious: the human action of *Paradise Lost* is simply more developed in its understanding of choice, guilt and repentance than what other epics, indeed other works, of neoclassical humanism can show. In an earlier chapter, I argued that neoclassical humanism was bound by its commitment to rhetoric to treat the motions of the will in a conventional way. Characteristically, humanists work with an ideal of free will as temperance. Milton's treatment of free will develops that so that it involves choice in a world that involves other people. He also took in what neoclassical humanism either did not lay hold of except superficially or turned away from, the study of volition in guilt and repentance. Luther, with his ideas of freedom and bondage, had come up with insights into how people really work as distinct from how they are supposed to work; but he wrote as a theologian, and his insights hardened into the institutional dogmas of the Reformation. While many humanists found themselves on the Protestant side, no humanist seems to have been able to lay hold of Luther's ideas with moral as well as religious understanding. At the same time, humanism, as it matured, increasingly tended to leave the motions of error and repentance to the special language and operations of religion. When Protestant humanists such as Grotius or Milton write as theologians on the atonement or free will, it is as theologians rather than as men they write; they do not illuminate the experience to which the doctrines address themselves. Nor do seventeenth-century churchmen of an Erasmian cast. Jeremy Taylor's chapters on repentance are an admirable Arminian exposition addressed to a reasonable and cultivated public; but, in comparison with *Paradise Lost*, they never seem to touch upon the real matter of the return upon the self. Similarly, Bishop Bramhall's acute, easy, forceful answer to Hobbes's *Treatise of Liberty and Necessity* succeeds splendidly except in telling us about ourselves.[46] Failures, or rather successes, such as these suggest why neoclassical humanism in its maturity increasingly left the Christian study of the will outside its scope and relegated it to the sphere of sacred truth.

The maturity of neoclassical humanism in English literature comes with the establishment – one can hardly avoid so deliberate a word – of Augustan humanism. Among the Augustans, the division of religious and humanist spheres settles into convention. It was the institutional or public side of Christianity which they treated. Swift was concerned with the Anglican establishment. When Pope satirised the pomp of prayer, it was a breach of manners and a sort of social affectation with which he was concerned. He implies a standard of true devotion of course, but the contents of true devotion, if not the forms, are a subject that lies outside his chosen scope. Dryden's contrition in *The Hind and the Panther* (I, 66–99) is unusual – I can think of no other such passage in Dryden or in the other Augustan figures I have mentioned – in being a dignified and moving utterance of personal devotion. Some excellent devotional poetry was written in the period, but it was not a form favoured by the representative figures of Augustan humanism. Johnson's judgement that the topics of Christian belief were unsuitable for poetry is notorious, and yet not really eccentric, considering the state of letters for which he speaks.

With the line of Augustan humanists, we can speak for the first time of a humanist institution of English letters; for with Augustan criticism, English letters became explicit about their vocation to humanise and civilise, to represent an urbane humanity in its central human concerns. That there were many other strains in the literature of the late seventeenth and eighteenth centuries besides the humanist one does not undermine the assertion that there is a consensus of literary principles among Dryden, Swift, Pope and Johnson of such influence that to speak of a literary establishment is not to overstate the case. Among Augustan critics, *Paradise Lost* had immense cachet, and I have already discussed how Milton's treatment of the creaturely middle state of humanity lent itself to the great Augustan commonplaces about human nature. Clearly though, *Paradise Lost* stands apart from Augustan humanism, above all in its managing to represent the Christian study of the will as a human action.

Nor in this does it stand closer to an earlier cast of humanism. It is indeed hard to talk with any definiteness of the state of humanism in England before Dryden. Certainly, classical literature was established as a humanising discipline in the universities and more thoroughly in the grammar schools. Conspicuously behind Jonson, Milton and Dryden stand the schoolmasters, Camden, Gill and Busby. Most writers of the sixteenth and seventeenth centuries would have had some humanist training in classical literature; yet this is not enough to make it sensible to talk of English literature in the sixteenth and seventeenth centuries as a humanist institution. No-one would want to call Herbert and Crashaw humanists as English poets on the grounds that they were fine Latinists. If we are to talk of the humanism of English letters, we shall have to find explicit pronouncements of a critical consciousness of a humanising vocation, and this before the Restoration is remarkably undeveloped. There are exceptions, Ben Jonson the most massive; but the tribe surrounding Jonson was not a school of humanism. There was, no doubt, much literary talk ranging from the sort of gossip to be found in Suckling's 'Sessions of the Poets' to acute ad hoc criticism of the sort represented by Carew's verse epistle 'To Ben Jonson'. There is no evidence, though, that any of the tribe of Ben held the sort of principles about the function of literature and the man of letters to be found, however sketchily, in Jonson's *Timber*. Most of them were gentlemen of letters. So, if we think of the English literature of the earlier seventeenth century, we can assert certainly that it was reared on a humanism of the classics but that in its conversation with itself, its literary scene and its productions, anything we might call humanist letters was on the whole elusive and diffident, glancing out ironically for example in the Horatian side of Marvell or more candidly in Cowley's attempts at the institutional humanist forms, the epic and the celebratory or reflective ode, but nowhere, except with Jonson, confident of its position as *magister vitae*. As far as humanism goes, then, the literature of 'the Gyant Race before the Flood' is irregular and indeterminate. There is nothing that helps us to place *Paradise Lost* and its perplexing way of making a humanist epic out of the Christian study of the will. If we cast further back to Elizabethan literature, we seem at first sight to hit a more promising state of affairs. There was nothing of such institutional weight as Augustan humanism. Still, the pieces collected in Gregory Smith's *Elizabethan Critical Essays* show an intense, if usually naive and derivative concern with the state of contemporary writing, and the various apologies for poetry sketch a conception of the function of literature. [47] Sidney's *Defence* is the most distinguished statement of these concerns, and it represents a genuine, if immature, humanism. We might consider *The Faerie Queene* as a product of that early English humanism. According to Spenser's letter to Raleigh, 'the generall end ... of all the booke is to fashion a gentleman or noble person in vertuous and gentle discipline'. [48] Here, then, is a poem that imitates a golden world and images virtues and vices for humanising and civilising ends. The interesting thing from our point of view, however, is that the first virtue of the gentleman is 'Holinesse', and remarkably the virtue touches the inner man. Christianity would naturally enough concern the public ideal of the gentleman and those public ideals of order that *The Faerie Queene* represents, and this would not be puzzling in a civilizing and humanising poem. Indeed, the Christianity would as easily fit into the public theme as it does in *Gondibert*. [49] However, Spenser's 'Holinesse' is attained through peculiarly private motions of the will in the Redcrosse Knight's encounter with *Despaire* and his subsequent repentance in the House of Holinesse. Here, then, we have a humanist poem, at least in principle, which nevertheless includes those motions of the will that play a central part in *Paradise Lost* and generally seem to have been inaccessible to genuinely humanist treatment. Perhaps then we should agree with the view that *Paradise Lost* was an old-fashioned poem for its time and that its humanism looks back to the sixteenth century.

Certainly, *The Faerie Queene*, through its allegorical treatment of virtues and vices, shares with *Paradise Lost* a certain moral innerness unusual in epic. However, this affinity does not really offer a precedent for Milton's treatment of his Christian subject matter. For one thing, Spenser's treatment of despair and repentance does not represent those motions of the will with the sort of human understanding to be found in *Paradise Lost*. Despaire's temptation turns on fairly conventional topics, and, though memorable, is not very persuasive. [50] In comparison with Milton's picture of the bound will in Book X of *Paradise Lost*, Spenser's treatment is fairly external. Again, Redcrosse's repentance does not get beyond fairly conventional metaphors for the transformation from bound self to free. There is the charming allegory of Charissa's being brought to bed in labour, her child being the rebirth of Redcrosse in the spirit (Book 1, canto 10, st. 16). This represents the operation of divine grace, which Spenser in the introductory stanza of canto 10 says is necessary for dealing with spiritual temptations. However, as a working-out of what is involved in repentance and the delivery of the bound self on the level of human volition, Spenser's treatment has none of the moral analysis to be found in *Paradise Lost*.

The natural line of development from Spenser's study of the will runs not to *Paradise Lost* but to Beaumont's *Psyche*. This Laudian epic of spiritual pilgrimage enormously enlarges upon Spenser's allegory of the soul's mortification, despair and final entry into heaven. Only in the most attenuated sense can one think of *Psyche* as a humanist production. It represents the inner life of the spirit in entirely religious, not to say ecclesiastical, symbols. Though these are often turned with delightful ingenuity, the poem treats sin and repentance in a highly conventional way, for all its extravagance. Beaumont's poem brings out and exaggerates how Spenser's Booke of Holinesse offers no real precedent for the treatment of volition in *Paradise Lost*. As far as I can see, Milton found his way to representing religious concepts as human motions on his own, and in this respect no more falls in with the humanism of an earlier age than with the humanism of his own.

Paradise Lost shares the impulse of the humanism of its time towards more critical ideas of what makes us human, but it also manages something otherwise beyond the range of neoclassical humanism in drawing a human likeness of sin and repentance. Perhaps our humanist criticism should rest content with pointing to this distinction of the poem in historical context. To urge the claims of Milton's study of the will further on our own humanism has perhaps more to do with bringing an argument to a conclusion than with the sort of clarification that allows the poem to speak for itself.

Nevertheless, it might help us to get hold of Milton's achievement if we brought George Eliot's treatment of wrong choice and guilt in *Middlemarch* to mind. Especially in her treatment of the Bulstrodes, she shares with the Milton of Books IX and X a kind of directness that seems to invite our recognition of what is being shown. Their narrative methods are quite different, she relating so much through analysis and commentary, he in the manner of classical epic, so sparing of narratorial presence. Yet both write as if the motions of the will were of absorbing interest, and elicit a grave but not unsympathetic understanding of human crookedness and solidarity between man and wife. In many ways, George Eliot's treatment is immeasurably richer. Bulstrode's hand in Raffles's death, like Lydgate's choice of Rosamond, involves a complexity of motive that the state of innocence rules out. Adam and Eve have no society but themselves to mould their wills. They do not have characters in the social sense that stamps Lydgate's and Bulstrode's actions. If, like Lydgate, they are carried away from themselves by others' suggestions, these never take the form of the talk of a community, with its oblique designs on the individual fate, that manages 'to get woven like slight clinging hairs into the more substantial web of [their] thoughts'.[51] Again the moral issues in *Middlemarch* are more accessible than all that is meant by the forbidden fruit. In his choice of Rosamond or his alliance with Bulstrode, we understand Lydgate's unwariness or inattention to what most closely concerns him more easily than Eve's, and we understand Bulstrode's dishonest self-communings more directly than Eve's or Adam's. As with their errors, so with their anguished realisations. At least Bulstrode's 'scorching' consciousness of social shame, which is the hell within for him, or Lydgate's miserable knowledge of how he has been made over to the mean and retrogressive society in which he had hoped to work as a free and energetic intelligence make less demand on our intellectual imagination than Adam's soliloquy of despair in Book X. Their psychological hell is a social condition, and we take hold of that more readily than Adam's self-enclosed guilt. In *Middlemarch*, George Eliot's study of the will is densely and exactly particularised in ways that make intelligent attention far easier than is the case with the bare and archetypal story which Milton has to tell.

Yet however thin in social representation, in other respects *Paradise Lost* may stand the comparison with *Middlemarch* where the study of the will is concerned. George Eliot draws the temptations and responses of her character with a subtlety that shows an exact understanding of how people work, but she does not eclipse Milton here in spite of the strangeness of his fable and the apparent simplicity of the divine command. Moreover, the social web of Middlemarch, though, or rather because, so finely drawn, has a way of taking the characters from themselves. Adam and Eve, just outlined as characters, are more immediately present to us as centres of self than Lydgate or Bulstrode. The way in which Adam and Eve can place themselves inside a universal scheme puts them at the same time in charge of themselves and their own experience. Bulstrode's anguish over his past, on the other hand, is chiefly fear of social disgrace. He can manipulate confrontation with himself and his conscience, but not social opinion. It is much easier to deceive ourselves in conversation with ourselves than with others. Bulstrode vividly represents that deviousness of the inner world, all the more vividly for his religious intensity; and yet the social direction of his honesty and dishonesty is self-trivialising. He cannot take hold of what he has done. Unlike Adam, he cannot properly grieve over himself, and he cannot make a return upon himself. Generally, anyone who sinks in Middlemarch is sunk indeed.

Nineteenth-century critics of religion such as Feuerbach, or Arnold, or George Eliot in her attempt to translate Christian ideas and images into secular moral life, considered that dogmatic Christianity alienated the life of the spirit. Certainly, the doctrinal casing of Luther's insights in Protestant theology or the legalistic reasoning of the Father in Book III of *Paradise Lost* seem to turn human understanding against itself. We cannot entirely detach the human action of *Paradise Lost* from its theological design. Repeatedly, I have had to admit that Milton's religious symbols and ideas cannot be entirely reduced to the sort of moral interpretation which I have been attempting, and, in admitting that, I have been saying that for all the human understanding with which Milton works out the action of his poem, the design to justify the ways of God alienates his human understanding from itself. But now, I should add a further admission. At the same time that it alienates, that is, wraps up the human concerns of the poem in the language and the operations of transcendental belief, Milton's universal theological scheme allows his characters – Adam anyway, Eve less so – to experience their choice, guilt and repentance deeply and inwardly. So far from alienating them from their own experience, it gives them to their experience absolutely. That, it might be thought, is precisely what is wrong with Milton's system: it exacts as human price the experience of error, guilt and repentance in their acutest form. I cannot agree. These seem to me elements of any human life, brought out, not produced, by Milton's system. They are still elements of life in *Middlemarch*, drawn into a web of social relations rather than a theological system. In some respects, the characters find themselves more fully in the social web of Middlemarch; but they are also lost to themselves in a way that Milton's characters in Milton's scheme of things are not. In *Middlemarch*, even the consciousness of others' centres of self made into a loving habit of will cannot really bring one back. The idea of living for others comes over as too good to be true in Dorothea, and it is not realised as a genuine ethical possibility elsewhere.

The moral scheme in *Middlemarch* is rational and secular, in *Paradise Lost* religious. Surprisingly, it is with the religious scheme that we find the more centrally human study of volition where the relation to oneself is concerned. I am not sure what to make of this observation; I certainly do not wish to generalise about the bearing of religious systems on the study of the self. That would take me on a critical enterprise quite beyond the scope of this book. Anyway, the human turn which Milton gives to his Christian system is after all his own. Nor do I wish to praise Milton's study of the will at the expense of George Eliot's. Her secular moral understanding of volition sets a standard of excellence. I have worked the comparison between them this way and that only to suggest how the seventeenth-century poet's excellences might find a place with the nineteenth-century novelist's in a humanism that cuts across century, genre and even system of belief.

Notes

1   *St Paul and Protestantism, Dissent and Dogma*, ed. R. H. Super (Ann Arbor, 1968), p. 16.
2   See Dennis Danielson, 'Arminianism in *Paradise Lost*', *Milton Studies*, 12 (1978).
3   *Christian Doctrine*, I, 8, *CP*, 6, 336. Cf. *Paradise Lost*, VI, 789–91.
4   John Leonard, *Naming in Paradise: Milton and the Language of Adam and Eve* (Oxford, 1990), pp. 147–56, has a subtle discussion of how Satan's words are so ambiguously framed as to elicit from, rather than introduce into, his fellow angels evil suggestions. But I cannot see a substantial difference here from the way in which he tempts Eve.
5   *Pro Plancio*, XXVII, 68, as Fowler notes.

6   Such is the view of A. J. Waldock, *'Paradise Lost' and its Critics* (Cambridge, 1966), pp. 77–9.

7   William Empson, *Some Versions of Pastoral* (London, 1950), p. 168.

8   *Some Versions of Pastoral*, p. 169.

9   William Empson, *Milton's God* (London, 1965), p. 69.

10   E.g. by C. S. Lewis, *A Preface to 'Paradise Lost'* (Oxford, 1949), p. 96.

11   *Milton's God*, pp. 77–9.

12   Empson, *Milton's God*, frequently adverts to B. Rajan's contention in *'Paradise Lost' and the Seventeenth-Cetury Reader* (London, 1947), p. 127, that sublimity is the pre-eminent characteristic of *Paradise Lost*.

13   *Johnson's 'Journey to the Western Islands of Scotland' and Boswell's 'Journal of a Tour to the Hebrides with Samuel Johnson LL.D'*, ed. R. W. Chapman (Oxford, 1924), p. 420.

14   XII, 33–7. Cf. *Eikonoklastes*, ed. Merritt Y. Hughes, *CP*, 3, 50–2, and see Joan S. Bennett, 'God, Satan and King Charles: Milton's Royal Portraits', *PMLA*, 92 (1977), 441–57.

15   *Milton's God*, pp. 36–7.

16   On how Satan's face draws his followers after him, see Christopher Ricks, *Milton's Grand Style* (Oxford, 1963), p. 89.

17   Ricks, p. 140, remarks on the recurring motif of the face.

18   Thomas Hobbes, *Leviathan*, ch.7, ed. C.B. Macpherson (Harmondsworth, 1968), p. 336.

19   Contrast Milton's grounding the image of God on freedom with Spenser's on love in 'A Hyme of Heavenly Love', lines 113–9, *Works of Edmund Spenser, Minor Poems*, I, ed. Charles Grosvenor Osgood and Henry Gibbons Lotspeich (Baltimore, 1943).

20   See J. M. Evans, *'Paradise Lost' and the Genesis Tradition* (Oxford, 1968), pp. 259–61.

21   Among those who see the Fall as the working-out of prelapsarian flaws are John S. Diefhoff, *Milton's 'Paradise Lost': A Commentary on the Argument* (New York, 1946), p. 56ff. (but see his 'Eve's Dream and the Paradox of Fallible Perfection', *Milton Quarterly*, 4 (1970), pp. 5-7, for another view); E. M. W. Tillyard, *Studies in Milton* (London, 1951), pp. 8–52; Arnold Stein, *Answerable Style: Essays in 'Paradise Lost'* (Minneapolis, 1953), pp. 75–118; Millicent Bell, 'The Fallacy of the Fall in *Paradise Lost*, *PMLA*, 68 (1953), 863–83; *PMLA*, 70 (1955), C. A. Patrides, *Milton and the Christian Tradition* (Oxford, 1966), pp. 105–6; Albert W. Fields, 'Milton and Self-Knowledge', *PMLA*, 83 (1968), 394ff.; David Daiches, *God and the Poets* Oxford, 1984), p. 39. Among those who contend for an instantaneous Fall are Wayne Shumaker, 'The Fall in *Paradise Lost*', *PMLA*, 70 (1955), 1185–7; Richard Heinrich Grün, *Das Menschenbild John Miltons in 'Paradise Lost'* (Heidelberg, 1956), p. 65; Joseph H. Summers, *The Muse's Method* (Cambridge, Mass., 1962), pp. 148–59; Stanley Eugene Fish, *Surprised by Sin: The Reader in 'Paradise Lost'* (London, 1967), pp. 216–32, 245–54; Thomas H. Blackburn, ' "Uncloister'd Virtue": Adam and Eve in Milton's Paradise', Milton Studies, 3 (1971), 119–37; Elaine B. Safer, ' "Sufficent to have Stood": Eve's Responsibility in Book IX', *Milton Quarterly*, 5 (1971), pp. 10–13; Peter Amadeus Fiore, 'Freedom, Liability and the State of Perfection in *Paradise Lost* ', *Milton Quarterly*, 5 (1971), 47–51; Stella P. Revard, 'Eve and the Doctrine of Responsibility in *Paradise Lost*', *PMLA*, 88 (1973), 69–83. Denis Danielson, *Milton's Good God* (Cambridge, 1982), pp. 126–7, forcefully argues for the freedom of the will before the Fall but implies that the Fall is already under way in the separation scene. Dennis Burden, *The Logical Epic: A Study of the Argument of 'Paradise Lost'* (London, 1967), pp. 85–93, and A. B. Chambers, 'The Falls of Adam and Eve in *Paradise Lost*', *New Essays in 'Paradise Lost'*, ed. Thomas Kranidas (Berkeley, 1969), pp. 118–30, argue that it can be seen as both theologically instantaneous and dramatically a process of error originating before the eating of the fruit. See also John S. Tanner, ' "Say First What Cause": Ricoeur and the Etiology of Evil in *Paradise Lost*, *PMLA*, 103 (1988), 45–56, for the view that Milton's threefold presentation of error ranges from instantaneous choice to historical contamination, and John M. Steadman, 'Man's First Disobedience: The Causal Structure of the Fall', *JHI*, 21 (1960), 189.

22   See Don Parry Norford, ' "My Other Half": The Coincidence of Opposites in *Paradise Lost*', *MLQ*, 36 (1975), 26ff.

23   See Joseph Summers, *The Muse's Method: an Introduction to 'Paradise Lost'* (London, 1962), pp. 97–8; also Burden, p. 184ff.

24   See Barbara Kiefer Lewalski, 'Innocence and Experience in Milton's Eden' in Thomas Kranidas, ed., *New Essays on 'Paradise Lost'* (Berkeley, 1969), pp. 92–6; Diane McColley, 'Eve's Dream', *Milton Studies*, 12 (1979), 25–45)

25 Danielson, *Milton's Good God*, pp. 126–7, 198–9, seems to consider both Adam and Eve to blame in this scene; Diana Benet, 'Abdiel and the Son in the Separation Scene', *Milton Studies*, 18 (1984), 129–43, holds that Eve is innocent and superior to Adam; J. M. Evans, ' "Mortals' Chiefest Enemy" ', *Milton Studies*, 20 (1984), 111–26, argues as I do for the innocence of both. Burden, pp. 82–92; Safer, Revard and Antony Low, 'The Parting in the Garden in *Paradise Lost' PQ*, 47 (1968), 30–35, assert Eve's responsibility and so exonerate Adam. Fish, who generally insists on the innocence before the Fall, does not excuse the separation.

26 See David Aers and Bob Hodge, 'Milton on Sex and Marriage', *Milton Studies*, 13 (1979), 17ff., on contradictions in Adam's feelings.

27 Cf. Russell E. Smith, 'Adam's Fall', *ELH*, 35 (1968), 527–39.

28 *Christian Doctrine*, I, 12, *CP*, 6, 395; see also Evans, ' "Mortals' Chiefest Enemy" ', p. 20ff., on unwariness.

29 Irene Samuel, '*Paradise Lost* as Mimesis', in *Approaches to 'Paradise Lost': The York Tercentenary Lectures*, ed. C. A. Patrides (London, 1968), p. 28.

30 Milton, *Of Education*, *CP*, 2, 396. Aristotle, *Nicomachean Ethics*, Book 3, 3, 1112a–1113a.

31 Philip Larkin, *The Whitsun Weddings* (London, 1964), p. 32.

32 *Preface to 'Paradise Lost'*, pp. 125–8.

33 *Christian Doctrine*, 1, 12, *CP*, 6, 394.

34 I am reading lines 1054–9 as if there were a semicolon after 'shame' and, in this, rejecting Fowler's reading in his note to these lines.

35 *Christian Doctrine*, 1, 12, *CP*, 6, 393. On the death motif and the implication of one self in another, see Jun Harada, 'The Mechanism of Human Reconciliation in *Paradise Lost'*, *PQ*, 5 (1971), 543–52.

36 See Fowler's note.

37 On concupiscence, see *Christian Doctrine*, 1, 11, *CP*, 6, 388–91. The notion that concupiscence disfigures appears already in *Comus*, lines 68–74, but the mutuality of looks lies beyond its moral scheme.

38 It was a commonplace of the humanist tradition that friendship meant equality. See Erasmus, *Adages*, 1, i, i to 1, v, 100, tr. Margaret Mann Philips, *Collected Works of Erasmus*, 31, (Toronto, 1982), p. 31.

39 For Milton's transforming the Aristotelian peripety into an inward turning point, see John M. Steadman, '*Peripeteia* in Milton's Epic Fable', *Anglia*, 81 (1963), 429–52, and Harada's development of the idea in 'Mechanism of Human Reconciliation'.

40 Fowler, note to lines 740–1; Harada, p. 544.

41 Cf. Sigmund Freud, 'Mourning and Melancholia', *Standard Edition of the Complete Psychological Works of Sigmund Freud*, ed. John Strachey, 14 (1914–16), (London, 1957), p. 246.

42 On the process, see Harada, pp. 546–8.

43 Harada, especially pp. 546 ff.

44 *Christian Doctrine*, 1, 20, *CP*, 6, 471–6; *Christian Doctrine*, 1, 19, *CP*, 6, 469; *Christian Doctrine*, 1, 20, *CP*, 6, 471.

45 Samuel Johnson's formulation of the moral of *Paradise Lost* in *Milton, Lives of the Poets* (London, 1906), I, 118.

46 H. Grotius, *Defensio fidei catholicae de satisfactione Christi adversus Faustum Socinium* (Leyden: 1617); Milton, *Christian Doctrine*, 1, 3 and 4, *CP*, 6, 153–202; Jeremy Taylor, *Unum Necessarium or the Doctrine and Practice of Repentance, The Whole Works of the Right Reverend Jeremy Taylor, DD*, vol. 7 (London, 1850); John Bramhall, *A Defence of True Liberty from Antecedent and Extrinsecall Necessity* (London, 1655).

47 Gregory Smith, ed., *Elizabethan Critical Essays*, 2 vols (London, 1904).

48 *The Faerie Queen*, Book one, ed. Frederick Morgan Padelford, *The works of Edmund Spenser*, ed. Edwin Greenlaw et al. (Baltimore, 1932), p.167.

49 See Sir William Davenant, 'Preface to Gondibert', in J. E. Spingarn, ed., *Critical Essays of the Seventeenth Century* (Oxford, 1908), 2, 32–34; and Chapel of Penitence in *Sir William Davenant's 'Gondibert'*, ed. David F. Gladish (Oxford, 1971), Book 2, canto 6.

50 *Faerie Queene*, Book 1, canto 9, sts 38–57. Spenser's treatment is of course splendid in the way which Paul J. Alpers, *The Poetry of 'The Faerie Queene'* (Princeton, 1967), pp. 3–35, explains; but rhetorical intensity is not what is at issue for our discussion. See also Browne's Spenserian treatment of despair and repentance in *Britannia's Pastorals*, Song V, line 521ff.,

Poems of William Browne of Tavistock, ed. Gordon Goodwin (London, 1904); see also Susan Snyder, ' "The Left Hand of God": Despair in Medieval and Renaissance Tradition', *Studies in the Renaissance*, 12 (1965), 18–59.
51   *Middlemarch*, ed. W. J. Harvey (Harmondsworth, 1965), p. 335.

Appendix

This is not a history of the criticism of *Paradise Lost* but a brief sketch of how critics and literary historians have met the problem posed for humanists by its religious scheme.

Eighteenth-century criticism probably comes closest to the sort of study of literature I have called humanist, though it does not lay claim to the title. At any rate, both Addison and Johnson deal with *Paradise Lost* as a criticism of life. A neoclassical discussion of epic could hardly avoid doing so, since the epic was supposed to be a didactic form and consequently to represent human life in an indisputably critical fashion. Addison conceded so much to Le Bossu as to discover a moral in the poem, and found it 'the most universal and most useful that can be imagined', 'that obedience to the will of God makes men happy, and that disobedience makes them miserable'.[1] Yet even if *Paradise Lost* does illustrate this moral (can one deny that *Paradise Lost* is didactic or that it enjoins obedience?), the problem of how it bears on human concerns is by no means solved. This emerges clearly when a modern critic contends that the poem 'is essentially a moral work, not a metaphysical one', and that it teaches obedience.[2] What exactly does the modern critic mean by 'obedience to God'? If he means merely that this was how Milton understood his moral, then one is still left with the question of whether Milton's religious moral makes sense outside his religious frame of reference. For Addison, on the other hand, obedience to the will of God probably meant obedience to the laws of nature and society enjoined by the Supreme Lawgiver – in short, to morality. It looks for a moment as though the religious moral were much the same as the moral concerns of mankind. The trouble is that the obedience by which Adam and Eve stand or fall is to a divine command that has little to do with ordinary duties because of its arbitrary terms and the peculiar situation of the human pair. Though Addison may rightly epitomise the moral of *Paradise Lost* as an injunction to obey God, a general moral sense does not follow without a certain absence of attention to the actual terms of the poem.

Of course, much of Addison's criticism, dealing as it does with the beauties and sentiments of the poem, points out how *Paradise Lost* does, in fact, represent human life. However, if the moral (the distillation) of the action is alien to human concerns, those beauties and sentiments will be incidental to the poem's design. This is the drift of Johnson's criticism, which takes over so many of Addison's observations but reverses his judgements. On the one hand, Johnson grants the usefulness of the poem's moral, extended from Addison's version to include 'the reasonableness of religion' along with the 'necessity of obedience to the Divine Law'[3]; on the other hand, the implication of his criticism is that he doubts the effectiveness of the moral's presentation in the poem. *Paradise Lost* treats 'the history of a miracle ... the probable therefore is marvellous, and the marvellous is probable. The substance of the narrative is truth; and as truth allows no choice, it is, like necessity, superior to rule.'[4] Because it deals with such unparalleled matters, the strength of the poem lies in sublimity of imagination rather than in just and vivid representation of experience. But the sublimity is also the poem's weakness, for 'the reader finds no transaction in which he can be engaged; beholds no condition in which he can by any effort of the imagination place himself; he has, therefore, but little natural curiosity or sympathy'.[5] For Johnson, then, Milton does not and could not succeed in bringing the truths of revelation into contact with the truths of experience except intermittently. Wherever he does, Johnson allows that he makes the most of his opportunities; but the opportunities are rare and incidental to his scheme.

In the sense that they are both concerned with *Paradise Lost* as a representation and criticism of life, Addison and Johnson share a humanist conception of literature. Johnson, however, brings out the difficulty which Addison passed over; but he overstates his case. The judgement that 'the reader beholds no condition in which he can, by any effort of the imagination, place himself' might apply to Shelley better than to Milton. Still, Johnson's objections are crucial for the humanist criticism of *Paradise Lost*. The point they urge is that, while one cannot help feeling that *Paradise Lost* is a grand production, while its handling of its theological and biblical material is admirable, the poem falls short as a criticism of life.

Arnold, though still within the scope of what I should call humanism, took a different line. His criticism moves away from Johnson's definite formulation of the poem's difficulties to more general concerns. It is, therefore, in my view at least, less crucial than Johnson's. Still, it bears on the issue of the religious as distinct from the moral nature of the poem, and is still important because it has been influential.

For Johnson, as for the eighteenth century in general, Milton's theology was broadly acceptable. Even Voltaire had it that *Paradise Lost* rescued the biblical narrative from ridicule.[6] The Romantic view, by contrast, was that Milton's theology was oppressive to the human spirit. Arnold made this view respectable: 'Milton was born a humanist, but the Puritan temper, as we know, mastered him'.[7] By 'humanism', Arnold meant the intellectual temper which he called 'Hellenism'.[8] By the 'Puritan temper', he meant not merely lack of amenity but also the dogmatic cast of a contentious spirit.[9] So, the theology of *Paradise Lost* was a Puritan recasting of Pauline inspiration in rigid doctrinal forms, and the representation of God there furnished him with a *locus classicus* of the substitution

of 'a magnified non-natural man' for '*the Eternal that makes for righteousness*'.[10] For
Arnold, the theological and supernatural matter of the poem could not command
assent, whereas for Johnson it could, even if it was scarcely enlivening.[11] Johnson's
objection was that it limited the human interest of the poem; Arnold's was that it
was at odds with the full development of the human spirit.

Johnson's humanism is concerned with the accurate representation of human
life; Arnold's humanism is committed to its free and harmonious expression.
Accordingly, his humanism, sometimes a matter rather of attitude and temper
and their cultivation than of a particular sort of critical attention, moves in a
wider and vaguer sphere than Johnson's. This does not mean that Arnold is
confused, though one may disagree with him, nor that the considerations that
he brings into criticism are beside the point, though one may prefer the closeness
of Johnson's judgements. Arnold made it his business to open the discussion of
Paradise Lost to the sort of criticism that takes in experience of the world
contemporary with the critic. To that extent, his humanism coincides with
Johnson's and belongs to the humanism described earlier. Arnold's criticism of
Paradise Lost is admittedly sketchy. It is typical that, far from repeating
Johnson's damaging reservations about Milton's sublimity, he should find the
permanent Milton not in what he says but in how he says it, in his grand style
and its power to elevate the mind.[12] Nevertheless, Arnold's stress on the spirit
rather than the letter is less unsatisfactory than it can be made to look. Much
subsequent criticism shows how his version of the humanist issue can be
elaborated with a close regard to the text. Walter Raleigh's *Milton* is an example,
though it shows how easily Arnold's humanism may become a bland attitude
and an urbane style. The theme of how an obsolete and inhumane theology
distorts Milton's narrative and censors his finer imagination and feeling receives
more solid treatment from Waldcock and Peter.

At this point, Empson enters with another sort of humanism. Most representatives of Arnold's sort of humanism have at least a literary interest in
religion, Arnold has a good deal more and none of them say Christianity is
pernicious, only that Milton's form of it is objectionable. Empson, however,
holds that Christianity is pernicious and that Milton's form of it is less objectionable than most. Empson, then, is a humanist in the most commonly-used
sense of the word.

> A humanist, as I understand the term, says 'This world is good enough
> for me, if only I can be good enough for it'; an anti-humanist, however
> noble in personal character, at least appears to be committed to saying
> 'Nothing but Heaven is good enough for me; I ought to be there already'–
> nobody but God is aristocratic enough for him. The attitude is not always
> combined with interest in Hell, but that seems to fit in to it very easily, as
> one of the aristocratic pleasures of Heaven.[13]

The Arnoldian complaint about the Christianity of *Paradise Lost* is that Milton's puritan literalism, cast in epic form, involves an unmanageable and theologically coarse representation of the divine. Empson's point is that Milton's literalism and the narrative consistency imposed by the epic form show the horrible truth about such doctrines as God's omnipotence, the Fall and the Atonement, while a refined theology would obscure them, or at any rate would not prompt the same searching scrutiny. For Empson, Milton's greatness lies in the dogged way in which he tries to conceive what God's justice meant and in his radical grasp of what it meant to be its adversary. The tactlessness, the gigantic embarrassments, the painful inharmoniousness, which for Arnoldian humanism are signs of a defective spirit, are for Empson signs of a human integrity wrestling with a monstrous tradition and with the strain itself becoming monstrous.[14]

Empson's book makes it hard to be comfortable about *Paradise Lost* as an orthodox and traditional poem – the line Empson calls dismissively 'neochristian'. But it will have become obvious that the humanist issue as I have posed it has become squeezed out of shape. The question was how, given its peculiar theological terms, *Paradise Lost* could justly represent human life. The eighteenth-century critical approach bore most directly upon it, but I allowed that Arnoldian humanism was relevant, if less directly. For clearly, human life cannot be represented justly by a spirit that is defective in humanity, and, if the spirit of Milton's theology is defective, then the representation will also perhaps be defective. With Empson, the representation of life is no longer the issue. He is concerned with *Paradise Lost* as the representation of Christian beliefs and with their wickedness. He thinks they lend the poem a barbaric power like that of Benin sculpture (so much for sublimity).[15] But this can only be considered in terms of the pathology of cultures, and there can be no question for him of Milton's providing a criticism of life. I do not wish to let the humanist issue be pushed onto Empsonian grounds. Clearly, a poem that sets out to justify God asks for a moral consideration of its theology. What interests me, however, is the poem's moral action, that is, the fall and restoration of humanity. Of course, theology bears on it, and of course Empson treats the fall as an action as well as a doctrine. But I think he is too taken up with Christian theology and neo-Christian critics to grasp what the poem is really about. As far as my understanding of humanist criticism is concerned, the important question is whether Milton's treatment of the moral action makes sense as a representation of human experience. If it should, then however Milton saw the matter, the theology of *Paradise Lost*, Empson's objections to its morality and Arnold's objections to its spirit are not the really important issues for humanist criticism.

Two post-Empsonian books may be thought to have some bearing on the moral action of *Paradise Lost*. The first is Dennis Burden's *The Logical Epic*,[16] which sets out to show how Milton develops his epic from the recalcitrant material of Genesis 'logically', that is as coherently and reasonably as possible (given the story he had to work with) in terms both of narrative probability in Aristotle's sense and of theology. But a narrative, however 'logically' developed within a given frame of reference, may bear little relation to reality – the example of science fiction comes to mind. While Burden's argument disposes of many incompetences that Milton's critics have enjoyed finding, and while it makes a good case for the fineness of Milton's shaping care and systematising intelligence, it does not in itself establish that Milton does not make the best of what may be a bad job, 'a monument to what the mind can achieve' (p. 201) but still perhaps a monument to dead ideas. Yet Burden's tone endorses what is not so much the system as the systematic mind, the virtues of system, orderliness, lawfulness, obedience. He thinks the fall was a failure in those virtues, and comments that, seen in this way, 'Milton's account of the Fall is ... a deeply human and moral episode' (p. 177). This is to contend that, however hardpressed by truth to scripture or theology, Milton succeeds in representing a serious issue of human life. It seems to me, though, that the same difficulty arises here as with Addison's moral. The obedience at stake is unlike any ordinary duty. Perhaps this is why Burden seems to recommend that we approve not so much the moral content of the narrative as the moral temperament of which it is the expression. The suggestion is that approval of such a temperament is the mark of the fit audience. Such approval need not mean self-approval, of course; but one's uneasiness that what Burden calls logical rigour is exercised in a field hedged off from real issues is not allayed.

The second book is Joan Webber's *Milton and his Epic Tradition*, which offers a gnostic interpretation of the poem.[17] For her, *Paradise Lost* is essentially a myth of evolving consciousness. Consciousness evolves by breaking out of the forms that constrict it into chaos; from that immersion in the destructive element, it proceeds to reintegration and extension of its powers. In the fall and the restoration of Adam and Eve, with their progress from innocence to self-knowledge, the pattern is clearest. But Webber, picking up on something that struck Empson, argues that God Himself evolves through the Son and His death from a self-justifying despot to a God who will be All in All.[18] Even the epic poet goes through this process. The successful epic is a challenge to the tradition, a subversion of it, a destruction and remaking of the form 'won from the void and formless infinite'. It is a salutary to be reminded of Milton's poetic radicalism. The poet who declared that his poem intends to outsoar the Aonian mount obviously meant more than a pious claim that he had a better subject than Homer or Virgil because it was Christian. Milton's lines are instinct with the sublimity that overcomes anxiety about one's rivals. Indeed, his reworking of the tradition is an epic like no other. Again, perhaps any powerful poem, certainly a poem that treats creation, will treat matter that does not behave according to the law of the excluded middle: 'a thing is what it is and not another thing'. In myth, one shape implies another, and, though the mythical framework of *Paradise Lost* looks like a rather conservative redaction of Christian doctrine, the mythical imagining will probably imply subversive shapes around the edges. Yet, to read *Paradise Lost* as if it were a poem by Blake or Emerson is a bit of a wrench. In any case, the unlocking of primal creative energies from the structure in which Milton has fixed them belongs to a level of interpretation that does not unpick the human action of the poem very finely.

Burden's approach is confined within the logic of Milton's theological scheme, whereas Webber's breaks it down to release a transcendental impulse. However, neither way of reading the poem really gets hold of the human action, where it seems to me that Milton's poem has the most interesting things to show.

I hope that this survey has made clear my conception of the humanist issue of *Paradise Lost*. While inevitably passing over many critical approaches to the poem, I have dealt with the most relevant to that issue, although none of them seems to treat it entirely satisfactorily. There is, however, another way of discussing the humanism of *Paradise Lost*. It can be discussed historically rather than critically. Critically, the question concerned the place of *Paradise Lost* in a permanent humanism, a question of whether the poem bears on general moral experience. Historically, it is a question of the poem's place in the tradition of neoclassical humanism. Clearly, an answer to the second question is not an answer to the first; but they are involved with one another and easily confused.

In the early twentieth century, Edwin Greenlaw and James Holly Hanford, disciples of the neohumanism of Babbitt and More, wrote about Milton's humanism. What they had in mind was the doctrine of temperance, thinking that *Paradise Lost*, like *Comus* and like Book Two of the *Faerie Queene*, was a fable about the virtue of self-control, the inner check of Babbitt and More. This is to say that Milton's humanism is more or less what most people mean when they talk of his Puritanism, a surprising conjoining of what Arnold had put asunder.[19] However, in spite of their peculiar use of the term 'humanism', what Greenlaw and Hanford meant is clear, and even if one finds their reading of *Paradise Lost* unenlightening and their history unsatisfactory, they do not confuse historical and critical issues. They assume the identity, *mutatis mutandis*, of their neohumanism and Renaissance humanism. Greenlaw makes an implicit case for the seriousness of Milton's narrative by interpreting the moral action in terms of temperance with reference to a general historical background of platonic idealism, the platonic idealism being, as he saw it, the historical form available to Milton of the perennial doctrine of the inner check.[20] Here evaluation, interpretation and the study of the historical context are each distinct yet each related.

With Douglas Bush, on the other hand, the critical and historical issues do become blurred. Since he has probably said what are perhaps still the most generally accepted things about Milton's humanism, it is important to see why this is so. He took over the neohumanists' account of the poem, but he placed it against an enormously expanded history of ideas and assimilated Milton's humanism to something he called 'Christian humanism'.[21] By 'Christian humanism' he meant a frame of mind which the Renaissance inherited from the Middle Ages, an ordering of things at once rational and Christian, in which human nature found its full and harmonious development. The notion of a 'Christian humanism' seems a happy one, an ideal tempering of the best elements of Christianity and of humanism and possibly a means of drawing together the theology and the moral action of *Paradise Lost*. Of course, one wonders if such a frame of mind really existed; but what matters here is the critical position which Bush adopts on his historical thesis.

The essential point is that he thinks 'Christian humanism' was something that existed in the past. It was, according to Bush, an outlook that came to an end more or less with Milton, when historical conditions became unpropitious and the intellectual currents of Europe set in the direction of the modern world and of what Bush sees as a generally regrettable state of intellectual affairs.[22] So, while he writes of 'Christian humanism' elegiacally and while he sees in it a reproach to the modern world, it is not for him since 'Christian humanism' is not something a modern intelligence can maintain, though it might wish to. Whereas Greenlaw or Hanford find that Milton's humanism is fairly close to their own, Milton's humanism and Bush's regret for it are worlds apart. As for Christianity, it sounds as if Bush thinks that time has made it impossible.

Actually, Christianity is not central to Bush's reading of *Paradise Lost*. It plays much the same role as platonism in Greenlaw's and Hanford's interpretation: it provides a structure for the moral drama of temperance and right reason. This emerges clearly if one reads *'Paradise Lost' in Our Time* alongside M. Mahood's *Poetry and Humanism*. For Mahood, the humanism of *Paradise Lost* is Christianity, a theocentric view of things that guarantees a truly human nature[23]; for Bush, the Christianity of *Paradise Lost* is humanist because the theocentric view of things underwrites neohumanist ethical views. Christianity is then more of a container of Bush's 'Christian humanism' than the actual contents. For all that, however, Bush seems to consider his sort of humanism unable to exist without the Christian container; for him it lives only in the history ideas.[24]

There is no reason why one should not write about a historically superseded intellectual outlook – and, insofar as Bush's historical account of 'Christian humanism' helps him to interpret the moral action of *Paradise Lost*, his approach is unobjectionable. What is objectionable is the tendency, which he helped to establish, to confuse the history of ideas with criticism, to assume that further elaboration of the Renaissance Christian outlook or of Milton's place in the tradition of 'Christian humanism' is the same thing as a critical interpretation, that the historical fact of 'Christian humanism' settles the question for a humanist criticism of *Paradise Lost*. What disguises this confusion is Bush's admonitory tone approving the past and deploring the present. He is apparently arguing for the permanent value of Milton's criticism of life; but a tone of voice is not an argument. In fact, Bush, as the historian of 'Christian humanism', hedges on what Arnold rightly saw as the real issue for criticism, that is for contemporary humanism: 'How does Milton's masterpiece really stand to us moderns?'[25] ('A French Critic', p. 186). That is the question we must ask if we are to understand what humanism has to do with *Paradise Lost*. If 'Christian humanism' sidetracks us from asking it, then we are not concerned with the real bearing of humanism on the poem.

Recently, the idea that 'Christian humanism' is an adequate historical explanation of what Milton was doing has come under attack. One still comes across nostalgic references to the last of the Renaissance humanists, but, after a long period in which Bush's thesis, though dated, remained unchallenged, the topic has been opened up for reconsideration, notably by Alan Sinfield in his *Literature in Protestant England, 1560–1660*, though I should add that his historical grounds for taking issue with Bush's thesis are not mine, nor does he write critically as a humanist.[26]

Notes

1   *The Spectator*, 369, *The Works of Joseph Addison*, ed. Richard Hurd and Henry C. Bohn (London, 1893), 3, 282.
2   Burton Jasper Weber, *The Construction of Paradise Lost* (Carbondale, 1971), pp. xxx, 172. The most thoroughgoing attempt to explain *Paradise Lost* as a parable of obedience, Richard Heinrich Grün, *Das Menschenbild John Miltons in 'Paradise Lost'* (Heidelberg, 1956), does so in terms of Barthian theology.
3   'Life of Milton', *Lives of the Poets* (London, 1906), 1, 118.
4   'Life of Milton', p. 120.
5   'Life of Milton', p. 126.
6   See 'An Essay upon the Civil Wars of France … And also upon the Epick Poetry of the European Nations from Homer to Milton' (1727), pp. 102–21, quoted in John T. Shawcross, *Milton: The Critical Heritage* (London, 1970), p. 49.
7   'Equality', *Essays Religious and Mixed*, ed. R. H. Super (Michigan, 1972), p. 296.
8   This is clear from the discussion of 'Hebraism and Hellenism' in *Culture and Anarchy*, ed. J. Dover Wilson (Cambridge, 1957), pp. 129–44; cf. 'The disinterested curiosity, the *humanism* of the Renascence are not characteristics of Milton' ('A Guide to English Literature', *Essays Religious and Mixed*, p. 246).
9   'Equality', p. 296; for the Protestant habit of hardening inspiration into dogma, see *St. Paul and Protestantism, Dissent and Dogma*, ed. R. H. Super (Michigan, 1968), pp. 10–16, where a speech from the Father in *Paradise Lost*, III, 203–12, is cited as evidence.
10   *St. Paul*, p. 10; *Literature and Dogma* in *Dissent and Dogma*, p. 215.
11   'Life of Milton', p. 126.
12   'A French Critic on Milton', *Essays. Religious and Mixed*, ed. R. H. Super (Michigan, 1972), pp. 182–6.

13   William Empson, *Milton's God* (London, 1961), p. 262; cf. *OED*, 'Humanism', 3: 'Any system of thought or action which is concerned with merely human interests (as distinguished from divine)'.

14   For basically the same reasons, even if they are transposed into psychological terms, the Milton of John Carey, *Milton* (London, 1969), p. 75, and John Broadbent, *Introduction to 'Paradise Lost'* (Cambridge, 1972), pp. 154–5, is great where he has cracked. See also Broadbent's earlier *Some Graver Subject: An Essay on 'Paradise Lost'* (London, 1960).

15   *Milton's God*, pp. 275–6.

16   Dennis Burden, *The Logical Epic: A Study of the Argument of 'Paradise Lost'* (London, 1967).

17   Joan Webber, *Milton and his Epic Tradition* (Seattle, 1979).

18   For myth of evolving consciousness, see especially pp. 10ff.; for God's evolution, pp. 113, 125–31.

19   James Holly Hanford, 'Milton and the Return to Humanism', *SP*, 16 (1919), pp. 128, contrasts Milton with the puritans, Bunyan and Baxter.

20   Edwin Greenlaw, 'A Better Teacher than Aquinas', *SP*, 14 (1917), pp. 196–217. See especially his summing-up of his procedure, pp. 216–7, and compare with Hanford, p. 142.

21   Compare Douglas Bush, *The Renaissance and English Humanism* (Toronto: Toronto University Press, 1939), p. 119, with the passages cited from Greenlaw and Hanford; *'Paradise Lost' in our Time* (New York, 1945), has a more religious accent.

22   *Renaissance and English Humanism*, p. 101: 'Milton is the last great exponent of Christian Humanism in its historical continuity'; p. 103: 'the last voice of an essentially medieval tradition'.

23   M. Mahood, *Poetry and Humanism* (New York, 1967), pp. 12–15, 195.

24   Joan S. Bennett's *Reviving Liberty: Radical Christian Humanism in Milton,'s Great Poems* (Cambridge, Mass., 1989) should be mentioned here. Her use of 'Christian humanism' is theological, unlike Bush's, but still different from Mahood's. For her, 'Christian humanism' means the sort of Christianity that insisted on the rational accountability of God and of Christian life. She places Milton's 'Christian humanism' in an exact account of the beliefs of his time, but still as a critic endorses his 'Christian humanism'. She writes of herself as a 'Christian humanist'. This seems to me critically coherent, though 'humanism' as I shall use it does not mean what she means.

25   Arnold, 'A French Critic', p. 186.

26   Alan Sinfield, *Literature in Protestant England, 1560–1660* (London, 1983).

Bibliography

Addison, Joseph (1893), *The Works of Joseph Addison*, ed. Richard Hurd and Henry G. Bohn, 6 vols, London: Bell.

Aers, David, and Bob Hodge (1979), 'Milton on Sex and Marriage', *Milton Studies*, 13, pp. 3–33.

Alpers, Paul J. (1967), *The Poetry of 'The Faerie Queene'*, Princeton: Princeton University Press.

Aquinas, St Thomas (1923–9), *Summa Contra Gentiles*, tr. English Dominican Fathers, 4 vols, London: Burns Oates.

Arbuthnot, John, et al (1950), *Memoirs of the Extraordinary Life, Works and Discoveries of Martinus Scriblerus*, ed. Charles Kerby-Miller, New Haven: Yale University Press.

Arendt, Hannah (1959), *The Human Condition: A Study of the Central Dilemmas Facing Modern Man*, Garden City, N Y : Anchor.

Aristotle (1946), *De Poetica*, tr. Ingram Bywater, *The Works of Aristotle*, ed. W. D. Ross, vol 11, Oxford: Clarendon.

— (1954), *The Nicomachean Ethics of Aristotle*, tr. W. D. Ross, London: Oxford University Press.

Arnold, Matthew (1963), *Culture and Anarchy*, ed. John Dover Wilson, Cambridge: Cambridge University Press.

— (1968), *Literature and Dogma*, ed. R. H. Super, *Complete Prose Works of Matthew Arnold*, vol 6, Ann Arbor: University of Michigan Press.

— (1972), 'Equality', *Essays Religious and Mixed*, ed. R. H. Super, *Complete Prose Works of Mathew Arnold*, vol. 7, Ann Arbor: University of Michigan Press.

— (1972), 'A French Critic on Milton', *Essays Religious and Mixed*, ed. R. H. Super, *Complete Prose Works of Mathew Arnold*, vol. 7, Ann Arbor: University of Michigan Press.

— (1972), 'A Guide to English Literature', *Essays Religious and Mixed*, ed. R. H. Super, *Complete Prose Works of Matthew Arnold*, vol 7, Ann Arbor: University of Michigan Press.

Aubrey, John (1949), *Brief Lives and Selected Writings*, ed. Anthony Powell, London: Cresset.

Augustine, St (1589), *Confessionum Libri Tredecim*, Rome.

Bacon, Francis (1905), *The Philosophical Works of Francis Bacon*, ed. and tr. Robert Leslie Ellis and James Spedding and ed. John M. Robertson, London: Routledge.

— (1937), *Essays*, London: Oxford University Press.

Baron, Hans (1968), 'The Querelle of the Ancients and the Moderns as a Problem for Renaissance Scholarship', *Renaissance Essays*, ed. Paul Oskar Kristeller and Philip P. Wiener, New York: Harper.

— (1985), *Petrarch's 'Secretum': Its Making and its Meaning*, Cambridge, Mass. : Medieval Academy of America.

Baxter, Richard (1974), *Autobiography of Richard Baxter*, ed. N. H. Keeble, London: Dent.

Beaumont, Joseph (1702), *Psyche: Or Love's Mystery in XXIV Cantos Displaying the Intercourse Betwixt Christ and the Soul*, 2nd ed. , London.

Bell, Millicent (1953, 1955), 'The Fallacy of the Fall in *Paradise Lost*', *PMLA*, 68, pp. 863–85; 70, pp. 1197–1202.

Benet, Diana (1984), 'Abdiel and the Son in the Separation Scene', *Milton Studies*, 18, pp. 129–43.

Bennett, Joan S. (1977), 'God, Satan and King Charles: Milton's Royal Portraits', *PMLA*, 92, pp. 441–57.

(1989), *Reviving Liberty: Radical Christian Humanism in Milton's Great Poems*, Cambridge, Mass. : Harvard University Press.

Blackburn, Thomas H. (1971), '"Uncloister'd Virtue": Adam and Eve in Paradise', *Milton Studies*, 3, pp. 119–37.

Boileau-Despreaux, Nicholas (1966), *Œuvres Complètes*, ed. Antoine Adam and Françoise Escal, Paris: Gallimard.

Boswell, James (1924), *Johnson's 'Journey to the Western Islands of Scotland'and Boswell's 'Journal of a Tour to the Hebrides with Samuel Johnson, LLD*, ed. R. W. Chapman, Oxford: Oxford University Press.

Bouwsma, William J. (1975), 'The Two Faces of Humanism: Stoicism and Augustinianism', *Itinerarium Italicum: The Profile of the Italian Renaissance in the Mirror of its European Transformations*, ed. Heiko A. Oberman and Thomas A. Brady, Jr. , Leiden: Brill.

—(1988), *John Calvin: A Sixteenth-Century Portrait*, New York: Oxford University Press.

Bowers, Fredson (1969), 'Adam, Eve and the Fall in *Paradise Lost'*, *PMLA*, 84, pp. 264–73.

Boyle, Marjorie O'Rourke (1977), *Erasmus on Language and Method in Theology*, Toronto: Toronto University Press.

— (1983), *Rhetoric and Reform: Erasmus's Civil Dispute with Luther*, Cambridge, Mass. : Harvard University Press.

Bramhall, John (1655), *A Defence of True Liberty from Antecedent and Extrinsecall Necessity*, London.

Broadbent, J. B. (1960), *Some Graver Subject: An Essay on 'Paradise Lost'*, London: Chatto.

Broadwin, Leonora Leet (1969), 'Miltonic Allusion in *Absalom and Achitophel*: Its Function in the Political Satire', *JEGP*, 68, pp. 24–44.

Brower, Reuben Arthur (1966), 'Dryden's Epic Manner and Virgil', *Essential Articles for the Study of John Dryden*, ed. H. T. Swedenberg, Hamilton, Conn. : Archon, pp. 480–83.

Browne, William (1905), *Poems of William Browne of Tavistock*, ed. Gordon Goodwin, 2 vols. , London: Routledge.

Bruno, Giordano (1975), *The Ash Wednesday Supper*, tr. Stanley Jakki, The Hague: Mouton.

Burden, Dennis H. (1967), *The Logical Epic: A Study of the Argument of 'Paradise Lost'*, London:Routledge.

Bush, Douglas (1939), *The Renaissance and English Humanism*, Toronto: Toronto University Press.

— (1945), *'Paradise Lost' in our Time: Some Comments*, New York: Cornell University Press.

— (1953), *English Literature in the Earlier Seventeenth Century, 1600–1660*, Oxford: Clarendon.

Calvin, John (1848), *Commentaries on the Book of Genesis*, tr. John King, 2 vols. Edinburgh: Calvin Translation Society.

— (1960), *Institutes of the Christian Religion*, tr. Ford Lewis Battles, ed. John T. McNeill, 2 vols, Philadelphia: Westminster Press.

Carey, John (1969), *Milton*, London: Evans.

Carlyle, Thomas (1908), *Sartor Resartus*, London: Dent.

Cavanagh, Michael (1971), 'A Meeting of Epic and History: Books XI and XII of *Paradise Lost'*, *ELH*, 38, pp. 206–22.

Chambers, A. B. (1969), 'The Falls of Adam and Eve in *Paradise Lost'*, *New Essays on 'Paradise Lost'*, ed. Thomas Kranidas, Berkeley: University of California Press, (pp. 118–30).

Charlier, Yvonne (1977), *Erasme et l'amitié d'après sa correspondance*, Paris: Société d'éditions 'Les belles lettres'.

Christopher, Georgia B. (1982), *Milton and the Science of the Saints*, Princeton: Princeton University Press.

Cicero, Marcus Tullius (1889), *Laelius. De Amicitia. M. Tullii Ciceronis: Scriptae que manserunt omnia*, Part IV, vol 3, ed. C. E. W. Mueller, Leipzig: Teubner.

— (1928), *De Legibus*, tr. Clinton Walker Keyes, Loeb Classical Library, London: Heinemann.

— (1928), *Pro Archia*, ed. James S. Reid, Cambridge: Cambridge University Press.

Cirillo, Albert B. , (1969), '"Hail Holy Light" and Divine Time in *Paradise Lost*', *JEGP*, 68, pp. 45–46.

Clark, Donald Lemen (1922), *Rhetoric and Poetry in the Renaissance: A Study of Rhetorical Terms in English Renaissance Literary Criticism*, New York: Columbia University Press.

Costello, William T., SJ (1958), *The Scholastic Curriculum at Early Seventeenth Century Cambridge*, Cambridge, Mass. : Harvard University Press.

Cowley, Abraham (1905), *The Poems of Abraham Cowley*, ed. A. R. Waller, Cambridge: Cambridge University Press.

Curry, Walter Clyde (1957), *Milton's Ontology, Cosmology, and Physics*, [Lexington]: University of Kentucky Press.

Curtis, Mark H. (1959), *Oxford and Cambridge in Transition, 1558–1642*, Oxford: Clarendon.

Daiches, David (1957), *Milton*, London: Arnold.

— (1984), *God and the Poets*, Oxford: Clarendon.

Danielson, Dennis (1978), '*Arminianism in Paradise Lost*', *Milton Studies*, 12, pp. 47–73.

— (1982), *Milton's Good God*, Cambridge: Cambridge University Press.

Davenant, William (1971), *Sir William Davenant's 'Gondibert'*, ed. David F. Gladish, Oxford: Clarendon.

Denham, Sir John (1969), '*Expans'd Hieroglyphicks': A Critical Edition of Sir John Denham's 'Cooper's Hill'*, ed. Brendan O'Hehir, Berkeley: University of California Press.

Diekhoff, John S. (1946), *Milton's 'Paradise Lost': A Commentary on the Argument*, New York: Columbia University Press.

— (1970), 'Eve's Dream and the Paradox of Fallible Perfection', *Milton Quarterly*, 4, pp. 5–7.

Dryden, John (1882), *The State of Innocence, The Dramatic Works of John Dryden*, ed. Sir Walter Scott, rev. George Saintsbury, vol 5, Edinburgh: Patterson.

— (1958), *Poems of John Dryden*, ed. James Kinsley, 4 vols , Oxford: Clarendon.

— (1961), *Essays of John Dryden*, ed. Walter p. Ker, 2 vols (1900); reprinted New York: Russell.

Du Bartas, Guillaume (1976), *The Divine Weeks and Works*, tr. Joshua Sylvester, ed. Susan Snyder, Oxford: Oxford University Press.

Duncan, Edgar Hill (1954), 'The Natural History of Metals and Minerals in the Universe of Milton's *Paradise Lost*', *Osiris*, 9, pp. 386–421.

Eliot, George (1965), *Middlemarch*, ed. W. J. Harvey, Harmondsworth: Penguin.

Eliot, T. S. (1932) *Selected Essays*, London: Faber.

Empson, William (1950), *Some Versions of Pastoral*, London: Chatto.

— (1965), *Milton's God*, 2nd ed. , London: Chatto.

Erasmus, Desiderius (1959), *On the Freedom of the Will, Luther and Erasmus: Free Will and Salvation*, ed. E. Gordon Rupp and Philip S. Watson, London: SCM Press.

— (1965), *Christian Humanism and the Reformation: Selected Writings of Erasmus*, ed. John C. Olin, New York: Fordham University Press.

— (1965), *The Colloquies*, tr. Craig R. Thompson, Chicago: University of Chicago Press.

— (1971), *The Praise of Folly*, tr. Betty Radice, Harmondsworth: Penguin.

— (1982), *Adages*, tr. Margaret Mann Philips, vol 1, *Collected Works of Erasmus*, vol 31, Toronto: University of Toronto Press.

— (1988), Epistle. 1211, to Justus Jonas, tr. R. A. B. Mynors, *Correspondence of Erasmus*, vol 8, Toronto: University of Toronto Press.

— (1988), *Enchiridion militis christiani*, tr. Charles Fantazzi, Collected Works of Erasmus, Toronto: University of Toronto Press.

Evans, J. M. (1968), *'Paradise Lost' and the Genesis Tradition*, Oxford: Clarendon.

— (1984), '"Mortals' Chiefest Enemy"', *Milton Studies*, 20, pp. 111-26.

Feder, Lillian (1966), 'John Dryden's Use of Classical Rhetoric', *Essential Articles for the Study of John Dryden*, ed. H. T. Swedenberg, Hamilton, Conn. : Archon.

Ferry, Anne Davidson (1963), *Milton's Epic Voice*, Cambridge, Mass. : Harvard University Press.

— (1968), *Milton and the Miltonic Dryden*, Cambridge, Mass. : Harvard University Press.

Ficino, Marsilio (1964), *Marsile Ficin: Théologie platonicienne de l'immortalité des âmes*, ed. Raymond Marcel, 2 vols, Paris: Société d'éditions 'Les belles lettres'.

Fields, Albert W. (1968), 'Milton and Self-Knowledge', *PMLA*, 83, pp. 392–9.

Fiore, Peter Amadeus (1971), 'Freedom, Liberty, and the State of Perfection in *Paradise Lost*', *Milton Quarterly*, 5, pp. 47–51.

Fish, Stanley Eugene, (1967), *Surprised by Sin: The Reader in 'Paradise Lost'*, London: Macmillan.

Freedman, Morris (1958), 'Dryden's Miniature Epic', *JEGP*, 57, pp. 211–19.

Freud, Sigmund (1957), 'Mourning and Melancholia', *Standard Edition of the Complete Psychological Works of Sigmund Freud*, vol 14, London: Hogarth.

Fussell, Paul (1965), *The Rhetorical World of Augustan Humanism: Ethics and Imagery from Swift to Burke*, Oxford: Clarendon.

Gerl, Hanna-Barbara (1974), *Rhetorik als Philosophie: Lorenzo Valla*, Munich: Fink.

Giamatti, A. Bartlett (1966), *The Earthly Paradise and the Renaissance Epic*, Princeton: Princeton University Press.

Goldman, Jack (1977), 'Perspectives of Raphael's Meal in *Paradise Lost*, Book V', *Milton Quarterly*, 11, 31–7.

Gray, Hannah H. (1963), 'Renaissance Humanism: The Pursuit of Eloquence', *Journal of the History of Ideas*, 24, pp. 497–514.

Greene, Thomas (1963), *The Descent from Heaven: A Study in Epic Continuity*, New Haven: Yale University Press.

Greenlaw, Edwin (1917), 'A Better Teacher than Aquinas', *SP*, 14, pp. 196–217.

Greville, Fulke (1968), *Selected Poems*, ed. Thom Gunn, London: Faber.

Grotius, Hugo (1617), *Defensio fidei catholicae de satisfactione Christi adversus Faustum Socinium*, Leyden.

Grün, Richard Heinrich (1956), *Das Menschenbild John Miltons in 'Paradise Lost'*, Heidelberg: Winter.

Guazzo, Stefano (1925), *The Civile Conversation of M. Steeven Guazzo*, first three books. tr. George Pettie, 1581; fourth book. tr. Barth. Young, 1586; 2 vols. , London: Constable.

Hanford, James Holly (1919), 'Milton and the Return to Humanism', *SP*, 16, pp. 126–47.

Harada, Jun (1971), 'The Mechanism of Reconciliation in *Paradise Lost*', *PQ*, 50, pp. 543–52.

— (1973), 'Self and Language in the Fall', *Milton Studies*, 5, pp. 213–28.

Henninger, S. K. (1975), 'Sidney and Milton: The Poet as Maker', *Milton and the Line of Vision*, ed. Joseph A. Wittreich, Madison: University of Wisconsin Press (pp. 57–95).

Hobbes, Thomas (1968), *Leviathan*, ed. C. B. MacPherson, Harmondsworth: Penguin.

Howell Wilbur Samuel (1956), *Logic and Rhetoric in England, 1500–1700*, Princeton: Princeton University Press.

— (1971), *Eighteenth-Century British Logic and Rhetoric*, Princeton: Princeton University Press.

Hunt, H. A. K. (1954), *The Humanism of Cicero*. Melbourne: Melbourne University Press.

Hunter, William B. , Jr (1936), 'Eve's Daemonic Dream', *ELH*, 13, pp. 255–65.

— (1959), 'The Meaning of Holy Light in *Paradise Lost*, III', *MLN*, 74, pp. 589–92.

— (1960), 'Holy Light in *Paradise Lost*', *Rice Institute Pamphlets*, 46, pp. 1–14.

Ide, Richard S. (1983), 'On the Uses of Elizabethan Drama: The Revaluation of Epic in *Paradise Lost*', *Milton Studies*, 17, pp. 121–40.

Jack, Ian (1952), *Augustan Satire: Intention and Idealism in English Poetry, 1660–1750*, Oxford: Clarendon.

Jacobus, Lee A. (1976), *Sudden Apprehension: Aspects of Knowledge in 'Paradise Lost'*, The Hague: Mouton.

Jardine, Lisa (1974), 'The Place of Dialectic Teaching in Sixteenth Century Cambridge', *Studies in the Renaissance*, 21, pp. 31–52.

Johnson, Samuel (1906), *Lives of the Poets*, 2 vols, London: Oxford University Press.

— (1969), *The Rambler*, ed. W. J. Bate and Albrecht B. Strauss, 2 vols, *Yale Edition of the Works of Samuel Johnson*, vols. 3–4, New Haven: Yale University Press.

Kates, Judith A. (1974), 'The Revaluation of the Classical Heroic in Tasso and Milton', *Comparative Literature*, 26, pp. 293–317.

— (1983), *Tasso and Milton: The Problem of the Christian Epic*, Lewisburg: Bucknell University Press.

Kessler, Eckhard (1968), *Das Problem des Frühen Humanismus: Seine Philosophische Bedeutung bei Coluccio Salutati*, Munich: Fink.

Knott, John R. , Jr (1968), 'The Visit of Raphael in *Paradise Lost*, 5', *PQ*, 47, pp. 35–42.

Koehler, G. Stanley (1975), 'Milton and the Art of Landscape', *Milton Studies*, 8, pp. 3–40.

Kristeller, Paul Oskar (1956), *Studies in Renaissance Thought and Letters*, Rome: Edizzione di storia e letteratura.

— (1975), 'Erasmus from an Italian Perspective', *Renaissance Quarterly*, 23, pp. 1–13.

— (1979), *Renaissance Thought and its Sources*, ed. Michael Mooney, New York: Columbia University Press.

Larkin, Philip (1964), *The Whitsun Weddings*, London: Faber.

Le Bossu, René (1970), *Treatise of the Epick Poem* (1695), *Le Bossu and Voltaire on the Epic*, ed. Stuart Curran, Gainesville, Florida: Scholars' Facsimiles and Reprints.

Leonard, John (1990), *Naming in Paradise: Milton and the Language of Adam and Eve*, Oxford: Clarendon.

Lewalski, Barbara Kiefer (1969), 'Innocence and Experience in Milton's Eden', *New Essays on 'Paradise Lost'*, ed. Thomas Kranidas, Berkeley: University of California Press (pp. 86–117).

Lewis, Clive Staples (1949), *A Preface to 'Paradise Lost'*, London: Oxford University Press.

Low, Anthony (1968), 'The Parting in the Garden in *Paradise Lost*', *PQ*, 47, pp. 30–5.

Luther, Martin (1955), *Selected Psalms*, 1, ed. Jaroslav Pelikan, *Luther's Works*, vol 12, St Louis: Concordia Publishing House.

— (1957), 'A Disputation against Scholastic Theology', ed. Harold J. Grimm, *Luther's Works*, vol 31, St Louis: Concordia Publishing House.

— (1957), *The Freedom of a Christian*, tr. W. A. Lambert, rev. and ed. Harold J. Grimm, *Luther's Works*, vol 31, St Louis: Concordia Publishing House.

— (1959), *On the Bondage of the Will, Luther and Erasmus: Free Will and Salvation*, ed. E. Gordon Rupp and Philip S. Watson, London: SCM Press.

— (1960), 'Preface to the Epistle of St Paul to the Romans', ed. Theodore Buchanan, *Luther's Works*, vol 35, St Louis: Concordia Publishing House.

— (1972), 'Lectures on Romans', ed. Hilton J. Oswald, *Luther's Works*, vol 25, St Louis: Concordia Publishing House.

MacCaffery, Isabel Gamble (1959), *'Paradise Lost' as Myth*, Cambridge, Mass. : Harvard University Press.

McColley, Diane (1979), 'Eve's Dream', *Milton Studies*, 12, pp. 25–45.

McSorley, Harry J. (1969), *Luther, Right or Wrong: An Ecumenical-Theological Study of Luther's Major Work, 'The Bondage of the Will'* ,New York: Newman Press.

Madsen, William G. (1958), 'The Idea of Nature in Milton's Poetry', Richard B. Young, W. Todd Furniss, and William G. Madsen. *Three Studies in the Renaissance: Sydney, Jonson, Milton*, New Haven: Yale University Press.

— (1968), *From Shadowy Types to Truth*, New Haven: Yale University Press.

Mahood, M. (1967), *Poetry and Humanism* (1950); reprinted New York: Kennikat Press.

Mason, H. A. (1959), *Humanism and Poetry in the Early Tudor Period*, London: Routledge.

Melanchthon, Philip (1969), *Loci Communes Theologici*, tr. Wilhelm Pauk, *Melanchthon and Bucer*, London: SCM Press.

Milton, John (1953–82), *Complete Prose Works of John Milton*, ed. Don M. Wolfe et al., 8 vols, New Haven: Yale University Press.

— (1968), *The Poems of John Milton*, ed. John Carey and Alastair Fowler, London: Longman.

Montaigne, Michel (1962), *Œuvres Complètes*, ed. Albert Thibaudet et Maurice Rat, Paris: Gallimard.

—(1965), *Montaigne's Essays*, tr. John Florio, 3 vols , London: Dent.

Mora, José Ferrater (1953), 'Suarez and Modern Philosophy', *Journal of the History of Ideas*,
    14, pp. 528–47.
Norford, Don Parry (1975), '"My Other Half": The Coincidence of Opposites in *Paradise
    Lost*', *MLQ*, 36, pp. 21–53.
Nuttal, A. D. (1983), *A New Mimesis: Shakespeare and the Representation of Reality*, London:
    Methuen.
Nygren, Anders (1969), *Eros and Agape*, tr. Philip Watson, New York: Harper.
Oberman, Heiko A. (1971), '*Facientibus quod in se est Deus non denegat gratiam*: Robert Holcot
    O. P. and the Beginnings of Luther's Theology', *The Reformation in Medieval Perspective*,
    ed. Stephen E. Ozment,Chicago: Quadrangle.
— (1971), '*Simul gemitus et raptus*: Luther and Mysticism', *The Reformation in Medieval
    Perspective*, ed. Stephen E. Ozment, Chicago: Quadrangle.
— (1974), 'The Shape of Late Medieval Thought: The Birthpangs of the Modern Era', *The
    Pursuit of Holiness in Late Medieval Religion*, ed. Charles Trinkaus and Heiko A. Oberman,
    Leiden: Brill.
— (1981), *Masters of the Reformation: The Emergence of a New Intellectual Climate in Europe*, tr.
    Dennis Martin, Cambridge: Cambridge University Press.
Onians, John (1984), 'On How to Listen to High Renaissance Art', *Art History*, 7,
    pp. 411–37.
Parks, George B. (1976), 'Pico della Mirandola in Tudor Translation', *Philosophy and
    Humanism: Essays in Honour of Paul Oskar Kristeller*, ed. Edward P. Mahoney, Leiden:
    Brill.
Patrides, C. A. (1966), *Milton and the Christian Tradition*, Oxford: Clarendon.
Peter, John (1960), *A Critique of 'Paradise Lost'*, New York: Columbia University Press.
Petrarca, Francesco (1496), *Opera omnia*, Basle: Amerbach.
— (1929), *Psalmi penitentiales: Pétrarque, les psaumes pénitentiaux*, ed. and tr. H. Cochin, Paris:
    Romart.
— (1948), 'On his Own Ignorance and that of Many Others', tr. Hans Nachod, *The
    Renaissance Philosophy of Man*, ed. Ernst Cassirer et al., Chicago: University of Chicago
    Press.
Pico, Giovanni (1948), 'Oration on the Dignity of Man', tr. Elizabeth Livermore Forbes, *The
    Renaissance Philosophy of Man*, ed. Ernst Cassirer et aline , Chicago: University of Chicago
    Press.
Plato (1871), *Alcibiades*, 1, *The Dialogues of Plato*, tr. Benjamin Jowett, 4 vols, Oxford:
    Clarendon.
Pope, Alexander (1950), *An Essay on Man*, ed. Maynard Mack, Twickenham Edition of the
    Poems of Alexander Pope, vol 3. , part 1, London: Methuen.
— (1963), *The Poems of Alexander Pope*, ed. John Butt, London: Methuen.
Rabelais, François (1929), *Gargantua and Pantagruel*, tr. Thomas Urquhart, 2 vols. , London:
    Dent.
— (1951), *Œuvres Complètes*, ed. Jacques Boulenger, Paris: Bibliothèque de la Pléiade.
Rajan, Balachandra (1947), '*Paradise Lost' and the Seventeenth Century Reader*, London:
    Chatto.
Revard, Stella P. (1973), 'Eve and the Doctrine of Responsibility in *Paradise Lost*', *PMLA*, 88,
    pp. 69–78.
Ricks, Christopher (1963), *Milton's Grand Style*, London: Oxford University Press.
Ricoeur, Paul (1965), *Fallible Man*, tr. Charles Kelbley, Chicago: Regnery.
— (1969), *The Symbolism of Evil*, tr. Emerson Buchanan, Boston: Beacon.
Ross, Malcolm Mackenzie (1943), *Milton's Royalism: A Study of the Conflict of Symbol and
    Idea in the Poems*, Ithaca: Cornell University Press.
Safer, Elaine B. (1972), '"Sufficient to Have Stood": Eve's Responsibility in Book IX', *Milton
    Quarterly*, 6, pp. 10–13.
Saurat, Denis (1944), *Milton: Man and Thinker*, 2nd ed. , London: Dent.

Schilling, Bernard (1961), *Dryden and the Conservative Myth: A Reading of 'Absalom and Achitophel'*, New Haven: Yale University Press.

Schultz, Howard (1970), *Milton and Forbidden Knowledge*, 1955; reprinted. New York: Krauss.

Schwarz, Regina (1985), 'Milton's Hostile Chaos . . . "And The Sea Was No More"', *ELH*, 52, pp. 337–74.

Seigel, Jerold E. (1968), *Rhetoric and Philosophy in Renaissance Humanism: The Union of Eloquence and Wisdom, Petrarch to Valla*, Princeton: Princeton University Press.

Shawcross, John T. (1970), *Milton: The Critical Heritage*, London: Routledge.

Shumaker, Wayne (1955), 'The Fallacy of the Fall in *Paradise Lost*', *PMLA*, 70, pp. 1185–7, 1197–1202.

Sidney, Sir Philip (1973), *A Defence of Poetry*, ed. Katherine Duncan-Jones and Jan van Dorsten, *Miscellaneous Prose of Sir Philip Sidney*, Oxford: Clarendon.

Sinfield, Alan (1983), *Literature in Protestant England, 1560-1660*, London: Croom Helm.

Sinning, Jens Andersen (1991), *Oratio de studiis philosophicis, theologiae studioso necessariis* (1591), ed. Eric Jacobsen, Copenhagen.

Smith, Gregory, ed. (1904), *Elizabethan Critical Essays*, 2 vols, London: Oxford University Press.

Snyder, Susan (1965), '"The Left Hand of God": Despair in Medieval and Renaissance Tradition', *Studies in the Renaissance*, 12, pp. 18–59.

Spenser, Edmund (1932-57), *The Works of Edmund Spenser*, ed. Edwin Greenlaw et al., Baltimore: John Hopkins Press.

Sperl, Adolf (1959), *Melanchthon zwischen Humanismus und Reformation*, Munich: Kaiser.

Spingarn, J. E. (1908), *Critical Essays of the Seventeenth Century*, 3 vols, Oxford: Clarendon.

— (1908), *A History of Literary Criticism in the Renaissance*, 2nd ed. , New York: Columbia University Press.

Steadman, John M. (1959), 'Heroic Virtue and the Divine Image in *Paradise Lost*', *Journal of the Warburg and Courtauld Institutes*, 22, pp. 88–105.

— (1960), '"Man's First Disobedience": the Causal Structure of the Fall', *Journal of the History of Ideas*, 21, pp. 180–97.

— (1963), '*Peripeteia* in Milton's Epic Fable', *Anglia*, 81, pp. 429–52.

— (1964), 'Mimesis and Idea: *Paradise Lost* and the Seventeenth-Century World View', *Emory University Quarterly*, 20, pp. 67–80.

— (1967), *Milton and the Renaissance Hero*, Oxford: Clarendon.

— (1974), *The Lamb and the Elephant: Ideal Imitation in the Context of Renaissance Allegory*, San Marino, California : Huntington Library.

Stein, Arnold (1953), *Answerable Style: Essays in 'Paradise Lost'*, Minneapolis: University of Minnesota Press.

Steinmetz, David (1980) *Luther and Staupitz: An Essay in the Intellectual Origins of the Protestant Reformation*, Durham, NC: Duke University Press.

Summers, Joseph (1962), *The Muse's Method: An Introduction to 'Paradise Lost'*, London: Chatto.

Svendsen, Kester (1956), *Milton and Science*, Cambridge, Mass. : Harvard University Press.

Tanner, John S. (1988), '"Say First What Cause": Ricoeur and the Etiology of Evil in *Paradise Lost*', *PMLA*, 103, pp. 45–56.

Tasso, Torquato (1930), *Gerusalemme Liberata*, ed. Luigi Bonfigli, Bari: Laterza.

— (1973), *Discourses on the Heroic Poem*, tr. Mariella Cavalchini and Irene Samuel, Oxford: Clarendon.

— (1981), *Godfrey of Bulloigne*, tr. Edward Fairfax, ed. Kathleen M. Lee and T. M. Gang, Oxford: Clarendon.

Taylor, Jeremy (1850), *Unum Necessarium or the Doctrine and Practice of Repentance*, *The Whole Works of the Right Reverend Jeremy Taylor, DD*, vol 7, London: Longman.

Thrale, Hester Lynch (1951), *Thraliana*, ed. Katharine C. Balderston, 2 vols, Oxford: Clarendon.

Tillyard, E. M. W. (1951), *Studies in Milton*, London: Chatto.
Toffanin, Giuseppe (1954), *History of Humanism*, tr. Elio Gianturco, New York: Las Americas Press.
Trinkaus, Charles Edward (1965), *Adversity's Nobleman: The Italian Humanists on Happiness* (1940); reprinted. New York: Octagon.
— (1970), *In Our Image and Likeness: Humanity and Divinity in Italian Humanist Thought*, 2 vols, London: Constable.
— (1979), *The Poet as Philosopher: Petrarch and the Formation of the Renaissance Consciousness*, New Haven: Yale University Press.
Turner, James Grantham (1987), *One Flesh: Paradisal Marriages and Sexual Relations in the Age of Milton*, Oxford: Oxford University Press.
Valla, Lorenzo (1948), 'Dialogue on Free Will', tr. Charles Edward Trinkaus, *The Renaissance Philosophy of Man*, ed. Ernst Cassirer et al., Chicago: University of Chicago Press.
— (1977), *On Pleasure*, tr. A. Kent Hieatt and Maristella Lorch, New York: Abaris.
Vickers, Brian (1988), *In Defence of Rhetoric*, Oxford: Clarendon.
Voltaire (1970), 'An Essay upon the Civil Wars of France . . . And also upon the Epick Poetry of the European Nations from Homer to Milton' (1727), in John T. Shawcross, *Milton: The Critical Heritage*, London: Routledge (p. 49).
Waldock, A. J. A. (1947), *'Paradise Lost' and its Critics*, Cambridge: Cambridge University Press.
Webber, Joan (1979), *Milton and his Epic Tradition*, Seattle: University of Washington Press.
Weber, Burton Jasper (1971), *The Construction of 'Paradise Lost'*, Carbondale: University of Southern Illinois Press.
Webster, Charles (1975), *The Great Instauration: Science, Medicine and Reform, 1620–1660*, London: Duckworth.
Weinberg, Bernard (1961), *A History of Literary Criticism in the Italian Renaissance*, 2 vols, Chicago: University of Chicago Press.
Weiss, Roberto (1964), 'Learning and Education in Western Europe from 1470 to 1520', *The Renaissance*, ed. G. R. Potter, *The New Cambridge Modern History*, vol 1, Cambridge: Cambridge University Press.
Williams, Aubrey (1953), *Pope's 'Dunciad': A Study of Its Meaning*, London: Methuen.
Woodhouse, A. S. p. (1949), 'Notes on Milton's Views on the Creation: The Initial Phase', *PQ*, 28, pp. 211–36.
Yates, Frances A. (1964), *Giordano Bruno and the Hermetic Tradition*, London: Routledge.

Index